What people are sayi

Everything Makes Sense

Everything Makes Sense is surcharged with heartfulness and artfulness and offers as well a deep store of thought-provoking verse and spirit-enlivening story-telling. The book is a tour de force worthy of the attention of anyone who has ever wondered what's really happening in the Game of Life. As I commented to the author, this book will likely be read for centuries.
Rick Chapman, author of *Meher Baba, the Compassionate One* and *How To Choose A Guru, An A to Z Guide To Telling the Real From the False*

I couldn't stop reading *Everything Makes Sense*, a deep and poetic book from an extraordinarily gifted writer. The book investigates human consciousness through the lenses of meaning and desire and should be required reading for all neuro-materialists holding onto the biological-robot/meaningless-universe meme.
Alec Tsakiris, host of the *Skeptiko* podcast and author of *Why Science Is Wrong ... About Almost Everything and Why Evil Matters: How Science & Religion Fumbled a Big One*

Everything Makes Sense is a thought-provoking book that challenges prevailing notions about the nature of intelligence and the limitations of physicalism. Author Tim Garvin invites us to immerse ourselves in deep existential questions about personal meaning and about our place in the universe. This book is a captivating read for anyone fascinated by the intricacies of the mind, consciousness, and the never-ending quest for understanding.
Dean Radin, PhD, Chief Scientist, Institute of Noetic Sciences, and author of *Real Magic, Entangled Minds*, and other books

Everything Makes Sense: A Close-Notice of Life and Consciousness is a vitally important book, offering a perspective on spirituality that informs and inspires. The thinking of Meher Baba and other spiritual leaders grace the book, along with rich thought experiments full of wisdom and beauty. The prose of this powerful book is artful, gripping, and insightful, and I enthusiastically recommend it as essential to everyone interested in spiritual enlightenment.
Jeffrey Long, MD, author of the New York Times-bestselling *Evidence of the Afterlife: The Science of Near-Death Experiences* and *God and the Afterlife: The Groundbreaking New Evidence for God and Near-Death Experience*

In this profound and hard-to-put-down book, Tim Garvin gently takes the reader on a journey of self-discovery. The simplicity of his method both belies and clarifies the depth of the questions he engages. Garvin patiently works through humanity's most-challenging questions in a way that is practical and relatable. In *Everything Makes Sense,* open-minded readers will find a manuscript that confronts the deep issues of life with a spirit of wonder and a sincere desire for truth. The book works both as a prologue to the thought of such great sages as Meher Baba, Sri Aurobindo, Sri Ramakrishna, and Swami Vivekananda, and as a follow-up study to more fully unpack their teachings. I recommend it highly.
Dr JD Long, Professor of Religion, Philosophy, and Asian Studies, and author of *Jainism: An Introduction, Hinduism in America* and *Discovering Indian Philosophy*

In this innovative and stimulating book, Tim Garvin takes the reader on a wild, witty, and wise ride into the depths of life. By exploring and illuminating the concepts of desire, meaning, and mysticism, he clarifies some of life's most profound issues: free

will, suffering, consciousness, reincarnation, karma. What's more, the writing is beautiful, with fantastic wordsmithing and creativity on every page. Everything, indeed, makes sense as Garvin integrates Meher Baba's comprehensive texts on creation, consciousness, love, and the nature of spiritual work.
Dr. Allan Cohen, clinical psychologist and author of *The Mastery of Consciousness: An Introduction and Guide to Practical Mysticism and Methods of Spiritual Development*

I read Tim Garvin's *Everything Makes Sense* with deep interest and believe his journey into the interior of consciousness will be loved, shared, and avidly read by the many seekers who are now awakening to the nature and purpose of life. *Everything Makes Sense* characterizes the universe as "the eternal busyness of God's manifestation, the something-seen and the something-seeing as well ... We are not only embedded in the being of God, we are ourselves made of God-stuff." When I met Avatar Meher Baba in 1965, He said, "You are God, as is everyone sitting here. You are just not conscious of your divinity. It is my job to create that awareness." Garvin's comprehensive philosophical and psychological insight supports this idea with an invigorating exploration of consciousness. His innovative ideas are presented in a simple, direct way and illuminate the conception that "the universe is a divine manifestation and that we are ourselves secretly God."
Naosherwan Anzar, author and editor of many books about Meher Baba, editor of the journal *Glow International*, and director of Beloved Archives

For any sincere seeker of Truth, *Everything Makes Sense* offers a path of contemplation that leads through the physical, psychological, and philosophical to the spiritual. The author eloquently and poetically directs the reader towards the purpose of life and consciousness. The writing reflects not only Garvin's decades of studying the great thinkers, but also his likely many lifetimes of association with the source of Knowledge. This book is a gift that will allow ready seekers to forego years of preoccupation with trifling intellectual distractions and get on with "close-notice of life and consciousness.

Peter Nordeen, historian of the life and work of Avatar Meher Baba, writer and producer of *God in Human Form* and other films for Meher Filmworks

Everything Makes Sense

A Close-Notice of Life and Consciousness

Everything Makes Sense

A Close-Notice of Life and Consciousness

Tim Garvin

BOOKS

Winchester, UK
Washington, USA

CollectiveInk

First published by O-Books, 2024
O-Books is an imprint of Collective Ink Ltd.,
Unit 11, Shepperton House, 89 Shepperton Road, London, N1 3DF
office@collectiveinkbooks.com
www.collectiveinkbooks.com
www.o-books.com

For distributor details and how to order please visit the 'Ordering' section on our website.

ISBN: 978 1 80341 432 4
978 1 80341 433 1 (ebook)
Library of Congress Control Number: 2023932252

A CIP catalogue record for this book is available from the British Library.

Design: Lapiz Digital Services

UK: Printed and bound by CPI Group (UK) Ltd, Croydon, CR0 4YY
Printed in North America by CPI GPS partners

For Cynthia
and
for everyone else

To penetrate into the essence of all being and significance and to release the fragrance of that inner attainment for the guidance and benefit of others—by expressing, in the world of forms, truth, love, purity, and beauty—this is the sole game that has intrinsic and absolute worth. All other happenings, incidents, and attainments in themselves can have no lasting importance.

Meher Baba

This cautiously bold beginning

Consider: any two people, if they are honest and patient, are compelled, by the nature of existence itself, to agree about everything.

That assertion, especially today, seems absurd. So here's a thought experiment: you and a friend commit to be honest and patient, then go for a walk to see if you can agree. That's a tree. There's a rock. Agreed? Agreed. Unless there's insanity afoot, agreement about the visible world is routine.

Next, one of you asserts: Chinese people are more hard-working than any other. Agreed? Well...

Because now you have both encountered the invisible world, which is the most of everything. How, you honestly inquire (that's the deal in this thought experiment), can you evaluate, measure, or even define the diligence of an entire population? You can't, so you both shrug. Opinion might want to muscle forward and assert itself, but honesty shrugs and so opinion, however reluctantly, must shrug too. We may not be able to agree about much, but at least we know this: the swordplay of opinion is helpless to generate agreement. And this: honesty is the force that sheathed those swords. And this: that we are profoundly, inevitably, maddeningly ignorant of what is going on in the invisible world. Which is almost everything.

Still this book will assert that everything makes sense, and further, that the sense everything makes is indescribably lovely. Is that, opinion? These pages will point toward the trees and rocks of experience as well.

One Question, Two Answers, and the Bike

Everyone's big question is always the same: what is all this? That is, what is life, existence, everything? For most of us it's a back-of-the-mind question, because we don't think we can answer it—or think we (or our betters) already have. Besides, how it gets answered by any one of us—or by any culture or era—is so variable we've mostly lost confidence in all answers. We might even think trying to answer the big question is presumptuous, or suspect the answer could turn us into either fanatics or desperados. That's because that question—what is all this?—has only two possible answers. One, existence has something to do with divinity (an idea notorious for producing complacency and fanaticism). Or it doesn't (which can produce despair).

On the no-God side we have the testimony of scientific materialism, and its cornucopia of iPhones and airplanes. On the God side we have libraries of disputing theologies. So why bother, because, anyway, we need to hit the grocery store, deal with those termites, look for a new job, and basically keep pedaling because, as we well know, unless we're moving forward, the bicycle of getting-along-in-the-world tips right over.

Still, for most of us there are moments when we lay the bike down, walk into a field alone, maybe at night, and think, well, I got a lot of what I wanted, some of what I didn't, and still, out here under these stars, this pesky loneliness is back. And again the question comes: really now, what is all this?

The question is generally not followed by an answer. And there's the bicycle. At least we know how to ride that. Also, we must. So up we mount, and off we go.

But if you find yourself returning to that field more and more these days, then come along.

Experience to thought

Writing down thoughts creates two problems. One is the problem of transferring experience to explanation. Problem two is the unhappy nature of explanation itself.

About the first: say you bite into an apple and then think to recommend its taste to a friend. You might say—need only say and can only say—try it, it's good. That's because even apple aficionados are helpless to usefully parse the subtleties of taste. Everyone can distinguish—on a chemically charged strip of paper, for instance—apple taste from orange taste, but no one can provide a verbal account of those tastes so that someone who has never tasted either can distinguish between them. There is a provoking bluntness about the meaning contained in words and the eerie vagueness of experience where taste happens. This bluntness, this inability of language to make evident and easily transmissible our lived experience, is why we communicate through the generalizations we call ideas. The difficulty is that the ideas about which we hope to construct agreement are seldom as simple as the taste of an apple. Instead they are compounds of ideas and have hidden in their layers ideas about which we may not agree. We are all Brazilians or Christians or pragmatists so at least we agree about...very little.

The fact that we communicate in ideas brings up the second hazard of thinking and writing thoughts—explanation itself. Explain a tree. Okay, it's that thing with branches and roots and leaves and— Wait, branches? What are those, now? Branches are those things that stick out from the trunk of the tree, and they have— Explain everything they have. Explain bark, then cambium, then mitochondria, then protein, then atoms, then quarks, then— And explaining stops, because, alas, explanation always finishes at the blank wall of the unexplained. Every explanation that satisfies only satisfies because we stopped questioning when explanation had served its purpose. How do you get to New York? Well, go north and east, and eventually you'll see a bunch of buildings, and that's New York. Every explanation requires only enough peripheral expansion to get us to New York, build an iPhone, or catch a mammoth. It's simple to see that all explanation, when examined, is founded on the unexplained.

Another issue with explanation, which will become more evident when we consider the notion of physicalism, is that explanations are offered to fill the void beneath inquiry, and thus must comply with and satisfy the inquirer's context. As in: a child cannot explain to his mother that the reason he hit his sister was that his hand moved.

Explanation can be understood as a penumbra of unthought thought that surrounds and supports the thought it explains. These unthought but linked thoughts are what create the vast meaning density we call intelligence and are why we can give each other hints. What's that animal with the long neck that lives in Africa? You mean *giraffe*? We were able to think of giraffe because the penumbra of connected thought surrounding *giraffe* includes long neck and Africa. On a map, you can know exactly where Kansas is and what it looks like if you know the shapes and locations of Missouri, Oklahoma, Nebraska, and Colorado. But if you don't know the shapes and locations of the states surrounding those states, you're still lost. Despite the immensity of our thought world, we are all swimming in a fathomless matrix of the unexplained. But we can catch the mammoth and build the iPhone, so we don't much think about it. Here we will though.

So apples and explanation make book writing, and reading, a fraught task. The best any thinking can do is point and proclaim, go that way, you'll see what I'm talking about. Though this book is boldly entitled *Everything Makes Sense*, clearly, so far, for humankind, it hasn't. These pages grant that all thinking, this thinking too, is merely a pointing, an effort to draw a clear go-that-way arrow, trusting that in the laboratory of your own being you can make the validating experiments.

Because when we're out in that field alone at night surrounded by either Something, or Nothing, we'd all like a bit more explanation.

Two primitives

A note as we begin: some of the thinking in these pages may at first seem regrettably philosophical. It's regrettable because philosophical thinking is too often merely spectating, a pointing-at, not a reporting-from. The thinking here though is not spectating and not scholarship either (a looking through the thought-lenses of other thinkers), but is instead *close-noticing*. Close-noticing sees what anyone can see when they bother to look. In that sense, these pages are nothing but a bothering to look.

Close-noticing can seem abstract but is really its opposite. Abstraction peers through the binoculars of intellect, which focus far from here and from now—as when, for instance, we consider history, that pieced-together assemblage of the past, or when we consider the mathematical conjectures of quantum theory, or when we examine life through the lens of other thinkers' thoughts. Close-noticing removes the far-focused binoculars of intellect and tries to see what is happening here and happening now. It is not an abstraction away from lived life but is instead a peering into it, and that peering, since we don't usually think that way, can seem abstract. (Phenomenology, the thought-system associated with Husserl, Heidegger, and Sartre, tried to see the world with as few presuppositions as possible, and was perhaps the first systematic effort to develop philosophy from close-noticing.) Close-noticing is witnessing existence as it is experienced. It is noticing what is happening within and without, with the fewest possible interpretive ideas screening and orienting that perception. Failure to close-notice is why we argue so much, and how opinion finds a nest in our thinking. If everyone were able to say only what they saw, everyone would be like the two guys on their honesty walk, contented shruggers. Anyway, the thinking here is generally that sort, the close-noticing type. Plus it's offered meekly and with a happy shrug. Whenever this thinking seems too philosophical, kindly imagine the thinker sighing, then wondering what's for dinner.

In the next few pages we are going to close-notice how thinking and living happen. That effort will serve us well when we begin to consider what we're doing here.

To avoid the notorious disagreements hidden in the far-noticing of generalization, we're going to start with the most basic thoughts possible, thoughts which have no penumbra of surrounding thought. We will borrow a term from philosophy here and call these thoughts our *ontological primitives*. (*Ontological* meaning having to do with existence itself, *primitive* meaning basic-most.)

So that: our first bit of close-noticing discovers that *meaning is*. Existence somehow means itself to us and does that continually, now and now and now. It's almost ridiculous to mention that meaning is, a bit like mentioning that we breathe. It's just what we are and do and doesn't require attention—which is why we usually don't think to mention it—or notice it. Meaning is the always-there stuff in which we're embedded in the way a fish is embedded in water. It's just the everywhere-and-always-stuff we're poking around in. If you walk into an empty room you can't say there's no one there because you're there. Meaning is just like that—some sort of always-there stuff. Whatever it may be—and that *whatever* is mysterious—we can at least hold that it's the isness-matrix we're all embedded in.

The meaning that presents itself to us now and now and now is different from what we think of as the meaning of life, which is a separate issue, one posed by the binoculars of intellect which wonders whether there is a point to all this poking around, a hidden substructure that we don't know about but if we did know about would delight or depress us. The thought here is simply: *everything that is, is because it means.* Even so-called meaninglessness is meaning. Meaning, we may say, is the cradle of being in which we are held.

On its surface, this claim is not extraordinary and is even a bit like Descartes's insight that since he was able to doubt, and since doubt was a form of thinking, and since thinking was a form of existence, then wonderful, he existed! A simple enough claim but also one that has electrified philosophy for centuries. The assertion here that meaning exists is as unastounding as Descartes' assertion and equally undeniable, and also, sort of offhandedly, grants that yes, if there's meaning, there's existence. But here that's beside the point. We want to know *what* meaning is, and *how* too, not whether it is. That it is is granted by—well, by its isness.

So the first primitive of this close-noticing is: meaning, which is the founding oddity of all existence.

Desire is the second primitive. It is, like meaning, discovered by close-noticing. I turn and notice a tree. How could I notice the tree without turning to look? How could I turn to look without wanting to? Everything we do or don't do, and everything we think, proceeds from desire, the push-puller within every moment of meaning. Even if I am sitting quietly beside a creek trying not to think, it is desire which holds me in place. Desire is no doubt full of nuance and hard to tease out clearly from the murk of meaning called mind, and, as will be discussed, is sometimes conscious and sometimes unconscious. But it is with us always as the current of motive force within. Beneath and in advance of every mood, attitude, and act is the force of desire. Whether we wave our hand or refrain from waving it, whether we glance or decline to glance, whether we reply or remain silent—in every moment of our existence we are in thrall to desire.

But this question: we may say, well, my heart beats, and my heart is part of me, and I don't desire that beating, so...But we don't beat our heart. Our beating heart is outside the force of conscious desire that, for instance, turns our head when we look at a tree.

Since we know desire only through meaning, then is desire just another sort of meaning? No doubt desire appears in a context of meaning, but it is interestingly different. It is a force of some kind, a pusher and puller, whereas meaning is the context of that force. We *want* our way through life and time, which is to say, through meaning. Whatever we are, we may at least hold that we are made of meaning and desire. *Meaning is the water of being in which we are suspended, and desire is the current that bears us along the river of time.*

These two elements of our being, meaning and desire, are most primitive because they have no precedent or constituent forces or notions beneath or causing them that we can directly experience. They are the bottom-most constituents of every moment of our existence. They are a sort of binary code on which everything is built. They are the stuff of being.

And they are marvelous. I look about me, and however empty the world may seem, its very emptiness means itself to me. I look about me, and however vague my wanting may be, it still persists as restlessness or discontent.

So that: we are curiously, unexpectedly, magnificently, and continually embedded in knowing and wanting, and these two are the most apparent and essential structures of being that under-stand all experience. We have discovered them by close-noticing, and it is from these two primitives that we can most usefully begin to consider the nature and truth—and perhaps the purpose—of life.

The hard problem(s)

Before we open a discussion of the hard problem, which is what contemporary philosophers lovingly call the issue of consciousness itself, it will be useful to create a distinction between consciousness and intelligence, which are often conflated as the same thing. In these pages we will separate them. Intelligence we will define as that station-of-meaning-receiving installed somewhere in our head. Its antenna of meaning-receiving, our body, feeds in the five-fingered meaning of sensation (sight, hearing, touch, smell, and taste) which enables us to notice the world outside us. Intelligence also and importantly includes the inner world and its desires. Bundle all experience, and we have what here we will name *intelligence, a compound of meaning and desire*.

The fact that sometimes this intelligence is conscious in us and sometimes this intelligence works in the dark of the unconscious (about which more later) makes it useful to consider consciousness the window or screen through which intelligence manifests—and not intelligence itself. Consciousness is conscious *of* intelligence. That's why it makes sense to refer to this sometimes-light-sometimes-dark window that sees intelligence by the name *consciousness*, and refer to the meaning and desire that it sees by the word *intelligence.* Which means that there are two hard problems. One, what's consciousness? Two, what's intelligence?

And, alas, there is even a third problem. Neither consciousness nor intelligence seem to be the whatever-it-is thing I am. I don't say, I *am* a thought, but instead I say I *have* a thought. This is not a peculiarity of language but has somehow to do with selfness, self-identity, I-ness—whatever those utterly mysterious terms may mean. (Few, if any, in the history of thought have plucked the notion of self from wonderment.)

Interesting, if a bit aside, is the fact that intelligence seems to be a property not only of the in-here stuff of my intelligence but also of the out-there stuff of the universe. The ordered world in me, my intelligence, receives order from an ordered universe, and this happens in both consciousness and unconsciousness.

Finally, this note: though in these pages we'll use the word *intelligence* for that meaning-getting-and-desiring something installed in us, it's good to note that many thinkers use the word *consciousness* to mean the same thing.

And here's an interesting oddity: the reason no one can explain intelligence is that it's always intelligence doing the explaining. Explanations, recall, are penumbra-thoughts beneath the thought being explained. The branches, leaves, and roots of the intelligence-tree are always just more unexplainable intelligence. Intelligence is always and continually the first-in-line unpenumbraed stuff of everything. If one reads widely on the subject these days in philosophical journals, or turns to the voluminous internet videos, there can be found many thinkers who speak about intelligence (which they call consciousness) with enthusiasm—and sometimes with a disconcerting confidence. They announce that of all problems available it is the hardest, and that they and their colleagues are earnestly at work on it, each morning trundling to the thought mine to extract more and more of the glistening ore of consciousness. Yet, alas, though consciousness (intelligence) is not antagonistic toward this effort, it is—and for thousands of years has been—austere, implacable, and mute.

Intelligence cannot be pried from the mine of being and inspected since the only pry bar available is intelligence itself. That's both a problem, and, as we shall see, the beginning of a solution.

The two types of meaning

At this point, it's useful to note that meaning comes in two varieties, a getting part and a holding part. First meaning arrives. Then it persists. As in: I turn and see the tree behind me. It means its being to me. That's the getting part. And when I turn away, the tree continues to mean its being as idea and memory. That's the holding part. This meaning-holding, this continuing-to-mean-being, is what creates the duration we call time. (Mark Twain: "Time is what keeps everything from happening at once.") It's also what creates that bundling of meaning we call intellect—the tree as idea when I'm no longer looking at it. And creates, as well, the disputes of generalization. (Interestingly, the power of meaning-holding is secretly part of meaning-getting. We'll get to that.)

Now then, want to witness a miracle? You're in one. Miracles are said to escape natural law, to be somehow unmoored from the tedium of cause and effect. Yet what of the mysterious natural law that creates the continuous eruption of meaning and desire that is our being? This unbroken pouring forth is the unpenumbraed and originating miracle of existence. (The term *miracle* is generally associated with divinity, but at this point it is meant only to express the unexplained—and unexplainable—isness of being.)

So that's the hard problem of modern philosophy, the consciousness problem, the what-is-all-this problem. Close-noticing has put us on the scent.

Somehow we seem to have skipped over the customary fork in philosophy between idealism and realism, realism being the view that the stuff of being is the bump-into material world, idealism being the consideration that bump-into stuff always occurs in and is known only in a field of mind. Every consideration of existence, Eastern or Western, has reached this point. Idealists favor the stuff that looks, the whatever-it-is stuff of intelligence. Realists favor the stuff that is looked at (though even they must concede that a good bit of that looked-at stuff is idea stuff—thoughts and emotions—and not just bump-into stuff). At this point, advocating the primacy of either idealism or realism is unnecessary because the two building blocks here proposed, meaning and desire, are preliminary to any position on the realism-idealism continuum, and from them we can construct a fairly complete picture of existence. Whether that picture is real or ideal, or whether those two terms lose their importance, will become evident.

Truth!

We generally think of truth as a sort of map-making, the correspondence of our thinking with what we experience. When our ideas (which are produced by meaning-holding) correspond accurately with the world's arrangement, we call them true. However much philosophy and epistemology might subtilize things, the meaning-holding sort of truth can be conceived as accurately noticing the world. So that: we say that bad ideas don't conform to the nature of the world, and true ideas do. We can build machines or dig a pit to catch a mammoth without thinking about all this, so normally we don't bother. Still, we sometimes build bad machines, and sometimes the mammoth gets away. That happens because our ideas don't always map perfectly. *Map* is, in fact, a shortcut word for *thought, existence,* and *correspond*. The mysterious power that makes us mapmakers is our mind's ability to get and hold meaning, not just from the out-there world but from the in-here world as well.

In the vast soup of existence in which we exist, meaning-holding ideas are buckets of meaning we carry about and mentally pour back and forth. They can get us to New York, catch the mammoth, and build the iPhone.

But how do those buckets get filled? They get filled by the second type of meaning, meaning-getting.

And meaning-getting creates a second type of truth.

The priest, the dinner speaker, and the murderer

Here's a tale logicians like to tell: John, the appointed dinner speaker, is late, so his buddy, a priest, takes the podium to fill in. The priest is a raconteur and tells the engaging story that when he was a young priest his first penitent confessed to a murder. John arrives, thanks the father, and, a raconteur himself, remarks that he has known the father for many years, and was, in fact, his first penitent.

Gasp.

It seems as if knowledge has been created—John's a murderer! That's because the facts of the tale were previously uncombined in a single mind. As in: you know that the first penitent was a murderer but nothing else. I know that John was the first penitent but nothing else. At that point, neither of us yet know that John is a murderer. But when we meet and confer we do know, because those two facts—known as premises—establish John's guilt. If those facts were always public there would be no *aha*. It would just be something everyone knew—John was the father's first penitent and murdered someone.

Combining uncombined premises in a single mind gives the illusion of new knowledge and has fascinated logicians, starting with Aristotle, for centuries. But if one person could know all the premises in existence, there would be nothing for that person to deduce. That person's knowledge would already be laced together in a vast fabric of thought. This is good to note since it helps clarify where the foundation of knowledge lies. It's not in the conclusions drawn from premises. It's in the premises themselves.

It's true, of course, that a single mind can know two premises, forget one, and by remembering it reach a conclusion that seems like discovery. This doesn't obviate the point—it just notices that by a single mind we mean a single moment of someone's consciousness.

The knowledge that lies within premises is not reached by deduction. And it's not the knowledge that we carry about in idea-buckets. The idea-bucket sort of knowledge is the sort we can ladle back and forth within us and between us with language. As in: *Carol, I really like elm trees.* Carol: *I like elm trees too.* How did our idea buckets get filled with elmness? We experienced an elm (whether in a book or a park doesn't matter here) and somehow got and held elmness within us. This getting-of-elm-meaning is prior to language, *otherwise there would be nothing for language to name.*

Meaning-getting is always preliminary to meaning-holding and is the source of all intelligence. How it happens is utterly mysterious. That it happens is utterly commonplace.

A good term for the meaning-getting that creates intelligence is *intuition*. The word comes from the Latin, *in* (meaning *within*) plus *tueor* (meaning *to look at*), so it's a looking that happens inside us and fits the use of the word as the source of meaning within the psyche. We sometimes reserve the word intuition for special depth of insight, but here we are urging its more foundational sense, the initial and primary operation of receiving-meaning. All meaning arises that way and only gets languaged (held in idea buckets) after that arising. Another good term for that sort of knowledge is *impression,* since intuitions are the impressing-of-meaning onto the stuff of intelligence. They are the *something-that-arises-and-means*.

Now this: in an interesting sense, even ideas, which are the holding part of intelligence, are forms of intuition (meaning-getting), since there is within them, unnoticed and usually unimportant to notice, a continuous gettingness now and now and now as they are held in consciousness. For that reason, *intuition, the meaning-getting aspect of existence, is the continuous and ever-present matrix in which all meaning, ideas included, is suspended*. It is the *Logos,* the foundation of all intelligence, and really is another way of noticing that meaning simply is, now and now and now.

Meaning-getting is the initiating miracle of everything.

Deduction, conjecture, and Descartes' farmer pal

Deduction holds unquestioned premises, and its conclusions are accompanied by a sense of certainty. Conjecture is different. Conjecture also holds premises and reaches conclusions, but its premises are held lightly in the palm, like nervous birds, and are granted the freedom to fly away at any moment. The conclusions of conjecture are tentative. Deduction asserts. Conjecture wonders. Conjecture is a form of guessing and is what scientists do. And mechanics and scuba divers. The scientist conjectures that the bacteria are eating the agar. The mechanic conjectures there must be an undiscovered bolt holding that plate in place. The scuba diver conjectures there might be a moray eel in that narrow cave. The scientist can't see the bacteria feed, the mechanic hasn't located the bolt, and the diver hasn't seen an eel, but all are full of conjecture. And ah, the bacteria have grown, the mechanic discovers the bolt, and that's a sneaky eel. Useful.

Conjecture is another term for what philosophers have referred to by the word *induction*, meaning a reasoning from prior experience (the sun has risen a million times so it's going to rise tomorrow). Giving it that name, though, implies it's a brother of deduction, so the word *conjecture* is better, since it points toward the secret in all idea knowledge: *even our seemingly infallible deductions are really forms of conjecture.* That's because the premises on which deduction depends arise from the first and only source of meaning, which is meaning-getting, our intuition, our moment-by-moment comprehension of the now. And, alas, this comprehension forever wavers like heat lines in the desert of consciousness.

The feeling of certainty depends on ignoring the meaning-mystery contained in every premise. Though this ignoring is natural and even essential for normality, it's still a form of ignoring, which is, oh well, a form of ignorance.

Is John a murderer? Only if the report that he confessed to the father is true, and also that he confessed truthfully. If we didn't see him do it, we have to wander a trail of believing to think him guilty. But since meaning arrives only through intuition, and since intuitions can be fallible (the railroad tracks don't meet in the distance), where's certainty? Alas, nowhere. Certainty is merely felt satisfaction and never something inherent in meaning. When I swing my feet out of bed each morning, how do I know the floor will still be there? How do I know I'll be married to the same woman? Many philosophers (Descartes, Hume, and others) have fascinated us by pointing out the conjectural nature of what-we-think-we-know. It was this uncertainty in knowing that Immanuel Kant said woke him from his dogmatic slumber to try to answer Hume and re-steady the ship of knowledge-getting. He left a tide of arguers in his wake.

How meaning-impressions arise and from where (and even why) is part of the gigantic *meaning-is* mystery. Intelligence is. And we are that. Somehow. The *somehow* issues from simple close-noticing. When we try to explore the penumbra or foundation of meaning—that is, to explain it—the handle we attempt to seize meaning with always turns out to be more meaning. Meaning can be explained by—well, damn—nothing whatever. Meaning is the context of everything. And utterly without an explanatory penumbra.

Meaning's origin, meaning-getting, is not only mysterious, but maddeningly unreliable—railroad tracks and fallible memory. It's all we have though—and is why argument about the nature of the world gets heated. And, incidentally, why we like reason so much. We'll get to that.

We don't normally notice the arising and persisting of meaning, or its uncertainty, because the second element of existence, desire, keeps us occupied. We are mostly, often desperately, busy with mammoths and iPhones. If Descartes had rushed out to his farmer pal and exclaimed, listen up, Josef! I just figured out that we actually do exist because, get this, even thinking about whether we exist means, hey, we must exist, since thinking can only happen in existence! Wow, hunh? Josef, a good-hearted fellow, nods, smiles, flicks the reins, and says, nice thought, Rene.

Lots of—actually almost all of—Western philosophy, and Eastern too, is this sort of thing, a rushing into the farmer's field with insights that don't assist in the plowing. It's the mind making maps of a world it can't see but imagines. It's the mind attempting to prove that consciousness exists or doesn't, that God exists or doesn't, that we should be good or who cares? These suppositions were inevitable after mankind had language and time to think. One guy on the corner could shout, watch out, everyone, God's angry and about to send a plague, and another guy on another corner (sometimes with an army behind him) could shout back, there's no God, let's loot the granary. Civilization gets messy and needs a skeleton of thought for support.

So far we have this: meaning-full intuitions arise in and flow through intelligence, which is both the getter and holder of this meaning (knowledge). Even if we are inclined to capitalize the *i* of the word *intuition* (or the *k* of the word *knowledge*) to indicate its august station as meaning's fundamental dispenser, we must still grant that the genesis of the meaning we receive through intelligence is utterly mysterious.

Here's why reason has an important place in human life. After we assemble our intuitive premises by the marvel of meaning-getting, then note intuition's meagerness and deceptiveness, we can employ reason, which is meaning-holding, to expose contradictions. The poets tell us that the ability to live with self-contradiction is healthy and courageous, but logical contradiction always signals error, plus builds bad iPhones.

So that: we live in a mysterious and continuously-erupting matrix of meaning, and the train of connected meaning which we call explanation rests and ends on a void. Mind looks for what works and goes from there. Deduction, sometimes called reason, adds no new knowledge and only seems to by combining previously uncombined premises in a single mind. Its use is in combing for contradictions. If in a single moment of consciousness one mind knew all the facts there would be nothing for that mind to deduce. Finally, the substance of knowing is always meaning-getting, which is intuition, which is what has always made scientists, mechanics, scuba divers, and plowmen good at their jobs.

For centuries, the light within these insights has attracted philosophers like moths, particularly today's philosophers of science. Though it's irritating that mankind is suspended over an abyss of uncertainty, it's also fascinating, since we are still able to create not only marvelous fabrics of thought but marvelous gadgets too.

Modern philosophers of science have devised an offset that deals with the uncertainty dilemma within conjecture. They call this offset *inference to the best explanation* (also probabilistic or Baysian thinking, after its originator, Thomas Bayes), which grants that, okay, the final truth is unknowable, but it's still more useful to guess that it's heat energy, not devils, that boils water. That way we can build nuclear reactors and don't have to paste pictures of Jesus on the towers. (It's not the time for science versus God, but we'll get there—and without the versus.) The doctrine of inference to the best explanation is, at bottom, an admission, a shrug, an admonition to press-on-regardless in best-we-can-do knowing.

An admission, an apology, and an encouragement

The apology is for the above bit of thoughty bush-hogging, which so far may seem like throat-clearing. That's also the admission. But throat-clearing, especially today with its cacophony of contending voices, is needed for clear thinking. The throat-clearing here is mind-clearing. Now that our minds are clear, we can begin to approach the real hard problem, not the revered hard problem of philosophers (consciousness), but the problem of what-is-good-to-do-all-day. And so we return to

Desire, and, hugely importantly, free will

We have established that every act done with what we call conscious will is done by following desire. Not only are we enmeshed in meaning, but we are led through the matrix of meaning by the bridle rope of desire. We seem to be free to choose our path through life, but hidden in the structure of choice is an invisible and utter bondage.

Some of the modern thinking around this topic involves neuroscience and the idea that the mind is a phenomenon of the physical brain, a cause-and-effect mechanism resulting from the electrical push-pull of molecular matter. Thus the mind too must be a cause-and-effect mechanism. Some thinkers, lamenting this bondage, appeal to the ideas of quantum mechanics, since that field postulates randomness at the core of material existence, a fact which they hold somehow rescues us from considering the will as entirely determined. But that postulate doesn't succeed in saving freedom of choice, since the randomness they applaud as the rescuer of freedom has no sway in the theater of choice, the phenomenal inner chamber where decision appears.

But what of the neurological assertion that the push-pull of chemistry in our material brains creates a cause-and-effect bondage? The protests of some thinkers hoping to rescue freedom is that so far we can only notice correlation between brains and thinking and have no clear understanding of the causation between those poles. Causation, they assert, clearly goes both ways. I take a pill and feel less pain. I want to raise my finger and do.

Yet free will can be seen to be an illusion long before we need to puzzle about molecular bumping or the correlation between matter and thought. In what we call free will there has always been an infinite regress discoverable by close-noticing.

Chocolate or vanilla?

I'll take chocolate.

Why?

I like it.

Did you choose to like it?

Ah.

Thus, as we stand before the ice cream counter, the hesitation we call choice is only a *sounding for preference* that waits to see which desire is strongest and will prevail. It is one of the foundational marvels of human life that the bondage of so-called choice is unavailable to experience—we'll make more of this eventually—and is available to thought only in reflection, only in a looking-back at the inner action of choosing. Then only can we understand—though never actually experience—that preference is not now or ever free, but always imposed from the matrix of desire that inhabits us.

Much of our doing arises and even continues beneath our notice, as in: I absentmindedly scratch an itch. Such acts do not involve conscious desire and thus do not challenge or support our notion of freedom. But when choice occurs with a deliberative pause—hummm, chocolate or vanilla? or hummm, should I use 24-inch or 16-inch centers in the stud wall?—that pause, when I consider it after the fact, seems to show that my mental consideration of alternatives means I could have chosen other than I did. But whichever flavor or wall design I choose, however much I may have weighed choosing the other, and however complicated and nuanced by fields of thought was my consideration, the decision that prevailed prevailed because the desire for that flavor or design was strongest—and its strength was not chosen but imposed. Choice follows the strongest desire and does not create that desire's strength. It accepts it. However tangled the thicket of consideration from which wanting emerges, the desires that emerge and become choice are always the strongest. And compel a perfunctory acceptance.

Finally, this last gasp objection: you like chocolate best, you explain, because you chose to like it best. We needn't confront the psychological impossibility of such a decision here. We merely need to ask whether you chose to choose to like it best. And then if you chose to choose to choose to like it best. That's the infinite regress. And no one stands before the ice cream counter infinitely long.

So that: choice is an illusion and not free, and, however delayed and nuanced by the hesitation of thinking, it is always completely determined by desire, which is not chosen but compelled.

Still, if you complain to a wise man that, alas, all are in utter bondage, the wise man—though he well knows what you say is true—is likely to clap your knee and say, *c'mon, brother, admit it, you are free*! This is because, despite the conclusions of thinking which demonstrate that we are entirely bound in the prison of desire, we are likewise bound in the inescapable theater of choice. The process of consideration we engage in before choice, however illusory, is an impossible-to-dispense-with feeling-state. There are no fatalist pedestrians in heavy traffic.

But this disturbing consideration: recognizing our bondage to desire seems to violate normality. If everyone is bound by desire they did not create or choose, then who is guilty? Who responsible? Are you telling me, sir, that the villain who murdered my mother is not guilty of a heinous crime and worthy of punishment! If we admit that each of us flails through existence pushed and pulled by thrust-on desire, can society be effectively ordered? Is all regret illegitimate? The ordinary idea-buckets of ethics and morality will not do here, since those buckets contain the crudity of *should* and *ought,* those ancient, implacable clubs that ignore entirely the desire-fix we are all in. We need more delicate thinking.

We'll find that thinking in what's to come. When we do, we will find that that thinking, instead of disturbing normality, enriches it. Our hidden bondage may be fatal to ideas of right and wrong, but it leaves intact the far more important notions of good and bad. Reunderstanding will is a massive reorientation—with massive consequences for society and for the psyche.

Now a few more preliminaries.

The marvelous consciousness-unconsciousness junction

When we try to hold consciousness, the *on* light, and unconsciousness, the *off* light, in our palm and carefully note their characteristics, we see that we can do this only for one of these poles, consciousness, because only consciousness is experienceable. Unconsciousness we know only by conjecture. It is the impenetrable darkness from which, we conjecture, all being rises and falls away. No doubt its conjecture is entirely natural to our being—as natural, in fact, as seeing a person behind a counter and feeling assured that his or her bottom half, which is not experienced in consciousness, is as existent as the visible top half. In my consciousness there is no tree. I turn and one appears. From where does it appear? It appears from a *somewhere* that I formerly was not conscious of. In these pages, we name that somewhere the unconscious.

Philosophy likes to raise its hand here to ask for epistemological details. That questioning began thousands of years ago and continues still. This discussion nods respectfully—but has business elsewhere.

This conception of the unconscious is, in other words, a way of noting that everything we are not currently conscious of we are unconscious of. This means, of course, that for human beings most of existence is entirely and unfathomably unconscious.

This idea of the unconscious is different from the psychologists' idea, which is mostly a way of conjecturing the existence of a holding place of desires that are unknown to us. The conception here includes those desires, no doubt, but also includes the no-tree state that follows the tree state, and in fact all being of which we are not currently conscious.

While we cannot directly experience the unconscious, we can get close to seeing it in action by performing a simple thought experiment. Answer any question with a spoken sentence—for instance, what did you do so far today? You might say, "Well, I woke up, went to the kitchen—quietly, since everyone was sleeping—and made a cup of coffee, which I enjoyed sitting in my chair by the window, then thought, time to get dressed, so I have to wake him up, so, oh well, I went back to the bedroom and touched his shoulder and..."

As you watch yourself speak that sentence, or any sentence, you have no consciously present idea of the sentence's grammar or how you intend to phrase it or when you intend to end it, yet it fountains from your being with masterful sense and order. Everything we do and have ever done is like that, an intelligent unrolling from the dark of the unconscious now and now and now. The meaning in speech issues from our being with full order and sense toward a perfectly grammatical end (usually) so that as we begin speaking a sentence it makes sense to conjecture that there must be an unconscious knowing somewhere in our intelligence. We have no foreknowledge of the precise words and tone of our sentence—where we will pause, where add emphasis—yet in speaking it we end up—quite eerily —making sense. We might think of sentence-saying as traveling along the span of the sentence as it unrolls in time so that sentences are the unconscious, somehow-prepared tracks of meaning we follow. But since we never experience the past or future but are always suspended in the present, a more accurate way to conceive of sentence-saying is that we are continually installed in a now-bound consciousness-cart, and sentences are tracks of intelligence that flow beneath us from darkness to light to darkness.

And this too: not only do sentences unroll beneath our consciousness-cart, but everything else does too. Our entire being is a track of intelligence that unrolls from the unconscious into consciousness and back to unconsciousness, and always now.

All this becomes evident in the simplicity of close-noticing.

We brought up the dual nature of our embeddedness in consciousness and unconsciousness to help us understand choice. Only by understanding our existence as occurring at the intersection of those poles can we begin to understand the nature of our lived experience—and also understand the resolution of our no-freedom fix. Clarity here will not only illumine the act of choice, but will lead us past the blindness of right and wrong to the land of good and bad. And begin to open the deepest secret in human experience.

How does the conscious-unconsciousness junction create the illusion of free will? It does this by concealing, in the dark of unconsciousness, the desires that bloom and flow through us in the now, in consciousness. Wave your hand. Or don't. Whichever you did, the desire that prompted or inhibited the action is dark *at the moment of action or inaction*. A feeling of assent accompanies some desires, and we permit their expression. A feeling of dissent inhibits others. Further, that feeling of permission or inhibition is itself not free, since it too is a feeling conditioned by desire. And the bottom-most desire, the energy-giving impulse that prompts action or inaction, *is always dark*.

I am overweight and decide to diet. A donut appears. If I push it away it is because the desire to lose weight prevailed. If I don't, it is because the desire for pleasure prevailed (or the irritated desire not to live as the prisoner of other people's evaluations). Choice sounds for preference, and this sounding, this sometimes delay at the consciousness-unconsciousness junction as our preferences emerge and clarify, is what we term choice. Unless someone has a gun to our head and orders us to choose chocolate, we consider choice free. But when we properly understand the act we call *choice*, we see that the assent or inhibition that accompanies choice is entirely desire-bound. When we refuse the donut, it's not because we chose to want to diet. If we accept it, it's not because we chose to want pleasure. One desire muscled its way past others because that desire had more strength. Every choice-deliberation ends in a moment of decision in which the strongest desire compels us, and, since that compelling is always dark and out of the keeping of consciousness, it seems free.

Understanding the bondage of freedom produces a massive—and inspiring—reconsideration of human life.

The plan of the next several pages

We have mentioned that some desires *muscle their way* past others. This insight leads to an appreciation of the strength of desire and is critical to understanding choice—and, as we will see, to understanding how to live. To get to that though, we'll first need to open some surrounding ideas.

First, we'll consider the nature of the ego, that always-present-but-always-elusive centralizing station of intelligence that is somehow suspended between consciousness and unconsciousness. Then we'll examine the oddity, and inevitability, of blame and guilt, those implacable twins that always squeeze through the door when we misunderstand choice.

Following that, we encounter the two blustery doctrines that oppose, obstruct, and even prevent the close-notice of lived life, namely physicalism and neo-Darwinism. Then comes a discussion of introspection and finally—after an encounter with two Mississippi detectives—we'll be ready to more deeply unravel the inner world.

And at last arrive at the central conjecture of these pages.

Where ego I go

Some desires flow through ego but are not thought of as egotistical. These produce offhand actions—brushing our teeth, sitting down, standing up—and ego here can be considered a centralizing station of desire, the inner pivot we experience the world from. On the other hand, some desires create, craft, and maintain our *front self*, the CEO of our seeing-and-doing desire-station.

So what's this front self? It is the conscious station of being we present to the world and ourselves. The most elementary inquiry (the chocolate-vanilla thought experiment) reveals that this front self is not, as it claims to itself and the world, in control of its being but is instead infested by desires and thoughts, which issue, one after the other, from the darkness of its unconscious. Though dark to the front self, this back-there-always unconscious self is possessed of a large and intricate intelligence. After all, it knows just what to promote or repress to keep things in order. (In neurosis it stagnates. In psychosis it fails.)

The back-there-always dark ego creates in the front self a complex of pride, self-justification, illusion, distorted memory, grudge, despair, blame, guilt, hypocrisy, sentiment, callousness, pretense, modesty, vengeance—and also gratitude, delight, hope, optimism, and kindness. In short, these parts, dark and light together, produce the continually self-tying knot of being that creates our who, our me, our first-named doing-thinking-emoting person. Our front and back selves construct a kind of junkyard boat, a pieced-together-from-scraps vessel that is launched onto the storm-tossed sea of an existence it little understands and continually misunderstands. This ego-boat has a thousand goals, but it's bottom-most purpose is to not sink, to not be humiliated, depressed, embarrassed, neglected, scorned, or made to look stupid. When it's successful (according to its own estimation), it feels superior. When it doesn't, it feels inferior. To whom does it feel superior or inferior? To other ego-vessels, which, like it, are floating and foundering in the sea of reputation. Whether we praise reputation as our most precious possession or scorn it as dependency, the ego's attention is helplessly fastened on the barometer of esteem. For that, the philosopher Sartre had a point—hell is other people.

The dark part of the ego, which psychologists name the personal unconscious and sometimes the shadow self, is made of tendrilled, twining, hard-to-separate and hard-to-see desires. These desires create the front self's foundation—and impenetrability. The ego's front self walks on stilts buried in its shadow where live the dark groomers and suppressors that create the ego's notorious craftiness. Their role is to somehow, anyhow, produce in the ego enough assurance, confidence, and get-up-and-go to get through the days and years of a life. Every psychological therapist worthy of that name has two patients simultaneously. One is the front self the patient is conscious of. The other is the shadow self beneath the patient's front self. As Carl Jung noted in *The Undiscovered Self,* failure to experience the patient's unseen shadow self reduces therapy to advice.

In both its conscious and unconscious parts, the ego is merely an invisible coach whose sole job is to select players (desires) that crowd forward from the bench of the unconscious, avid to get in the game. The players jostle and elbow for the coach's attention because they know there are plenty of other players eager for the ball. This ego-coach is thought to be a commander but is really a servant that must and does select for play the most powerful desire-soldier able to push its way forward and present its claim. However subtle and seemingly intelligent, egotism is essentially an ordering of the soldiery of desire. Where the strongest always wins.

A by-note: the structure of egotism seems to be uniquely human and not so much a part of the animal or plant kingdoms. It takes vast intelligence to navigate even clumsily through the welter of our own and other people's impressions and expectations, and it is likely that only our fullest human consciousness is up to the task. (Dogs are on the way, though, as when, for instance, they slump in sheepishness after being scolded for gobbling your untended sandwich.)

The psyche is a mass of desire-layers that support and repress each other, and its shifting matrix makes living giantly subtle. I refuse dessert, then notice someone noticing my refusal and note too, and happily, their jealousy and admiration. Though she is contentedly married, I tell her how nice she looks, and she, though she is contentedly married, responds with flirting pleasure.

We sometimes consider the ego's chief work to be self-confidence, which we may describe as desire fountaining smoothly from the self (in both its unconscious and conscious parts). Yet smoothness of desiring is hardly the height of value. A handsome movie star enters the ballroom and contentedly receives his accustomed notice, blithely ignorant or even indifferent that the room contains three Nobel laureates. We are aware that confidence is not, by itself, the essence of value, since we revere dignity, which is confidence accompanied by understanding. The word we use for confidence without understanding is *cocky*.

It's worth noting at this point that our pushed-along-by-desire egotism is notoriously invisible. That's because desire, and, for that matter, all thinking, is notoriously invisible. That's why considering the ego and its crowd of desires can seem hopelessly conceptual. At least at first. Eventually though, we can begin, through simple close-noticing, to see desire in action. We can more and more clearly experience, despite desire's invisibility, its powerful and evident thingness. Though we cannot experience the unfreedom of choice, we can be conscious of the desire that compels us to action. Admittedly, it sometimes takes a bit of special attention to pry invisible desire from its hiding place, but that is not intellectual work. It is the work of close-noticing. By resolute looking, we can experience the thingness of desire—which means, however slippery and hard to parse desire may be, it can be truly or falsely mapped.

Now then: we began with meaning and desire as our most basic, close-noticed, ontological primitives, revealed free will as a sounding for preference, moved on to considering the consciousness-unconsciousness junction, and finally described the dark-light ego as our natural station. Forward now to

The durable weirdness of blame

Blame is an emotional force, a finger-pointing feeling-state that takes its instruction from thwarted desire. You forgot to close the door again! In blaming you, I ignore entirely your helplessness in forgetting to close the door or perhaps your helpless willfulness in wanting to have more fresh air or even your helpless purpose to give me offense. In short, I ignore your bondage in desire. Guilt is the brother of blame, since when I neglect to close the door I can feel guilty only if I overlook my own desire bondage.

Both blame and guilt are themselves a species of desire, an impossible—but entirely natural—desire that things be otherwise. Exposing the necessity within desire seems to make the customary ordering of human relationships through blame and punishment unhappily unjustifiable.

Here there is prickly terrain indeed, and we must go forward barefooted (without presupposition) to feel the nuance of this understanding. What can it mean to live in and with the truth that all are bound? This is a fraught idea, since if we know the truth of our bondage as an idea only, as a conclusion reached by the mereness of thinking, we must witness Ronald, that rascal, once again forget to close the door and must then be compelled to deny in ourselves the righteous indignation such selfishness demands! What a fix, to recognize through thinking the unintelligence of blame and yet find that unintelligence artificial to our emotional center. Plus, if Ronald defends himself by declaring he is not free, we mainly want to throttle him—which, says smiling Ronald, is more of the same mistake.

To understand the solution to this emotional impasse we must examine the mechanism of desire itself, because it is desire that creates the acts we feel responsible for and desire that sanctions the blame that scolds. We must examine the arising of desire at the junction of consciousness and unconsciousness. We find that there, as desire manifests within us, it exposes only the tip of its nose and never its full body to view. Desire's tip-of-the-nose manifestation in the act of choice is what makes the feeling of freedom possible—and natural. Only by hiding its power is desire able to disguise itself as free instead of revealing its authentic structure—as coercion from the dark of the unconscious.

The incompleteness of our seeing is a kind of instantaneous and incessant amnesia and is what makes the feeling of freedom possible. We discover our bondage only through reflection and never in the moment of doing. Which is why *character* is important to good living and the good ordering of society. Character can be understood as the *inner hall where desire must present itself before it is permitted satisfaction.* It's the home of what we vaguely, and with often tedious self-satisfaction, call *conscience.*

For instance, chocolate pudding. Ah well, I think not. For instance, a lovely woman to woo. But she is a happily married mother. Conscience is inner consideration, and not some force alien or antagonistic to desire. It is, in fact, desire itself. A larger, deeper, wider desire appraises the lesser desire brought before it and judges its worth. I love pudding, but, more deeply, I want to remain healthy and thin. I long for intimacy with a woman but, more deeply, I don't want to destroy Sally's happiness.

A problem notorious to conscience, of course, is that, since it is made of desire itself, it is maddeningly unintelligent. The Nazis ask where my brother is hiding, and, since I want never to lie, I tell them. I refuse to steal a loaf of bread, and my child starves. Here conscience cleaved to honesty and ignored or was unaware of the deeper desires of loyalty and love. We approve of conscience (desire evaluating desire) in the case of Sally and the ice cream but not in the case of the brother and the bread.

This inner hall of character and conscience is the evaluation that some act or thought, in ourselves or in another, is either approved or sanctioned. But since we have shown that all action that issues from the conscious-unconsciousness junction, our always standing-place, is compelled by desire-following, how can the sanction of guilt and blame be legitimate?

It cannot.

But even when blame and guilt are exposed as ontological errors, character and conscience will continue as humanity's guides. But only when that guidance issues from a better understanding of the psyche will conscience cease to be a clumsy hoeing in the delicate garden of being. Interestingly, blame and guilt are frauds for the same reason that modesty is a fraud—they have not discovered the depths on which they stand and from which they issue.

Though conscience is fraught with complication, its structure points conclusively and importantly to the fact that in human life *desire is layered.* And has sizes. Every strong thinker throughout history has contemplated how humanity might have better desires. And wondered what makes some desires better than others. It is the *sizing of desire* that gives us clues about the nature of the universe itself and helps us expose and understand not only the error inherent in blame and guilt, but also the deep structure of the psyche.

An exploration of those depths is coming, but first we must dispense with the two most popular—and mesmerizing—conceptual frameworks currently on offer for existence-explaining. These twin thought systems are *physicalism* and *Darwinism*. As we will find, they are not particularly close-noticed bodies of thought. Still, though we must eventually set them aside as incomplete, they have been useful and even necessary in the development of humankind.

The doctrine of physicalism

Science, that exuberant explainer-destroyer, attempts to grapple the vagueness of existence to earth by a doctrine currently called *physicalism* (a more modern term for materialism). We have previously noted that there is a vogue among contemporary thinkers to call discussions of consciousness the hard problem. The irony is that consciousness is hard for scientists to account for because they have for several hundred years been convinced that the best map of existence is drawn by considering the universe as material (whatever that might mean—and about that physicalists are enthusiastic guessers) and that what we call consciousness is a somehow-emergent rider on waves of matter (however that might happen—and physicalists have no guesses about that). This is not unexpected, since matter bits are, after all, the most evident and measurable parts of existence. No wonder, then, that physicists, chemists, and biologists have come to ply their trade in that surround.

This system of thought works great for building iPhones but is flaccid in accounting for emotional states. Using an iPhone to call your grandmother is one thing. Wanting to is entirely another. Still, as neurologists examine the brain and find areas of gray matter excited by this or that emotion, they confidently posit that that excitation caused the emotion. Through brain scanning, they have even recently noted a microsecond delay between a neurological firing and a consequent thought or feeling, leading some scientists to greater comfort in asserting that the firing, since it was preliminary by a few microseconds, caused the conscious response. (Other scientists note that unconscious thought could be preliminary to the observed firing.) Still, some neurologists, a minority so far, wonder whether thinking causes brain excitation instead of the reverse, since, after all, it's undeniable that causation in the brain goes back and forth. Pills can change your mood, and you can blink if you want to.

Whether the mind functions the brain or the brain functions the mind can't be decided from neurological watching. The interplay between what we call physical and what we call mental is subtle indeed. (Philosophy calls this the mind-body problem.) What is undeniable is that the intelligence inherent in existence cannot be purely material, that is, a substance independent of, but somehow productive of, mind. The stuff of mind is clearly distinct, however mysteriously, from the stuff of matter. Even if a computer (a material thing) could display the answer to every question of fact (the capital of Bolivia, the length of the Nile), it could not itself understand what it had displayed. One philosopher, John Serles, captured this in a much-discussed thought experiment called the Chinese box, in which someone sat inside a room (or box) and received Chinese script from one slot, consulted a Chinese-English dictionary, and fed the English translation out of the other slot. For the people outside, the mysterious box seemed to be able to understand and translate Chinese. The fellow inside didn't though. He was just matching symbols up. Like a computer.

When you think of a computer as billions of on-off electronic circuits, you realize that even if the computer can display "Washington is the capital of Bolivia," it has no idea what that means. Meaning arrives when we read its statement and think it not only wrong, but likely infested with arrogant colonialism. In the two-part structure of existence, the thing seen and the seeing thing, meaning happens only in the seeing part. Meaning happens in minds.

Some argue that the cloud of electronic connections surrounding each item displayed on a computer screen is intelligence. They claim that the on-off firing of electronic circuits in a computer is just like the firing of neurons in a human brain. The more detailed neurological maps become, the more some computer scientists become convinced that computers must be able to think, if not yet, eventually.

But however much neurology notes that this or that area of brain activates when this or that thought occurs, and however much neurology smudges the distinction between matter and mind by substituting the term *brain* for mind—as in, brain receives inputs from the optical nerve and creates the landscape you see—it is helpless to account for intelligence (meaning) itself. Matter is something—one of many somethings—that intelligence is conscious of. Intelligence is meaning, and meaning occurs only in mind. A crowd of electronic synapses in either a computer or a brain are not meaning. Only intelligence means.

No doubt matter and meaning are intricately entwined. No doubt there's lots of correlation between brains and meaning, but explaining meaning through neural sparking is like explaining a basketball game through the stretching of tendons. No doubt the fizzing within our brains is intimately related to what we are thinking, but neurons, molecules, atoms, and quantum bits are not that thinking. Considering meaning and brain activity as equivalents violates the law of identity.

Still, for more than 200 years the physicalist thought-system has mesmerized science. This is not merely due to looking where the light is good—at the material world—and not merely because looking closely at matter has produced the extraordinary wealth of the modern world. It is also because materialism has helped free humanity from the perversity of myth and superstition. And that's a boon not easily forsaken.

The above seems to dismiss in one paragraph the notion currently called strong AI, a body of thought that presumes some sort of intelligence possible to computers, which someday might become more than the one-thing-after-another firing of electronic circuits—in short, become conscious. Really, the question is this: could the whatever-it-is stuff of intelligence, so far embodied only, as we conjecture, in living things, one day embody itself in machines? Could the whatever-it-is of intelligence somehow transfer itself to man-made electrical circuits? In that case, however possible or impossible, it still makes sense to suppose that intelligence itself would not be those circuits, but instead be the whatever-it-is ghost of intelligence that has come to inhabit them.

We may empathize with those who hold that electrical circuits themselves *are* this intelligence, since it is the same two and two make four proposition that has mesmerized neurologists. Our brains are electronic matter, right? And we are intelligent, right? Ergo, the electronic matter of machines might someday become intelligent. This is beguiling thinking, but it includes the odd, and evidently, for some, hard-to-discover error of not noticing that the electrical pulses arising from any computer system are not, in fact, meaning at all until they reach a mind. All computer displays and instructions—calibrations, guidance circuits, chess moves—are not meaning unless someone is conscious of them, and then the meaning is not in those displays and instructions but in the apprehending mind. Meaning itself, which is to say, intelligence itself, is solely a property of mind.

It's simple to see that by limiting our thinking to the physical alone we cannot get to meaning and mind. It is just as simple to see that if we start with mind the physical is included, because it's part of what the mind sees.

The everything-is-matter view mesmerizes by convincing physicalists that thinking itself is, however mysteriously, produced by the matter of the brain, and so the only useful effort of thought is to discover which matter locus (the corpus callosum! microtubules!) is responsible for producing consciousness. This assumption, this invisible—and, for physicalists, undeniable—explanatory mind-lens is like a glued-on pair of intellect-binoculars its wearer cannot notice and hence cannot remove without a kind of psychic surgery.

Of course, the being-captured-by-an-explanatory-idea-before-thinking-begins problem is the plight of most thinking and is why the effort here is to cut away the accumulated dross of unexamined thought and get at the bottom-most bottom of our experience. Which is why we began with meaning and desire. To the binocular-wearers among us, these pages are a gentle, if unhopeful, reminder that intelligence is first and foremost a seeing. Which minds do.

All philosophical and man-on-the-street thinking has, since the beginning of thought, noticed that there are two poles in existence—one, the stuff seen, and two, the stuff seeing. That the concentration of modern science on the first pole has obscured and even denied the second is marvelous but understandable, like watching a puppet show and forgetting the puppeteer. Then is forgetfulness of the second pole of being, the seeing pole, tantamount to ignoring half of existence?

As we shall see, forgetfulness of seeing ignores far more.

No doubt the existence of meaning, of intelligence, is a hard problem indeed. It is, in fact, the primary problem of all philosophy. It's the what-is-all-this question that drives us to that lonely field at night.

So that's physicalism, the powerful stuff-noticing, gadget-making system of thought that leads, well, to stuff and gadgets. It produces marvels but is limited by its stuff-and-gadget approach to knowledge. It tries to imagine intelligence, where meaning lives, as the bumping about of matter bits, without noticing that noticing itself (intelligence) is the matrix in which everything that exists is embedded.

It should be noted that those committed to a belief in strong AI will have read the above thoughts with building exasperation because giving up the hope that machines may one day become conscious seems to give up a future of vast technological adventure. It can be offered, however, that understanding understanding is a compensation, and adventure, far vaster.

Finally this: the reason for the resistance of many scientists to any interpretative scheme other than physicalism is understandable. It has been science—careful thinking from evidence—that has dispelled the injurious notions of priests and shamans and freed mankind from prejudice, illusion, myth, and superstition. Scientific destruction of belief has left us achy and unmoored, no doubt, but what to do? If the universe is empty of ultimate meaning, apples are still sweet. Perhaps, we are, like the earth, or like a melody, immortal enough. Do these thoughts console? Or do they merely pull a cover over despair and offer courage as consolation? Is courage the only dike against being drowned in meaninglessness?

Come along.

Darwin, that troubled and troubling genius

Physicalism's twin is the theory of evolution (constructed by Charles Darwin), one of the most trenchant and persuasive explanatory systems to arise in the modern world. Now that molecular biology has arrived (genes, DNA, protein, etc.), the theory is termed neo-Darwinism, but the thought-system is still committed to the idea that random mutation through time produces new life forms which survive or perish according to their fitness. Life, the theory holds, arose naturally from chemical debris, not by a wave of God's wand. Then, after somehow achieving consciousness, life moved progeny by progeny through advancing grades of form.

This account, made particular and convincing by Darwin, but supposed by many previous thinkers (and simultaneously by his contemporary, Alfred Wallace) seems undeniable in the face of the paleontological evidence. The earth is a graveyard of developing species. Though neo-Darwinism addresses the issue of consciousness only indirectly, it does posit that the bottom-most desire driving consciousness is survival, which is to say, the power for any biological entity to last long enough to produce progeny. Its thinking has created the field of evolutionary psychology, and that field of thought has produced notions about our inner nature. Enthusiasm for evolutionary psychology has diminished, but we'll consider it, since it illumines certain problems in all psychology. First though, let's consider how the theory of evolution fares in the materiality unknown to Darwin, the world of molecules and genes that supposedly produce the required random mutation through time.

Darwin had only to recognize that variation happens and, given the vastness of time, he thought it likely that these variations could produce more and more resilient life forms as those life forms produced better and better adapted progeny.

He did not wonder much about life's beginnings, except to speculate in one of his letters that life might have begun in some warm pond. He was troubled mostly by the Cambrian explosion, an eruption of forms without paleontological evidence of prior forms. (He hoped and assumed those missing forms would be found—they haven't been.) We also know (also from his letters) that he was troubled by the power of his explanation, since it seemed to obviate the need to posit a supporting and creating divinity, thus leading to the repudiation of most high-minded thought systems.

But today, as neo-Darwinism has sought to integrate the discoveries of molecular biology, the objections to Darwin's theory are many-fronted. First, given the now-evident complexity of genetic information in DNA—our genome has around 23,000 genes, and some life forms have far more—if the mutation in these genes were purely random, workable life forms would be astronomically unlikely. Francis Crick, one of the co-discoverers of DNA, so much lamented the impossibility of random mutation producing a living being that he conjectured that life must have arisen on another planet and been seeded on earth by an asteroid, a theory now named *panspermia*. (Presumably, noted his critics, the miracle of life originated on a planet with an infinitude of warm ponds for life-sparking.)

Mathematicians assure us that simple combinatorial calculations (factorial mathematics) applied to gene biology yield exponential results far greater than the number of particles in the universe (estimated at 10 to the 81st power). Recent work in molecular biology has demonstrated that in order to create a functional protein 150 amino acids in length (smallish for proteins) evolution would have to sort through 10^{77} unworkable forms (some mathematicians, and Crick himself, posit numbers higher than 10^{200}). Further, this change wouldn't have to happen just once, but trillions upon trillions of times in every species. Thus, the chance of any survival-enhancing genetic mutation in the genome of any particular person or animal vanishes into practical impossibility. Botanist Hugo de Vries, early in the twentieth century, put it this way: "Natural selection may explain the survival of the fittest, but it cannot explain the arrival of the fittest."

Further, mutation is never one-at-a-time change but must always be lots-at-a-time change (the saber-toothed tiger's elongating tooth required rehinging the jaw and the development of an accommodating lower jaw), and this extends the improbabilities.

Further, increment-at-a-time change does not itself produce survivability. A tooth an eighth of an inch longer would not make a puny tiger a gene-promulgating hero. (This has been called the half-a-wing problem in evolution discussions.)

Further, the variations evident in the individual life forms making up each biological species (human included) are vast. And since these differences must be accounted for by each species member's non-shared DNA, a far less vast set of genes must account for the infinite variations in color, size, and texture of tails, petals, skin, flesh, and bone.

Finally, if the attraction-repulsion causation of material chemistry is the cause and director of life's corporeal growth, it's hard to see, and as yet entirely unexplained, how 23,000 genes or even several trillion trillion trillion could push and pull the multi-quadrillions of atoms and molecules in life forms into the various living beings that populate the earth. It seems we are compelled to imagine that genes are traffic cops that somehow, from their post in a fertilized cell, direct and distribute the countless atoms and molecules that pass them. This direction must be, of course, completely physical—which means by touch or by the emission of chemicals that touch—because, after all, atoms and molecules are entirely stupid and would simply lie inert if not impelled. As in: now then, you, oh carbon molecule, sir, kindly move .0000732 nanometers north by northwest 43.55091 degrees to meet the oxygen molecule I have stationed there to await you, then proceed to your new home in the fourth vertebra. Hubba hubba and bon voyage! How Captain Gene is able to bump into place the molecules and atoms in the bloodstream or cell or mitochondria is utterly marvelous, and its supposed physicality-only functioning remains unimaginably mysterious. Experimentation shows that if you pour chlorine and sodium into a glass of water you get salt, and on that event and events like it science imagined biological development. It's not only that if you pour 10^{25} carbon, hydrogen, and oxygen molecules into a glass of water things are more challenging, it's that molecules are conceived as utterly dumb and can only wander around unless pushed or pulled. Biologists name this wandering Brownian motion and point hopefully to that as the somehow mechanism that underlies metabolism. But even if there were one gene per molecule in every living being, how does that gene provide the guidance-impulsion that directs atoms, proteins, and fatty acids to their appropriate home in the body? On this, biological physicalism is mute. Why then hasn't it thrown in the towel? Because, alas, for science, physicalism is the only game in town.

If we halt, as most scientists do (almost a professional requirement for the untenured in universities) at the speculations of Darwin, we are left with a system of thought that is more and more challenged as too crude. But progress in thinking is always slow, even philosophical and scientific thinking, since even the most learned grip new thought with the hands of the old thought they know and favor—and to which their career and reputation is pledged. Physicist Max Planck has been paraphrased as remarking that scientific progress proceeds funeral by funeral as the old thinkers and their staunchly defended ideas die off. There is even research documenting that when an eminent scientist dies, papers challenging his or her thought begin to appear with more frequency. When a large tree falls, the vegetation beneath it sees the light.

Honest investigation is confronted by twin threats. The religious fear that their stronghold of doctrine and world esteem will be exposed as simplistic. Scientists fear that should they even begin to suspect that the object of their study, the cosmos, is produced by a divine interferer, their reputation will suffer. Though confidence in neo-Darwinism is flagging, scientists are understandably reluctant to abandon it, because their opponents are religionists with horrific histories. The most simple of these are called creationists (who rely on religious texts). The more subtle are called intelligent design theorists (who like molecular biology and probability theory). And both—so say the scientists—have a hopeful eye on God.

But even if only some of these thinkers have religion motivating them, the mainstream scientists opposing them have the customary reaction of thinkers to those who are willing—so hold these scientists—to suspend critical thinking in service of their emotional needs. After all, bringing God on board usually means we bring on board his magic wand, and science (and reputation) goes out the window. Plus we get all those ancient conundrums like: Who is God and what does he want? Why suffering? How to get these fools to convert? Evolutionary science is unsurprisingly reluctant to concede its shortcomings, since on the other side of that concession is an army of needy, disagreeing, and sometimes disagreeable people brandishing the pitchforks of dogma—and sometimes steel pitchforks too.

But religion aversion is not entirely or even chiefly the source of their defense of Darwinism. Their main reason for supporting Darwinism is that if life did not evolve from random, survivability-enhancing mutation through time, then how to explain it? If mind did not emerge from a giant particle-based clockwork, and if life did not climb the ladder of evolution through survivable mutation, then how does everything happen? Darwinism may be falling apart under the onslaught of new thinking from molecular biologists, but where to next?

Now a bit about the psychology that developed in the wake of Darwinism—evolutionary psychology. This theory holds that the primary impulse that has guided evolution and psychic development is the desire for power and progeny and that these desires are hidden and made palatable by morality and tact. That idea-set, in order to account for the good will we feel for the humble and wise, and for our occasional aspiration toward truth, wideness, and altruism, offers that the yearning for truth (good mapping) is part of the power impulse. After all, good existence-mapping helps us catch more mammoths. So at least as far as mammoths go, we can reasonably assert that the power impulse has conditioned us to love truth.

But what about good will toward our fellow man? Evolutionary psychology makes sense of that by recognizing that individual altruism—your behavior toward me and mine toward you—could not have developed in evolution because of the cheater problem. Group altruism though—as in drone bees sacrificing themselves for the welfare of the hive—makes good genetic sense. There's a compulsive drive in genes, say the neo-Darwinists, to replicate. How these genes, which are essentially lifeless bundles of atoms, actually enact cause in mind is subsumed under the endemic-to-biology *somehow.* They reason that since all desires must be natural to and developed from the overmastering impulse of all life—to survive and produce progeny—the causal *somehow* of genetic working, though mysterious, is justified and required. Because here we are.

But while the life-is-a-struggle-for-power doctrine has an initial persuasion, it ties itself in odd knots as it attempts to explain our attraction to the selfless ones among us. What is it in our natures, in all eras and cultures, that disposes us favorably toward the humble and kind? Are we attracted to the selfless because they are less threatening, less likely to kill us or refuse us grain? This reason for attraction makes sense for the frightened and weak, but kings and queens love the humble too. Thus, we must make a further assumption—rulers unconsciously calculate that their power will be best served by humble subjects. The queen's indignant denial of such low motives is what we must expect—after all, she's unconscious of the urging of those sly genes. Really? Is it the love of power that impels us to prize statesmen over politicians? Is any wholesome welcome we feel for our fellowman, any love, at bottom an effort to get a leg up? And, by the way, do the humblest get to make more babies and catch more mammoths?

Simply put, modern thought's life-as-power-struggle explanation of existence has ignored and left unmapped the higher ranges of feeling and thought common in all cultures. Its fabric is a so-far impervious, sometimes contemptuous, weave of physicalism and neo-Darwinism, and both these systems have forsaken conjecture about the purpose of life—or concluded there is none. No doubt there is heroism in taking the stand that only the brave and intelligent can endure the angst of meaninglessness. Still, we may rightly wonder whether any thinking that trades the possibility of ultimate meaning for the triumph of emptiness-endurance has made the proper bargain.

Those two theories, one of the mechanism of existence (physicalism), the other of life's development (Darwinism), are contemporary science's chiefest props, and their influence is felt in almost every scientific effort. Though careful thinking exposes voids and uncertainties in their suppositions, can we devise a better explanation without throwing their researches overboard and taking refuge in the unexplanation of religion?

To answer that, we must examine more closely (close-notice) the actual structure of consciousness. And for that we must make a space for the only tool available for such an examination—introspection.

Introspection, the seeing inside

As earlier noted, the ego is composed of both ontological primitives, meaning and desire, and its working is furtive. It's furtive because it operates mostly in the unconscious, but also because it's an effortless, motive-masking liar that needs to promote this in order to repress that, and repress that to support this.

In considering the ego-nexus, we confront the confounding dilemma that has driven science into the confines of physicalism—namely, the evidence of the meeting of the self with experience, called meaning, is invisible and available only through introspection. Introspection is sometimes seen as the navel-gazing office of the effete or at least the exclusive business of artists. But introspection is employed continually by everyone in normal living and is in essence simply the notice of what we are thinking and feeling. Though its uncertainty is perplexing, it is the only source of good mapping of the world where the most of everything happens, the world inside us.

But, alas, pressing on the ego to extract its motives is like pressing on a piece of ice—the pressure of mental examination makes it skitter away. Most of egotism is hidden from consciousness in the darkness of unconsciousness—for the good reason that the desires that parade through the ego are in fierce and continual argument. The ego's masterful elusiveness makes sense in that too close an examination could confuse the naturalness of its working (like the centipede in the poem that forgets how to run after wondering which leg moves after which).

Desire is what drives the ego from one moment to the next, sometimes guilty, sometimes exultant, sometimes remorseful, sometimes vengeful. Desire is the existence-imposed feature of our intelligence that determines the ego's nature, structure, and expression. Reports of meditators escaping the sensation of selfhood and entering an egoless state are not to be dismissed, but we remind ourselves that these meditators always appear among us again the same selfy person as before and at dinner ask us to pass the salt. That fabled state, whether called satori or samadhi or spiritual trance, is not permanent. What is permanent is the ego and desire, and it is there that we must explore.

The inner being is generally held to be the province of psychology, but psychology's much-lamented paucity of hard evidence (a result of the psyche's unmeasurable invisibility) has left it in a quandary. It can't see its subject with instruments as the "real" sciences do and thus must endure the sometimes smirking watch of its hard science peers. This led first to behaviorism (a field today dried up by ineffectuality) and more recently to correlating neurological brain states with inner experience and to altering mood with drugs. This comes under the umbrella of: lots of need, no time to quibble, best we can do. And fair enough. After all, the undeniable back and forth causation between the brain and inner experience has already led to useful interventions, sometimes surgical, sometimes pharmaceutical. Because physicalist science insists that only repeatable, deniable, and measurable evidence is worthy of consideration, the only recourse psychology has had to respectability is to sigh, get out the sensors and cameras, and coddle college sophomores into clever experimental scenarios.

But instruments can so far only measure the world outside our intelligence. The brain too is outside our intelligence—and it is intelligence itself that psychologists want to know about. That's why, for psychology, physicalism is an imposed blindness. Their world is the invisible world of felt experience—the world, as philosophers put it these days, of qualia (experienceable stuff). Psychology as science is hesitant to employ in-sight, available only through introspection, since within the psyche, that vague soup of meaning and desire, there are few measurable contours. And alas, those available through brain state monitoring are, so far, trivial correlations (this section of the brain lights up when we are angry—ah!).

The trouble is that the inner structures of being are so invisible, immeasurable, and submerged that we can only come to grips with them through the dingy periscope of introspection. Still, introspection is a *form of seeing*. Employing it, we must abandon the precise measurement possible only in the physical world, but we needn't abandon the most precious of all our investigative equipment—our intuition, the ground and floor of all meaning. The mysterious that-which-gets-meaning organ of consciousness, which is intuition, which is the source of all intelligence, will remain our trusty companion.

We can fortify our resolve by reminding ourselves that even that which seems most clear and evident, the material world, is far from either—and is likewise seen through its own dingy periscope, which we might term the periscope of extrospection. The results of extrospection are themselves continually under dispute and, like all meaning, rest on a void of ignorance. In the inner world we will no doubt encounter the endless disputation (sometimes well-meaning, sometimes self-serving) of the enthusiasts and counterfeits who abide there, but we are compensated for the tedium of that struggle by having arrived at last at the first-most fountain of life.

Is recognizing our dependence on the source of all meaning as within us somehow limiting and unfortunate? Worse, does opening to the within give sanction to the supernatural? No and no. Opening to the inner world does, however, open us to the super-material. That world, the inner world, offers a promising, and necessary, beginning, since only in that world do we find the structures of being that condition and direct our lives.

It's easy to see that the intelligence of intuition is already much employed in everyday living and found to be practical, useful, and indispensable. We rise each morning embedded in meaning available to us through the elemental process of intuition, the faithful here-you-are offer of ordinary being. We rise where we slept (usually) and things are as they were (usually), and if they are not that difference too is an offer of the meaning-getting of intuition. If, for instance, I wake to find my slippers no longer beside my bed, I can suspect theft, a mischievous animal, someone's trickery, or a faulty memory. I needn't be Sherlock or Descartes to conclude that: I've been robbed, that damn dog, there's a prank afoot, or I didn't leave them where I thought I did. I simply know, and the reason for this knowing is that the world as intuition receives it is somehow (an essential, continual, and unfathomable *somehow*) constructed of connected sense, and this sense-connectedness is inherent in both worlds, inner and outer.

Thus we enter the inner world wary but fearlessly, arm and arm with our ancient and faithful companion, good sense. And at last begin an examination of

Disposition and the hierarchization of desire

This beginning recap of our so-far close-noticing: the two ontological primitives, desire and meaning, create the ego and its station at the consciousness-unconsciousness junction. There we experience choice, the sounding for preference, as desire sorts and shifts before decision. Our thoughts and actions feel free but are nevertheless invisibly conditioned by the desire and meaning that create our intelligence. Intelligence is mysterious, and its origin must remain mysterious, since explanation, by its nature as thought, ends empty-handed at the last penumbra of surrounding thought. Finally, although the last mystery, the moment-by-moment enigma of intelligence, has no explanatory penumbra, many lesser mysteries imposed by errors in thinking can be uncovered so that the contours of the last mystery begin to emerge. We cannot explain the sun of all being, but we can clear the underbrush so that the dark wood where we stand is better illumined.

Since meaning is continually served forth on a platter of desire, and since no one is able to think independently of desire, we are happy to name most thinking opinion, which here we will consider to be a dispositional attitude that is invisibly created and supported by desire.

We must pause at the use of the word *dispositional* to avoid gliding over the issue at hand. To have a disposition, mindset, attitude, outlook...These terms name a comportment natural, inevitable, and generally unexamined, which is why we mostly ignore that we are captured in a disposition. Each of us acts, thinks, and exists according to a disposition, so that it is into disposition itself, the source of opinion, that we must introspectively seek and sort for truth, for good existence-mapping.

Disposition, and its expression in thought as opinion, is a seeing of the world through the lens of desire. That we inwardly recognize and accommodate the mandatory murk of disposition is evidenced by the lack of astonishment that in all nations even our high court judges have political (desire-flavored) leanings, a condition tantamount to acknowledging that they have already at least partly made up their minds. In many nations, we agree without protest to house these judges in impressive Grecian-columned buildings, since we appreciate that only such architectural grandness can generate the social assurance required to counter what we all know—the robed men and women within are, like us, bound in desire, and the columned buildings that house them are veneer. The verdicts of courts are, after all, known as opinions and change over time as the spirit of the age changes. The most useful posture is to recognize that opinions are like rugs—they give us a place to stand, but do accumulate dirt, and from time to time need to be taken outside for some sun and a good beating.

Disposition is the lens-freight of mind each of us bears to see and do life, and it is marvelously subtle, invisible, elusive—and 100 percent persistent. No matter how long, high, or sublime a spiritual trance may be, we are deposited always back into the humdrum of a disposition.

Which is made of desire.

So far we have established that meaning-getting (intuition) is the existence-mandated starting place of all reflection (meaning-holding). It's interesting to note that when we look at a tree, our intuition (meaning-getting) offers treeness effortlessly and for free. The meaning-holding of a tree-thought is not only more pallid than tree-seeing, it requires the extra work of memory—and is more prone to mistaking. Clarity is hard because both meaning-getting and meaning-holding must run a gauntlet of desire to arrive in consciousness—but meaning-holding has to cross more distance. Both see what they want to see. But meaning-holding is more removed from its source and has to see farther.

Well, what a fix for meaning! Which is to say, what a fix for humanity. And for each of us. But an inspiring fix. Because hidden in the dilemma of the obfuscating desires of disposition is a remedy. Which is: *there are little desires and big ones.*

And that makes all the difference.

Desires little and big, and honesty, and humility

Desire is the culprit behind all mis-taking, which is to take wrongly. The more bound we are by small desire the more inaccurately we take the world. Certainty? Never. Error? Certainly. But always: small desires assert a viewpoint which impairs our ability to notice and map accurately. Larger desires produce better maps (more truth). Scientists, judges, plowmen, and mechanics all know we think better by, as we say, not forcing an outcome. It is the little-and-big structure of desire that provides for each of us a sometimes vague, often troubling, continually perplexing, but also enduringly available truth ladder that can be climbed by the sounding of preference called choice.

We do this by letting the meaning-is of existence, our intuitive impressions, assemble themselves in consciousness without constricting their appearance by submitting to the desire for a preferred outcome. Instead, we let the *surrender of honesty* be the undersoil of their appearance.

Surrender? Honesty? How quickly does introspection pluck from the murk of interiority such massively penumbraed terms!

What means this surrender? What is the nature of honesty? This is why philosophy is generally so tedious. As consciousness begins to ponder itself it encounters the previously invisible mass of unconscious meaning that aided its mammoth-catching and baby-making. It finds that to understand this idea it must first understand that one and that that idea can only be understood in terms of...And so philosophers have customarily resorted to achingly careful systems to coax us word by word along the trail of their thinking. Poetry uses words as well but darts about the tedious terrain of philosophy on the wings of compression. Yeats' potent line, "Love has pitched his mansion in the place of excrement," says in ten words what a philosopher might say in 10,000. In these pages we will adopt an intermediate course, opening philosophical thought from time to time, but also relying on our reader's gleam of intuitional sense. And we'll use poetry too. After all, understanding through the mereness of language is always confined in a circle, every word defined in terms of other words until at last we come back to the beginning. Language-using is first and mostly intuitional, a meaning-getting enterprise in which words themselves are merely markers of the intuitional sense they convey. We escape from the encirclement of words by becoming conscious of the sense toward which they point.

Now then: surrender means to give up, and giving up is both a letting go and an acceptance. When we open in honesty to the meaning-isness of existence, what is let go of and what is accepted? We let go of small desire by accepting large desire. What is the desire within the surrender of honesty that permits this? Can it be, as the Darwinist might hold, that beneath honesty is the desire for power, the desire to see clearly in order to survive? Is the desire for better existence-mapping sufficient to explain all ranges of feeling? Or are there feelings and desires that cannot be subsumed under the desire for survival? Alternatively, are there levels and grades of the power desire that can transform our understanding of the nature of power?

As we grapple with this issue, we encounter a state of being that provides the clue and solution to these conundrums—a state most prized by all cultures and eras and which is in fact the culmination of the state of honesty. This state is humility. The word comes from the term *humus*, meaning lowly, of the ground, the dust beneath the feet. Humility may seem to be honesty's elder, but they are essentially twins and conjoined at birth. How then is intelligence constructed so that humility is attractive, valued, and productive of truth?

We can begin to comprehend humility by contrasting it with its imitation, modesty, the tactful front presented to ease and make palatable some evident superiority over others. Through modesty we are announcing our accomplishment and power and simultaneously assuring others that we do not intend to exploit it by demanding its recognition, at least any further than by assuming the mask of modesty, a mask which is, of course, both a disguised advertisement of superiority and a useful social lubricant. Modesty's disguise as humility offers both the modesty artificer and his or her audience comfort, the audience since it covers their inferiority, the modest since it attributes a valued nobility to what is ignoble. Why ignoble? Because modesty conceals our vanity, and we know inherently, in ourselves and in others, that vanity is weakness, since in the vain is a felt insufficiency that requires support, and what is in need of support is not strong in itself. Vanity reflexively denies its need for support, but since all vanity is self-measurement by the size of others, the vain have a roving eye for height. (By instructing children that they are to be proud of themselves we do not mean to instruct them to display a pride that belittles the inferiority of others, but that they must have the courage to recognize their worth.)

Humility is not a state of mind affected by or produced for the appreciation of others. It is a state arising from within and is independent of seeming. Interestingly, and frustratingly, *it cannot be produced by effort or will.* It appears when the screen of desire consolidated in the front self of our disposition has dissipated sufficiently so that we are able to let-be-what-is—and to be content with that letting-be. The humble stand unpretended. (Consider the perfect etymology of the word *pretend,* meaning *to tend before,* as in: *I tend to my pride with modesty before it can express itself.*) Modesty is forgery and testifies to humility's value. No one counterfeits worthless coin.

Humility is not confined to any particular religion or set of ideals. In an atheist or devotee of whatever God, humility is the same force in the within, a releasement and a concession. If the atheist is asked to what he has conceded, he might answer, however vaguely, the universe—or being itself. The devotee, however vaguely, might answer God. But both, atheist and devotee, in so far as they have noticed humility, have caught the scent of honesty.

At this point, we cannot fully reveal the geography and source of humility since it involves structures of being not yet illumined in these pages. As the discussion continues, we will eventually consider the desire that produces both humility and honesty—and consider as well whether that desire is a species of the desire for power over others.

For now, let's reacquaint ourselves with the eternal predicament of all mankind: that we are dipped into existence, coated with enough meaning-getting ability to so-so live, and set loose to scramble through a one-thing-after-another world where all explanation fades into mystery at its periphery. We must get about, do life, and somehow survive, without ever fully knowing what's going on. And since we must, we do. This press-on-regardless feature of intelligence sets the stage, provides the structure, and even mandates that we construct an always-rickety but good-enough front self to navigate through time. We call it being confident, believing in yourself, all that. Still, the ship of our front self, our ego (ahoy!—nautical imagery ahead) is anchored by chains of pride, buffeted by winds of envy, driven by storms of ambition, bored through by doubt, and scorched by doldrums of emptiness.

It's worth noting here that of all these natural perils, it is the discontent of emptiness that has the central place in our dilemma because it is the majority of our time-felt experience. We move through an interminable train of desire-fulfillment, each one hyphenated to the next by the same persistent emptiness. It is that emptiness itself that is the predominant feature of our lives. The void of discontent beneath and between each desire fulfillment creates a soreness that cries for solace, and yet, as we try to answer that cry, we can offer only gratifications too trifling for the need. Moment by moment, meaning faithfully arises. Moment by moment, desire lures us toward an uncertain future where we may find the next apple or adventure—and maybe Nothing.

A predicament—but one in which there are clues and directional arrows. The inevitability of our felt emptiness is a clue. The nature of humility and the gradual releasement of small desire is a clue. The greatest clue is that desire has sizes, that some are more satisfying than others, and that, perhaps, there is a highest desire.

As the nature of the psyche becomes more evident, the contours of higherness will emerge.

The lynch mob and the nature of higher desire

Consider: what sort of desire is it that could make a man in a Jim Crow lynch mob shout, "Wait a second, guys! Are we sure he raped her? Maybe she's lying." To say that such a man wants justice is too conceptual. What is the nature of the felt urge within such a man?

Let the members of the lynch mob gather round him: "Do you mean to say you'd side with a colored man over a white woman?"

What desire force in this man could now repeat, "How do we know she's not lying though?"

As we imagine this scene, we stand at the edge of a volcano. We see desire flowing through those who would kill in anger (from small desire), and in our hero (possessed by larger desire) who would not, and in ourselves as we yearn for release from this restless cruelty. And we might wonder again whether the desire for power alone is sufficient to account for this complexity. The lynch mob's anger might be explained by a Darwinian power struggle, but not our hero's bravery. Are we to imagine he is motivated by a desire to be mayor and impress the women? We also sense that our own distraught outrage is not some gaudy plumage in the power-sex parade.

Clearly it is the man's nobility, or honor, or honesty that produces his courage. But if life is merely a power struggle, where do these forces come from? And why do we like them so much? To answer that we must pry deeper into the fabric of being than Darwinism can do. We must examine what honor is in itself, what threads of meaning and desire it pulls together to make its stand within us. Though Darwin's theory has been useful in ushering us from the simplicities of old thinking, it seems unprepared to escort us into the higher ranges of consciousness.

The search for these higher ranges is not simple, at least for those of us who stand in the dark wood of ordinary being. We may sense that wideness of seeing and largeness of desiring are clues, but how complex is that terrain! We see that our heroes, whether military, political, artistic, or spiritual, are bound in desire that is not only vast but also various. Genghis Khan looked past the oxcarts about him and saw from China to Europe. Michelangelo saw David within the stone. Saint Francis saw radiance. That brief catalog suggests desire's size, complexity, and range.

But which desires, we desire to know, are largest and best? What is best—and also possible—to want? And how can we know?

As we begin this exploration—and it is an exploration of the inner world—we come to many recognized qualities and states, but the ones these pages will elaborate are (some already partly elaborated): empathy, humility, egotism, consciousness and unconsciousness, freedom, blame and remorse, and then, more subtly, recognition, acceptance, and sameness. And love. This list may at first seem oddly arbitrary, but the discussion that follows will demonstrate its inevitability. No thinking is sufficient to color the entire range of the inner world, since it is endless and endlessly complex, but the above list is ample enough to create a psychic geography and help us get at the nature of higher desire. A good place to begin is with

The astonishment of empathy

What is the locus of most-meaning in the universe? Unsurprisingly, it is the human face where, most surprisingly, we are able to note the being, state, and disposition of another. The names we have given this power of meaning-getting—empathy, sympathy, instinct, intuition, understanding—merely name the mystery and simultaneously shield us from appreciating its peculiarity. This neglect is, of course, as normal as the inattention of the centipede to its legs. Pressing our minds too closely to almost any structure of existence is a bit of a monkey wrench in the business of living.

How is empathy possible? How is it that we are able, in time and across space, to receive an impression of the inner state of another? We do not know exactly what someone else is thinking, but we generally and clearly know how they are feeling. We read them. Some of our fellow creatures are able to read others more accurately, and we call them sensitive. Sensitivity is rare and prized and why we often admire literary people and why acclaimed fine art costs so much. Yet sensitivity is not solely the province of artists. Sensitivity is, at bottom, the meaning-receiving power of the intelligence we have called intuition and is installed in crickets, elephants, and human beings. (Some brows will furrow at crickets, no doubt. But crickets shrug.)

Mistakes in the intuitive reading of other people are possible (psychologists name this mistaking *projection*), but still we generally know how other people feel—and sometimes how they think. In actual fact, we read their minds by glancing at them—that ironic smile, that ironic smile tinged with regret, that seething pride-protecting anger, that sexual interest masked by indifference, that self-confidence disguising insecurity.

When psychologists discuss empathy they sometimes remark that we get clues from the body language and facial comportment of others, and we then, with the computational power of our brain, draw conclusions about the other person's state. (Today most psychologists are conditioned to say *brain* instead of *mind,* but, as mentioned earlier, though brains are somehow connected to the meaning-power of intelligence, meaning-states themselves happen in minds, not in brains.)

Head tilt to the right, mouth purse, eyebrow lift, compute! Skepticism! That would mean that empathy is a near instantaneous deductive process. Instantaneousness is not the issue, since we can easily imagine near light speed electrical impulses zooming about the brain. But deduction, as shown earlier, is a premise-combining process—I know that John is the first penitent, you know the first penitent is a murderer, and when we confer we know John's a murderer. But how do we know John is the first penitent? How do we know the first penitent is a murderer? How do we come to know what that eyebrow lifts means, or that reluctant smile, or that eye-rolling guffaw, or that quiet attention? The only real recourse psychology has ever had is to hold that these insights are somehow contained in instinct or the unconscious. Which only names the mystery.

No doubt the raising of an eyebrow is a clue, and, when considered in the formality of abstract thought, eyebrow-raising seems simple enough. But eyebrow-raising is never simple when expressed in the immense variety of lived experience. It is vastly subtle and might mean irony, sarcasm, delight, surprise, and so on. An eyebrow raise might even be meant to convey a supposed sarcasm that its expresser, as a bit of wit, understands that I will recognize as mock sarcasm so that we can share the joke that he might, though never would, in that instance intend actual sarcasm. In short, the flavors of mind which pass instantly back and forth between people are so subtle and various they are inexpressible by generic two millimeter eyebrow lifts.

Further, how do we come to know these inner states of others? Do we study our own face in a mirror, grimace with reluctant irony and think, ah, reluctant irony! So that's what she was feeling! No, instantaneously and mysteriously we *get* other people. And it's impossible that we get the meaning within people from the fractional movements of their mouth or eyebrows, since if we do, then how did we learn that that one millimeter uplift of the mouth (a smile) represents simply humor or kindness, and not petulant sarcasm or tactful distain or wistful memory? The supposition that empathy is somehow learned, that when our mother smiled at us above the crib and did not simultaneously strike us, we understood that she meant well, crumbles into nonsense as we consider the infinite subtlety and variation of human feeling available through empathy. We might assume goodwill by the notice of an upturned mouth, but how about perfunctory goodwill, guilty goodwill, how about an upturned mouth disguising frustration or agitated impatience? The problem is to see and say: how do the meaning-states of another person transmit themselves to me from that person's outward appearance? How do I, through physical clues, reliably become aware of their invisible mind?

A by-note: even if feelings are learned—that is, recognized as a species of already-known feelings—somewhere along the trail of learning there must be unprenumbraed first feelings that are/were simply grasped whole and without likeness to other feelings, since at that point there would have been no feelings yet for the grasped feeling to be like. Thus, the vast complexity of feeling states we collect through empathy cannot be wholly a compound of previously understood feeling states since that leaves ununderstood how those previous feelings states were originally grasped. The accumulation idea implies that every time we receive some new type of impression from another person, an impression not based on any previous state, it is accompanied by explanation, either verbally or through action (a smile without a slap, a kiss without a kick). Which doesn't happen.

In an important sense, the source of empathy is the question inherent in all meaning-getting. The infinitely various meaning contained in empathy is only the highest peak of meaning-getting, since it is, after all, the consideration of the most developed storehouse of meaning, the human intelligence behind the human face. But whence comes any meaning whatsoever? The word *learn* contains a subtle fraudulence when used to explain the nature of meaning-getting since it neglects, and is utterly unable to clarify, the process of the experience it names. *Learn* refers to the accumulation of meaning, but what is the nature and constituent process of this accumulation? What is it in the nature of meaning-getting that permits not only the accumulation of meaning we call learning but meaning-getting's very appearance in consciousness? How we respond to the human face is no different (and equally unexplained) from how we respond to a coffee cup. No doubt the information passed from a coffee cup to my intelligence is less full than the information I receive from the human face, but the meaning-getting from both is an offer of an intelligence that issues naturally from existence (and, by the way, not some sort of imagined, created, or directed act). Again, to assert that the vast sensitivity of the unconscious is responsible merely hands off the puzzle. The coffee cup appears, and, amazingly, we grasp its offer of meaning. Carmen smiles, and, amazingly, we feel the world within her.

From these thoughts we see that the origin of empathy is not the essential question. The essential question is the origin of meaning itself, which is, of course, a species of the trusty hard problem which seems always to raise its hand from the back of the class and querulously repeat, *but you haven't answered my question yet*. The action of meaning-getting is always miraculous (unexplained and unpenumbraed) and only becomes most evidently miraculous when we consider the action of empathy, meaning's most developed manifestation. The real question is not how we get meaning from a face, but how we get meaning from anywhere. In short, what is this meaning-getting intelligence in which we are continually embedded?

A hard problem indeed.

An interesting feature of meaning-getting from the face of a human being, or from a coffee cup, is that meaning-getting ceases abruptly when we close our eyes. It was likely this feature of empathy that convinced humanity for centuries (and now convinces contemporary psychologists) that it is somehow physical clues that an empathizer is responding to. But physical clues, eyebrow raises, a one millimeter chin lift, a two millimeter mouth purse, are, as shown, immensely interpretable and thus uncertain. Even if we consider physical clues the sole meaning signal on which empathy depends, still the meaning that arises from these clues is not imposed deductively by some fierce computational cross-checking in the mind (or brain)—mouth purse plus eyebrow lift equals skepticism—but instead arises wholly as: Zuberi is jealous and mad but wants us not to notice. This impression from Zuberi is not deductive, not composed somehow from a near infinity of physical clues from which we marvelously, instantaneously, and accurately deduce his inner state. Instead, we see his state, and whether this seeing is conscious or unconscious is unimportant. It is as if the meaning-field that is our being receives from the other, through the medium of sight, the meaning-field that is the other person. (These pages will eventually have a name for these meaning-fields.) When we close our eyes, reception stops because meaning-getting across space stops. Sight is merely the portal through which our meaning-intuition must pass.

Empathy, when we permit it to manifest as the primordial fact it is, is simply the most obvious and disconcerting example of our always-embeddedness in an unexplained and unexplainable meaning-world. The mystery at the heart of empathy is the first-in-line mystery of meaning itself. And, alas, as we dig for meaning's origin, we must helplessly employ a shovel made of the very meaning we are exploring for—the well-known dilemma of knowing knowing through knowing, of trying to see beneath our seeing. Which is why, in the littered landscape of meaning in which we continually exist, we must open ourselves to the disconcerting-at-first but invigorating-at-last utter ignorance of meaning's source. And we must *make a guess*. We must conjecture. If our conjecture is inclusive and clear, we can begin to get on with the business of living—and begin to figure out what that business might be.

As we will see, around that conjecture a rich, deep, thorough, and useful theory of life can be developed.

Now—as a breather from hard thinking—we will detour to the fair land of Mississippi where we will accompany two detectives to a murder scene (always fascinating to the unmurdered). The detectives and their struggles will illumine many of the items on our list of topics—ego, consciousness and the unconscious, humility, recognition, acceptance, sameness, blame, freedom, and remorse.

Two Mississippi detectives

Consider: Two detectives, both white, enter a murder scene to question the possible suspects, a beautiful white girl and a middle-aged black man. The first detective notes that the white girl presents a front of helpful patience but also notes that her smile is determinedly formal. He further notes that the black man stands with folded arms and a frown, which the first detective considers normal and even slightly admirable in that the black man is unafraid to present his apprehension that these white cops might arrest or frame him. The other detective experiences a prettiness-flustered gratitude for the white girl's helpfulness and sees the black man's frown as suspicious, perhaps guilty. (The girl did it.)

Neither detective is reasoning. The world they see is the world apparent to them. They see this world through a lens of meaning-getting-and-holding (intuition and thinking about it) conditioned by both previous meaning-getting-and-holding and by desire. They are both bathed in intuition, that instantaneous compound of intelligence that delivers their workable knowingness, the way a fish is bathed in water. This is the I-know-what-I-know common sense we all rely on and mostly share. The *mostly* reminds us that the first detective is more sensitive than his partner, that his intuition is wider and produces a more accurate map of reality. The second detective encountered both suspects simultaneously with the first detective but was dazzled by the girl's beauty and suspected the black man.

The first detective's seeing saw what his partner's seeing did not. His intelligence was not the deductive, premise-putting-together kind, but rather the immediate kind that intuitively (empathically) receives sense. If the first detective had to explain his insights, it might seem to the second detective that the first detective had reached his conclusions through deduction—as Sherlock seemed to when explaining to Watson that someone was of this or that profession, with or without a spouse, had recently ridden a train, and so on, all by noting the condition of shoes, cuffs, and handkerchiefs. But Sherlock only seemed to be deducting because Watson (and the reader) required the stepwise progress of explanation. Sherlock and the first detective and, in fact, all of us receive information directly, by seeing people and letting meaning arise. Some of us see more, but all of us see some. The two detectives have stepped forth in these pages to help us see the how of that some and understand why it is sometimes not more.

Meaning arises somehow (that irascible somehow!) through intuition, and it makes sense to hold that some intuitions are wider, truer, and deeper (more full of accurate noticing). It makes sense to hold that intuition can be layered, can be compounded and added to, so that we can have new and deeper insights about life and people. This deepening of intuition, this making intuition more accurate, is not a premise-putting-together process, but rather a fuller seeing.

Now we let our helpful detectives demonstrate how meaning arises and how to get more of it.

It's evident that the second detective's impressions were conditioned by his disposition—he was allured and flustered by the girl's beauty and considered the black man's hostility a mark of guilt. This is because, we now reveal, he has an aversion to black people.

The second detective's biography: his father was a Mississippi dirt-farmer who seduced and married his mother, a local beauty. His father grew yams and hired a neighboring black man to help him. The second detective, as a child, became best friends with the black man's son, Charlie. They made a rope swing over the swimming hole, caught crawdads with bacon on a string, played marbles, trapped a skunk in a cardboard box and paid the price. His father accepted his son's friendship with a black boy, since this was the Jim Crow old South where rural black and white kids were often permitted to play together—until earning began and the social-power differences between the races separated them. Besides, Charlie's dad was a good worker and cheap.

One fall the price of yams fell, and his father fired Charlie's father. There was an argument in the yam field over three months unpaid wages. The argument ended when the second detective's dad struck Charlie's father with a hoe and sent him to the hospital. The sheriff came by but left without filing charges. The next day Charlie's house burned to the ground, and Charlie and his family left the county. The second detective was consoled by his mother for the loss of his friend and told to forget him. But did Dad burn their house? Of course not, said his mother, and offered a sad smile as assurance. And the small boy second detective was gradually able to submerge both his longing for his pal Charlie and his suspicion of his father's cruelty. He did this by nurturing an attitude of resentful revulsion of black people. We will not examine here the day-by-day, week-by-week layering over of his love for Charlie, except to note that the falling away and covering over of child-like Charlie-love is the must-have-happened case with every racist. Little kids mostly like everyone.

The second detective's life continued. Now he has now caught the beautiful-girl murder case and steps helpfully forward in these pages to guide us in understanding the psyche's working.

This much we have—the purity of the second detective's impression-receiving ability was spoiled by desire. His attraction to female beauty shunted away suspicion, and the belligerence of the black man amplified his ever-ready hostility toward black people. Desire, that always and elemental structure of consciousness, prevented him from receiving accurate impressions. As earlier shown, knowing always sees through a lens of wanting, and so a circle begins. Desire conditions the meaning we receive, and that conditioned meaning in turn guides our wanting, which has already been shaped by conditioned knowing, which...No wonder it's hard to think straight.

Recall that honesty is an efforting produced by surrender to larger desire. How in the second detective can honesty prevail?

Say the second detective were at some point confronted with evidence that the girl did it—her DNA on the knife, the stolen bracelet discovered in her safety deposit box, and photos of the black man a hundred miles away at the time of the murder. How might the second detective react? He might, one, assert that his infatuation for the girl and his prejudice against the black man is just fine and who cares and anyway a girl that beautiful probably had good cause for murder, and the black guy, if he didn't do this crime, I bet did other stuff. Or two, come to see that his attitude almost resulted in a miscarriage of justice and change his mind by becoming aware that his infatuation with beauty and his hatred of black people obscured the truth. (That phrase, *change his mind*, contains the fascinating and habitual error of supposing that minds change through decision. They don't, because they can't. Disposition is a function of desire, which, as demonstrated, can only seem to be chosen.)

But what if the second detective accepts the girl's guilt and some mood-force in him deepens, widens, relents—and he is flooded with something larger? In short, what if he is overtaken by remorse? Describing this remorse as a deepening and widening is at first perhaps even more nebulous than describing the taste of an apple. But also just as real. What is the inner largest of remorse and how is it possible? What is the nature of consciousness so that small desire can be subsumed by larger desire? To understand that we must examine the always-cradle of desire, the palm in which desire manifests, the first ontological primitive, meaning itself. We must consider how meaning means.

We'll get back to our Mississippi murder but first comes the deepest dive, into

The ocean of meaning, learning, recognition, and sameness

Though the what of meaning cannot be lifted into view, since it's always meaning that's doing the lifting, we can consider its how. And from that *how* form good guesses about its understructure—and its source.

So now comes a foundation, not of meaning itself, but of its process. Now comes a bit of close-noticing.

When a coffee cup means itself to me in the morning, I am utterly unastonished. The event of its appearance occurs in the great ordinariness of meaning-getting. Like all things-that-mean, my coffee cup is held forth by the trillion hands of the meaning-penumbra that upholds it. I know that it is made of something, ceramic or metal. I know the meaning-penumbra of ceramic and metal—molecules and so on. I see the cup's shape and color and location, and my memory of this cup and other cups and their use to me are part of its penumbra. There it is, my coffee cup, my familiar pal.

Then I notice the coffee cup in the hand of my spouse, and something interesting happens. I see that my spouse's cup is not my coffee cup. But it is like it.

But how?

It's clearly not the same as my cup, since it's over there and my cup is here, and even if it's made by the same manufacturer, it's not entirely the same color, since it's reflecting light differently, and it's not the same weight or shape and on and on. It's utterly different from my cup. But is like my cup. So what's the deal with anything being like anything else?

Likeness is such an everyday operation of meaning-getting that we don't much notice it, and now that we have we may impatiently wonder why we should. The reason we should is that likeness is *the glue that sticks everything together.*

It's also how we learn.

The likeness of things is not a property of those things, but of our apprehension of them. Clearly, nothing is actually the same as anything else, so that, just as clearly, the sameness of things is a property of our intelligence.

Interestingly, our sameness-making intelligence is what makes learning possible.

Here's how that works. The increase and enlargement of meaning occurs through *association,* the one-thing-like-another structure of the meaning-world we inhabit. This is because the action of all knowing, both the getting type and the holding type, is the action of *recognition through sameness.* As in: I see a coffee cup or human face and am not utterly confounded—because they are *just like what I have seen before.* As we will see, this sameness business has a lot to do with prejudice, creativity, and even the Eastern concept of maya.

The term *recognition* used above is, of course, nothing but another term for meaning itself, but is useful here since it offers a sense of the action in time of meaning-arising. When we recognize anything, what is inherent in the action of our intelligence? The coffee cup means itself to us and our ability to apprehend and recognize it as a coffee cup is a result of its sameness to our already-held—thus previously acquired—coffee cup idea. (And sure, it's evident my spouse didn't have to arrive with a different coffee cup for sameness to be in operation. Sameness operates even when I look away and then back at my own cup without astonishment.) I know coffee cups as coffee cups because I know coffee cupness. All meaning, as it arises, is held in familiarity, so that *the present rolls forward in the arms of the past.* Everything in our meaning-field exists as meaning because it has been recognized in terms of what already was/is in that meaning-field.

The enlargement of that meaning-field, which we call learning, depends on sameness—because *nothing can be noticed unless it is recognized.* Constituent in the word *recognize,* of course, is the very sense that comprises sameness—to cognize again. It is that *again* which implies sameness to what was noticed before.

The idea of sameness may seem like an abstract observation but instead is merely the close-noticing of the meaning's operation. Sameness is the power within, and structure of, all meaning gotten and all meaning held. Sameness is inherent in every idea, impression, and intuition. It is the invisible structure of meaning. It was likely the action of recognition through sameness that gave Plato his idea of Forms, that there is some power in intelligence that enfolds this tree as tree and the next tree as tree, and so on, so that, as Plato might have put it, the tree idea within me emerges from intelligence to engage every newly appearing tree in the welcoming arms of treeness.

Learning is the expansion of sameness, as when someone who has seen only oaks encounters an elm and adds elm to treeness. What comes-to-be is always held in the sameness-bucket of what has already been. But if learning is dependent on sameness recognition, are we then compelled to know the new only in terms of the old, and are we thus condemned to a vast sterility of sameness? If every meaning-thing (idea, impression, intuition, notion, insight) can only enter our meaning-field by way of its association with previously held meaning, is everything we learn merely a synonym of what we already know? It makes sense that it might be, since we know well in ourselves and from history the implacable power of prejudice, racism, and tribalism, the children of Emperor Sameness.

A nicety in this discussion is the question of how the first meaning-element of all arose, since, in an empty field of consciousness-intelligence, there is no meaning-thing already held that can enfold or associate itself with the arriving bit of meaning. It is not that I would not be able to recognize a tree without first noticing plants, since I may have seen a stone and thus have associations ready to enfold tree as perhaps greatly different from the stones that already populate my meaning-field but still a dimensional object of the out-there and hence a thing with likeness to what I have already experienced. But what if I had experienced nothing whatever? What if my meaning-field were entirely empty (the philosopher Locke's *tabula rasa*)? If more-meaning-getting (learning) relies on the welcome of new meaning through sameness, on what does the very, very first moment of knowledge-getting rely? How can knowledge arise in an entirely empty intelligence, since in an empty intelligence there exists nothing yet for any meaning-impression to be like? How did the first moment of knowledge-getting occur in any bit of conscious intelligence whatever—in electrons, if you're a panpsychist, or in the earliest life form if you're a biologist, or in infants, if you're a child psychologist? How could meaning have begun in a blank intelligence if knowledge is the accumulation of knowledge-elements through sameness? These pages will eventually develop an answer for this conundrum.

It's always the morning after the fight

Our beingness consists in flowing from one meaning state to the next cradled comfortably in the arms of sameness. I'm watching the coffeemaker sputter. My husband enters. We quarreled last night, and I sense he's tentative and sullen. Should I offer him coffee? I squelch generosity since I'm still angry myself. But generosity, however reluctant, prevails. I open the cabinet and take down his coffee cup. He sees this. He slumps. We gaze at each other, waiting to see what will happen. We both shake our heads. We smile, then chuckle. The fight is over.

These states of beingness flow between human beings continually and are the all-we-have of existence. The rest, even bump-into-stuff, comes from thinking about these states. And in these states, sameness is the sine qua non, the without which not, of all meaning. It is not merely that I contentedly recognize the man across the kitchen as the same man I married, or that I recognize the coffee pot as the same one I left on the counter last night, and not merely that I woke in the same bed, and feel the same way about the fight we had, but that absolutely everything, the wall, the sink, the toothbrush, means itself to me through the agency of sameness. If the toothbrush was unlike anything I had ever seen, how could I recognize it? Even if the article in my toothbrush holder is one morning not at all toothbrushy but instead seems to be a little dragon or even an unidentifiable stuff-lump, that whatever-it-is thing is recognizable as a something. It appears to me through the agency of likeness—a little dragon, a little odd stuff-lump, which is like other stuff-lumps or dragons I have seen or imagined. Everywhere I look, I am embedded in sameness, this the same as that, that the same as this. Nothing appears in consciousness unless it is recognized, and nothing can be re-cognized unless it resembles what we know.

In deduction there is no new knowledge but only the sterile circle of tautology (a is a). Yet in an important sense that makes sense all knowledge is tautology since whatever becomes known is known by way of resemblance to what is already known—and, alas, the knowableness of the newly known occurs because of resemblance, which is sameness, which is its hidden identity with the already known. The known widens to incorporate the unknown, and the unknown becomes known by resemblance and recognition. The making-conscious of the waiting-to-be-known is the widening of intelligence through recognition, and this recognition is possible only because of the sameness-seeing power inherent in intelligence.

From this line of thought we are led to conclude that, since all knowing is possible only through sameness, all knowing is a form of tautology, and that learning is only the widening of intelligence to include concealed sameness. *Intelligence, which we are, and which ants and elephants are, knows (and learns) by becoming more conscious through the power of sameness recognition.*

Just as sameness is embedded in knowing, so too is a notion, however vague, of wholeness. If we trace the resemblance of this to *that,* then want to know what that newly-discovered *that* resembles, then want to know what the last *that* is the same as, we inevitably come to some *final sameness* that everything else is the same as.

Relevant and informing here is an interesting modern phenomenon having to do with the online encyclopedia Wikipedia. If a user clicks on the first link in the main text of any Wikipedia article, then clicks on the first link in the subsequent article, and so on and on, in 97 percent (in February, 2016) of all Wikipedia articles the user finds him or herself in the article on philosophy. The remaining 3 percent of articles land on an article without any links, or reference non-existent pages, or get stuck in loops. All roads lead to philosophy, that is, to the vast-most idea we have, the idea which stands beneath and encapsulates every other idea. Which is what the final sameness does.

That final sameness we can think of as the wholeness beneath all sameness. As sameness accumulates—as intelligence learns—it creates more and more wholeness, more thises like thats. Sameness is, in a sense, magnetized by the wholeness that draws it. And yet that wholeness remains forever elusive. A botanist studies a tree and knows more and more and still his knowledge is incomplete. Even if he were to descend into the hallways of uttermost being, into the structure of bark, for instance, where quarks and muons and Higgs bosons zipped overhead, his tree knowledge would remain incomplete, since it would be bound in the present only, and more, the force impulsion within those particles would remain invisible. The nature of knowledge is reflection, and in reflection is a profound mereness. *Thought is not the thing it is a thought of, and thus it is not the fullness of being, but only its map.*

That map, though, is where sameness first reveals itself.

Zeno, clever fellow

How meaning arises we don't know, but we do have some notion about how it functions. In the proposition that *a* equals *b* we note an equivalency-transition of *a*-ness to *b*, which, of course, is no transition at all but merely a recognition of the *a*-ness of *b*. As mentioned, no thing outside intelligence is equal to anything else—no stones, thoughts, or people are identical. We can say that *a* is equal to *b* only in mentation. This utter separation of the mind world from the bump-into world is what inspired Zeno to confound Greeks with the paradox that Achilles could never beat the tortoise in a race if the tortoise was granted a head start. Achilles, at every moment of time, would always be required to reach the point that the tortoise had just been, and, in the time that it took, the tortoise would have advanced a bit farther. After we prove that Achilles can't win, he does anyway, so we must then consider where the paradox arises. It arises because a map is not the thing mapped. It is consciousness *of* the thing and always an approximation. Equality—and sameness too—occur only in mind. Achilles doesn't care what Zeno *thinks*—he wins anyway. (A note for the interested—the mathematics of calculus overcomes the impasse of infinite divisibility by the clever use of the concept of limits.)

Whatever the cause, source, or nature of meaning, and whether panpsychism is correct and everything is a form of intelligence, or whether, as some think, only metabolizing life is, we can at least comfortably hold that meaning itself relies on the property of sameness to know and learn, and standing behind sameness is its father, the final sameness, the everything-laced-togetherness of wholeness.

Another feature of knowing worth mention is that the bits of meaning that create the meaning-penumbra of something known—like a tree—are mostly unconscious. The branches, roots, and bark that form the penumbra of treeness for me do not need to be held in consciousness for me to successfully mean tree. Further, if those surrounding meaning-bits move into consciousness, they too have a meaning-penumbra, bark of a type, branches of a kind, some sort of roots.

Thus one property of knowing is its reliance on sameness, and another is that all sameness is made of penumbraed parts. This parts-wholes business is a familiar study in philosophy, called mereology, and dates back to the Presocratics. In a sense, parts are magnetized by the whole around which they gather, and are somehow attracted and fixed in place by the sameness of which they are parts. Every tree idea is pregnant with its faithful children, roots and leaves, and when brought into the Solomon's court of mind resists division. Though all ideas are divisible into their parts, their parts remain submerged, holding their idea across the conscious-unconsciousness divide into the light of consciousness with invisible hands secreted in the unconscious. This feature of ideas, that its parts are hidden supports, means that ideas may be wrong if their as-yet-unmanifested parts are wrong (bad maps), which is why thinking our way out of a problem—or into one—is fraught with mistaking. Which is why here we have chosen to build inch by inch from only two primitives, meaning and desire.

We'll leave this bit of metaphysics suspended here, but before proceeding it's natural to note that theologists have always held that God is one, which is, after all, sameness, the daughter of wholeness, which is oneness. So maybe there's a clue here. Unless, of course, sameness is merely part of the mechanism of always-existing, uncreated existence-intelligence, and even, maybe, it was this natural and always-there property of mind that gave those ancient, hopeful thinkers the idea that, since sameness is the one-thing-like-another essence of knowing, God must be the original and final one thing-that-everything-else-is-like. Unless it's just a property of the universe, which who knows, so, in short, the fact that sameness points toward wholeness does not demonstrate that either are God. It's an interesting fact though.

As a by-issue, note that both the sameness essential to knowing and the adding to knowing called learning, imply unity (this and that share a sameness). An oak is like an elm, since they are both trees. But also and simultaneously sameness implies duality, since sameness is impossible without twoness—the oak is like an elm, and the oak and elm are two. Thus sameness establishes both unity and duality at the same time.

To recap, the principle is this—sameness is necessarily inherent in all meaning, because the nature of intelligence is that it sees the coming-to-be-known in terms of the already-known.

If the discussion ended here, it wouldn't be worth much. It might even be depressing to acknowledge that we are fastened in the repetitive rhyme of sameness. But we aren't.

The lone ranger of desire to the rescue

Rescue from the sterility of sameness arrives because though we must entertain all that is new in the banquet hall of recognition, that hall also welcomes another visitor, desire.

No meaning arrives without desire. You don't see the tree unless you look. You know where you are, and it is from there that you want. These two powers, meaning and desire, can be separated in thought but are never separated in the action of being. So though the world means itself to us through the recognition power of sameness, and though, because of this stale and continual offering, a sterility opens to us at every moment, we are simultaneously and perpetually confined in meaning's sister, desire. These sisters, meaning and desire, are not identical twins, but are more intimate than even these, since the sister of desire can only want what her sister sees, and the sister of meaning can only see what her sister wants.

But sometimes one sister is more insistent than the other, and the more insistent sister is always desire. (New thought may open us to deeper desire, but it was desire that opened us to that new thought.)

And it is precisely this restlessness, this one-elemental-primitive-ahead-of-the-other condition of existence, that produces change, development, growing depth and wideness, and what we blithely call creativity. Restlessness calls both children and adults to greater maturity. Restlessness is the need that drives the ones we call geniuses into the dark forests of being. Restless desire is continually rattling the cage of form, producing the need to know more and to want more satisfyingly. This imbalance is a fundament of existence and is the push-puller of all action, thought, and feeling in the psyche. Because of the infinity of things to know and want, restlessness, the source of our discontent, seems endless. Yet hidden in restlessness is its remedy, which is: *some desires are stronger than others and more—some desires are larger.*

This needn't be asserted. It can be noticed.

The unforeseen architecture of magnanimity

That some desires are stronger than others is evident from the simple fact that some desires get expressed in action by overcoming others that oppose them. I am cold and, after a struggle with inertia, I rise to search for my coat. My desire to be warm was stronger than my desire to not-move.

But what can it mean to hold that some desires are larger? What is the architecture of the psyche so that largeness can be a property of desire? Terms like *nobility, transcendence,* and *magnanimity* present themselves here—but can only suggest. They fail to mark our notoriously amorphous inner terrain with a precision that produces insight and agreement. Still, their suggestiveness offers hints. *Magnanimity,* for instance, is a compound of *magnus,* great, and *animus,* or spirit, and so points to inner largeness. In essence, desires enlarge through deepening, and deepening is possible because meaning-getting-and-holding, the cradle of desire, can widen through greater and greater association—the moreness produced by the increasing notice of sameness—and that developing wideness provides a station and structure for the largerness of desire. As in: I am insulted and react with bitterness, then notice the insulter's embarrassment and feel sympathy. The widening of my awareness permitted the deeper, more expansive—hence larger—desire of sympathy to supplant the smaller desire of recrimination.

It's worth mentioning that Darwinists have noticed largeness as well (which they call altruism) in that bees and ants sometimes die for the hive. Which gave them an idea (the Darwinists, not the bees)—good will for our fellow beings is genetically conditioned, a predisposition installed in the psyche as a force useful in promoting group survival. So that: a wealthy fellow who hoards corn during a famine is tapped on the brain by the altruism gene, which unconsciously provokes him to invite the villagers to a feast. (This conjecture, of course, overlooks the oddity of a material thing, a gene, mysteriously crossing the body-mind divide to produce psychic force, a curiosity which is part of the built-in conundrum of physicalism.) But evolution hardly needs an altruism gene. Things could proceed just fine, thank you, if the commoners seize weapons and assault the villa—which is what they generally do. Greed is plenty of psychic architecture to keep the species going.

And even if we are willing to hold, for instance, that it's not genes, but instead some sort of psychic force independent of materiality, a force part of a Jung-style collective unconsciousness, we are still left with the conundrum that greed—and lust too—is sufficient to produce the next generation. And no one thinks of greed and lust, and any of the other so-called vices, as part of magnanimity.

Yet magnanimity is. So whence is it? (Why comes later.)

Let's consider an example that might suggest its outline. Your friend claims a stone weighs 30 pounds. You claim it weighs 20. You weigh the stone and find your friend correct—the stone weighs 30 pounds. You magnanimously concede he was right. What is the psychic event within you that produces that concession? What, in fact, is concession? *Concede* means to yield or give way and so points beyond itself to further structures of the psyche. What is yielded? What is given way to?

It's good to note, in the case of the stone, for instance, that it is not my truer view of the world (the stone weighs 30 pounds) that represents my magnanimity. I could, for instance, concede my friend was right and feel humiliated. Only if I grant my friend's rightness without jealousy or reluctance do I express magnanimity. As disappointingly rare as that state may be, in ourselves, our friends, and our public figures—so rare, in fact, that many distrust it as illusion—we can all imagine and value its possibility if not its existence. What then is the architecture of the psyche that might produce such a state and that creates in us admiration for it? And can we, in understanding that architecture, come to better understand the sizing of desire?

Earlier, we left incomplete the discussion of humility and its counterfeit, modesty, since we had not yet developed the psychic understructure required to make sense of them. Now we take that up.

This beginning note: thinking about the inner world is always conjectural. For one thing, most of it is hidden in the unconscious and mostly and frustratingly unavailable to measurement. Thinking is only reflection, and the inner being is lit so poorly that it reflects dimly at best and distortedly at worst. All introspection can do is to create more and more conviction as the ideas it develops interconnect, validate, and clarify. But introspection, unlike deduction (in which, as shown earlier, the conclusions are inherent in the premises), can never reach certainty. But it can reach a useful confidence, and, as we shall see, useful confidence is a powerful, elementary, and crucial world-and-psyche-changing force.

As soon as ideas like magnanimity appear, other ideas—ego, the power impulse, reputation, selfishness, pride—present themselves, and, like the idea of magnanimity, remain vague. Ideas are, after all, merely outlines of the invisible and formless inner world. Yet those terms, which we all intuitively, if vaguely, recognize as opposite from magnanimity, share this commonality—they are a wanting for the self. Though the term *self* too is amorphous, we can at least comfortably hold that magnanimity, though itself a form of desire, is somehow different from the desires that create the normal traffic of selfness. When I contentedly accept my friend is right about the stone's weight, I am magnanimous. If I announce that he is right but harbor resentment, I am selfish. If I announce that he is right so that he will suppose me magnanimous, I am selfish again. In magnanimity—in which there are no doubt shades and stages—there is happy concession and easy submission, and the disposition that produces that ease and happiness is what we are here trying to unearth. (The terms *happiness* and *ease* point out that magnanimity is not a strained compliance with external guidance, as in: I must be honest, so I am compelled to admit you are right about the stone's weight. It is instead a willing and contented submission, and the felt indifference of that submission results from my indifference to reputation.)

It is sometimes argued that our disapproval of selfishness is misguided because it inhibits mankind's greatness and also naturalness. Social conditioning, it is argued, promotes a hypocrisy that hides not only selfishness but also the deeper ranges of our being. To prevent chaos, group living requires the social conditioning of good manners, a sort of false magnanimity, and this counterfeiting—so scold the philosophers Nietzsche and Rousseau—promotes self-repression and emptiness. Yet when considered more deeply, it's evident that the argument for selfishness is really an argument for honesty instead of an argument for cruelty or greed.

If there is a difference between the magnanimous self and the selfish self, it makes sense to consider first, whether such a division is more than imagination, and second, to consider, if it exists, what it portends for our understanding of the psyche. We might also wonder whether such a division fits comfortably within a Darwinian view of life. After all, whatever its underlying structure and source, since magnanimity could easily be held as less useful than force for gene-propagation, it must then be only a spurious appendix of evolution produced by genetic drift. If life is about mammoth-catching and babies, then magnanimity, fairly useless in all that, must have arisen accidentally. It found a welcome place in life, the Darwinist might hold, because we are naturally pleased that that kindly fellow over there has no plan to interfere with our roast mammoth and baby-making.

How it could have continued in the species presents a problem though, since it hardly seems likely that the most magnanimous get to make the most babies.

The idea of magnanimity clarifies as its contraries surround and inform it. All cultures and creeds are fond of listing so-called vices—lists which vary in length and variety—and, since seven is a good number for sins (according to Pope Gregory I), this thinking will choose these: lust, greed, anger, selfishness, hatred, jealousy, and pride. These seven sins, as they are called, are magnanimity's opposites. All of them, from first to last, are servants of small desire, and so are not wide or thoughtful—in short, are not large.

The difficulty in this discussion is that evidence of magnanimity lies solely within each individual's inner experience and about experience argument is tedious and useless. Those without experience can happily deny. Those with experience can happily shrug.

The best we can do is offer again the 30-pound thought experiment, which, if it does not point to common experience, at least points to an experience we can commonly imagine. When we admit without humiliation that the stone weighs 30 pounds, we recognize in the *without humiliation* part of that inner event some sort of release, detachment, welcome, freedom—something good and happy to feel, something big. What station of the psyche can imperturbably concede error, and how is that station different from the mind-station that feels the humiliated sting of diminished reputation? All of us have felt in ourselves and seen in others evidence of this station, and, however fragmentary and impure, whether illusion or real, whether embraced or denied by doctrine, we have sensed its value.

Our experience or imagination of this psychic station shapes a notion of its opposite, the self, the ego, the desire-disposition. This invisible ball of knowing-wanting that is installed somewhere in our heads is a scampering-about inner thingamajig famously on the lookout to manicure its reputation and satisfy its desires, which it does mostly by viewing the world through the lens of the above seven dispositions. All this discussion about the disposition-self-ego just states what we all commonly know—we're out to get what we want and action central is the vaguely-felt ego through which desire continually pours.

But sometimes, and importantly, this ego station relents, releases, quiets—one of those terms or their kin—and experiences an unaccustomed inner largeness, as in: indeed, I now see—and without perturbation—that the stone weighs 30 pounds.

For some at least we have just taken a paragraphs-long tour to state the obvious—we value largeness. But we have taken the tour through close-noticing, not through the admonitory advice of a doctrine. Largeness is just a lying-around fact of life.

No doubt, to hold that some desires are larger than others involves us in one of the most trenchant of all human debates, the consideration of value. If some desires are larger are they also better, and if they are, what can *better* mean? Philosophy and theology have wandered this terrain for centuries—and today even science has raised its voice here. Tracing those historical paths is the work of scholarship, and this thinking, while noting a here-and-there echo of its discoveries with prior thought, is satisfied to rely on close-noticing. After all, the more entangled thinking becomes with previous explanation, the more distant its view. Also, let it be announced and urgently urged, that at this point in our thinking we remain indifferent to any and all isms, creeds, faiths, philosophies, or spiritual suppositions. This thinking simply wants to know.

The more we consider largeness of spirit, the more it becomes evident that it is not produced by the ordinary impulse for power. That impulse might imitate magnanimity, but imitation is easily exposed as a counterfeit intent on renown or esteem. Something in us is drawn to high-mindedness but not spite, to dignity but not resentment, to statesmen but not politicians.

It's good to remember that even the clearest naming exhibits the disappointing mereness of all thought—it is only a pointing-to-experience and not experience itself. But in that mereness we can find clues to the geography of our depths. To what state of being do these names point?

To make that state more vivid,

The second detective takes his final bow

Several pages earlier we left the second detective as it dawned on him that his judgment of the black suspect had been wrong. And we related that he had experienced an impulse of remorse.

Recall that the second detective grew up in the south where the black people didn't speak like him, where black people exhibited obsequiousness and resentment by turns, where black neighborhoods were poor, unsightly, and sometimes dangerous, and, in short, where blackness was associated in the white man's mind with contemptible otherness. Though the second detective loved Charlie, this welter of impressions made the submergence of his father's crime, however painful, easy to sustain.

But now—the black man is innocent! The white girl guilty!

Let us introspect the within of the second detective as he discovers the white girl's guilt, admits his mistake, and then becomes aware of what led him to that mistake, a concealed disposition of conditioned enmity. We must proceed cautiously because here we meet with hidden structures of the unconscious. How are feelings concealed? What is the nature of remorse? Lifting this psychic structure into the view of thought is like lifting a fish from water—it gasps for its natural home, the flow of the dark within that produces our consciousness. Yet as the fish of the second detective's remorse breaks the surface of his mind to taste the clear air of consciousness, it is welcomed there not as a creature of dark but as a companion of air and light. The remorse he feels as his revulsion toward the black man melts is not accusatory but somehow welcoming, deepening, and enlarging. That *somehow* is what we are considering. Somehow the dark fish of his egotism was removed from its natural home—to a home even more natural.

We have shown that recognition is possible only through sameness. How then did sameness operate in the second detective? We may say that he saw, or that it came to him, or that it dawned on him, or that some disposition in him relented or gave way or released—all these are best-we-can-do phrases that attempt to awaken in us a comprehension of the phenomenon that occurred in the second detective—a recognition that he had excluded in himself a profound sameness, his sameness with black people. And he felt remorse.

Let us see and feel with him.

At first perhaps the second detective feels confusion, then, as he realizes that his reputation might be sullied, he feels chagrin. Then comes self-accusation, then unfocused anger. (Anger at our disposition is always unfocused since our disposition lies always unseeably beneath the surface.) He speaks sharply to his wife and daughter. He is unmanned by his harshness and goes for a drive, driving fast, toward nowhere. He finds himself in the countryside, turns onto a forested road. He parks beside a pond, sits on its edge, and gazes at the empty water, beneath the empty sky. Emptiness presses like a weight until, gradually, sadness appears. He does not resist—he senses its truth and use. Vaguely, something in him hopes and opens. He recalls his sharp words to his family, his wife's alarm, his daughter's hurt. Sadness grows. He has not cried in years, not even in movies, and now feels tears close. The black man's face rises in his mind, the black man's fear and anger, and now wildly, unexpectedly, he sees his boyhood pal, Charlie, his laughing face, his careless trust. And tears do come. He weeps. He weeps fully and well and feels in himself the deep delight and rinsing freedom of his tears. When the weeping subsides, he is left bewildered and shaken. And yet not. There was clarity in the weeping, and freshness, and there was comfort. There was welcome. He is filled with longing, to enfold his daughter, to hold his wife, and yes, he will make a search for Charlie and see what became of him and his family and help him if he can help him. He will find the black man. He will apologize as well as he is able and hope to be strong enough to expect no forgiveness. He means to mean well more and more and more.

Ah, well. We leave him to his thoughts. He has served us well. Safe travels, second detective!

The sizing of desire, and heart, and head

Above, it was reported that the second detective felt remorse. But what of guilt? Though we generally use the terms *guilt* and *remorse* with some degree of useful sense, distinguishing fulsomely between them is difficult since that distinguishing requires the notice of an inner terrain that for most remains stubbornly obscure.

In general, the psychic geography suggested by the difference between guilt and remorse maps regions we think of as head and heart. In the West we think of the center of emotion as residing in the chest. We touch our sternum when we feel moved. In Yiddish, we feel verklempt as our chests thicken with feeling. In the East, the heart center is considered the locus in the chest of one of the seven chakras (energy centers). Both cultures think of head as somewhere above that center. Like everything within, these areas are invisible and can only be felt for. And while we sometimes think of larger desire as residing in the heart and smaller in the head, we also know there are spiteful hearts and broad-minded thinkers. To understand the difference between guilt and remorse we need to develop the geography of the inner being.

The difference between head and heart points to the same feature of intelligence that we discovered in the 30-pound thought experiment—that intelligence is layered, that some inner stations are wider, deeper, larger, and that largeness somehow dissolves, supplants, and subsumes smallness. How this happens and why that is significant in the psyche is what we are considering.

It's worth noting that the sizing of desire and the strength of desire interweave to create the complex of human experience. I am writing a letter, and someone asks to borrow my pen. My desire to write is strong but less strong than my larger desire to cooperate—so I pass the pen over, but reluctantly. And in that reluctance is the felt strife of living, the back-and-forth between strength and size in the desire world that produces the tangles of human valuation in everyday living (and in the courtroom).

Though vague, the terms head and heart are at least useful in suggesting the inner layering of the psyche. This layering helps us understand sentimentality, in which head poses as heart, and also dignity, in which heart takes a stand beneath the vacillation of head. In general, whether heart is considered a pulse of meaning from higher ranges of thought or whether a pulse of higher feeling, heart is commonly understood as a higher mode of being, and points again to the existence of higherness itself. It points to a vast inner terrain whose working is subtle and mysterious, compounded not merely of intuition, intellect, and desire but of these elements, in both conscious and unconscious form, that shift, blend, and ceaselessly dance as they do the work of our life-living. To see this clearly is to witness life pouring through us, to see the rising and falling away of meaning and desire, to be in and with the isness of being.

The twin quicksands

If I assert that the stone weighs 20 pounds before my friend and I find a scale, something interesting about my psyche is revealed: I have made a claim. I was willing to express an opinion in opposition to my friend's and then submit that claim, however timorously or confidently, as: You are wrong, sir! The stone weighs 20 pounds! Thus, since I was ignorant of the stone's actual weight, I strode boldly forth on the plank of opinion over the void of my own uncertainty. It makes useful sense to hold that my willingness to make that claim is the result of the power force in me, a force installed in all life to promote survival. Thus, we clap Darwin on the shoulder and declare, well done, sir!

But what if I am unwilling to walk the plank of opinion so unwarily? What if I say to my friend, you say the stone weighs 30 pounds? You may be right, but I confess I am doubtful. Shall we try the scales? Here I have not presumptuously strode forth on a plank cantilevered over uncertainty. I have merely put one foot hesitatingly forward, and when the needle reads 30, my appreciation of physics needs more adjustment than my self-esteem. It may even be that when my friend makes his 30-pound claim I merely nod, and, whether doubtful or not, remain indifferent about expressing an opinion. The young, as we know, are enthusiastic plank-walkers of opinion—which makes good Darwinian sense since they have confidence to get and babies to make. But many of the old also find themselves proudly cantilevered over uncertainty. These we call foolish. We say that their good sense, their world-mapping facility, has been hijacked by desire. We say they are bent on vindication, not truth.

The 30-pound thought experiment is an attempt to illumine the invisible, formless, opinion-urging ego force in us which brags and vaunts when right-seeming and blenches and falters when wrong-seeming. This me-self is structured by desire that not only has strength but also has size. And from desire's sizes we can get a sense of so-called high-mindedness.

It's worth noting that anyone who attempts to understand high-mindedness in humankind must be alert for two quicksands awaiting them. Simple-minded homage is the quicksand of the hopeful. Simple-minded cynicism is the quicksand of the discouraged. And both these sinks are bound beneath the surface in a symbiotic embrace since each is made energetic by its opposition to the other. Cynics shake their heads and insist high-mindedness is illusion. The hopeful shake their heads and condemn cynics as lost. The magnanimous ignore the debate.

The discussion of the largeness of desire, which is magnanimity, leads naturally to a discussion of humility, and that discussion leads, just as naturally, to a discussion of love.

Humility and coffee cups

Humility and love are both so pedestaled in the mind that understanding them can provoke doubt or sentimentalism. Both these attitudes occur because of our inability—wonderfully concealed by nature—to recognize the oddity that love and humility are *immune to will*. Admonition can change conscious behavior—the front self personna is a form of behavior—but cannot penetrate the nine-tenths of the self which is unconscious. No one in human history has ever heard the advice to be more humble and said, *Okay then, I will,* and done it. No one in history has ever heard the advice to be more loving and done it. Humility and love are stations of being maddeningly elusive to conscious will because, important to understand, *they do not issue from our ego self.*

Which is a clue to the structure of both the psyche and the universe.

When we close-notice love and humility it becomes evident that both are present in every moment of ordinary life and that it is only at their height that we think to name and revere them. Earlier, in the discussion of sameness and recognition, we saw that to encounter a coffee cup (or anything else) and not be startled by its appearance, we depend on re-cognizing its coffeecupness—that is, on permitting the idea of coffeecupness to inform the object in the cupboard or in our spouse's hand as just another one of those things I know as a no-big-deal coffee cup. Any particular coffee cup is welcomed into my meaning-field through the agency of sameness recognition—and hidden in that sameness recognition are the rudiments of both humility and love. We might conjecture that it is not coincidental that the word *like* in English names both a love state and a sameness state. As in: I like you because you are like me.

At bottom, it makes sense to understand humility as a species of noninterference in meaning-getting. The essence of humility is to let-be-what-is. And in an important sense, each moment of our lives depends on that letting-be. I turn and a tree appears. I accept it as an out-there thing that is as it is and do not contend to myself or others that it is an intelligence agent in clever tree disguise. Such imagination we understand as insanity, and the absence of that imagination, which is the absence of isness-distorting desire (fear is desire), is what determines our workmanlike going-about-the-day. In that going-about-the-day is the customary, immediate, and unspoken humility of encountering the world without distortion. That encounter, and all the ordinariness of living, depends on my acceptance (which is the essence of letting-be) of the isness surrounding me and within me. Acceptance is the essence of humility. In that sense, humility is the basis of all consciousness, since it is by accepting the world that we know and want our way through it.

A synonym for humility, considered as the bottom-most essence of all experiencing, is love. When pedestaled in the mind, love is that out-there ideal whose possibility lures and whose absence accuses, but its basis is identical to humility's basis and ingredient in every moment of consciousness.

It is the welcome of the world.

Oddly then, since all action and thought proceed only by and through this welcome, this love, even love's opposite is one of its forms. We hate this because we love that. At its most elemental level, love is acceptance, welcome, recognition. When I pick up a pencil to use it, I feel for the pencil a species of love. The pencil has entered my meaning-world, and its being offers itself to my purpose. Though I am unaware of the least pulse of gratitude for its existence, my withness with the pencil and its offer of use to me is silent testimony that the pencil is loved. I love my clothes, my hands, car, and food. The lion loves the gazelle. The worm loves the earth. Love can be understood as the binding force of recognition and acceptance that tethers us to existence. It is the force within our intelligence that produces each moment of meaning-getting-and-holding and desire. It is the unitary action of the two ontological primitives, so that each moment of existence can be properly understood as the substance and action of love. Though it is only at its height that we enthrone love as most valuable, it has been our companion all along. It is the habitual and unnoticed welcome of being and is inherent in all meaning gotten and in all meaning held, as well as in all that we desire—and in our hatred of what thwarts our desire. The force that binds intelligence to existence is the simultaneous action of meaning and desire, and that rudimentary force is usefully understood as love.

Though we use the terms love and humility in different contexts—humility suggests the relation of the self to the world, and love suggests the force active in the self as it experiences—both terms point to the same feature of intelligence which may be termed letting-be, welcome, or trust.

So that: humility, kindness, charity, and large-mindedness do not suddenly appear within us when we somehow become good, but develop from the primordial structures of being that make intelligence-consciousness possible. They are ingredient in the structure of being. Love and humility are the essential withness on which all consciousness depends. Humility empowers me to see the pencil. The welcome of pencilness into my world is love.

And both are forms of desire, or, put simply, of interest in existence. The difference that makes all the difference is in the fullness and development of that interest, in the sizes and shades of that desiring.

As we discover that love and humility, in their primitive-most forms, are the hidden powers that make intelligence possible, we recall as well that underlying both of them is the previously discovered notion of sameness, the feature of intelligence that empowers all that means itself to us. And they say, don't they, that God is love and also one, which is the final sameness, so who knows, maybe there's God too and more, maybe he's love! And then everything is wonderful and meaningful.

Before we celebrate this trail of thinking, let us note that this means, oddly and maybe perversely, that everything is the expression of love, that hatred is love, that anger is love, that thought is love, that love is mistakes, emptiness, and sorrow, and pornography, tears, release, loss, bravery, war, and utterly everything.

Plus down here with the second detective things are gritty and hard, and there's no graspable God, and we remind ourselves that even if the universe is somehow structured by love, maybe that's just how things are. Maybe things are cruising along with love and sameness at the bottom but no great overmastering, overwatching, and controlling divine consciousness behind things. Love, sure, but no help, and then you die. In short, if love is at the bottom, is God, whatever or whoever that may be, there too? And how to know, and more—how to live so we can and do know?

These are not the complacent questions of religion. They are the questions of seekers and are mature, sensible, and honorable. They require answers in kind.

To make full sense of the states of humility and love, we must open again the subject of freedom. Because only by fully comprehending the nature and bondage of what we call *will* can we deeply grasp the what and why of those states, and also the state of inner largeness, and more, finally get a grip on the hardest problem, the what-to-do-all-day problem.

And get a sense of what sort of universe this is.

That tireless problem of freedom

Recall that, as shown earlier, choice is an illusion (though psychologically essential and life-smoothing) that can be described as a sounding for preference which is not free but imposed from the unchosen, unchoosable, and mostly unconscious desire-disposition. Which means that everything that seems to be willed by us—the entirety of our going-about-the-day, our hesitation here, our enthusiasm there—is determined by forces out of our keeping. Which means that all our doing, however free-seeming, happens under the eerie and implacable blanket of an amnesia installed in us by the marvel of the consciousness-unconsciousness junction. Which means, at first rather uncomfortably, that all our notions of responsibility are based on illusion. But this illusion, as we shall see, *is essential for natural living and conceals an even greater naturalness.*

This unfreeness conception is ferociously opposed to normality and is why it has been unrecognized for centuries, except by the few. Because if choice is imposed, are not pride and blame forever unwarranted?

It's not only unnatural to accept this, for most of us it's impossible. That's because our doing-willing and our reflection about our doing-willing occur in two separate parts of our being. One is our do-this do-that going-about-the-day part. The other is the part that thinks about our going-about-the-day. In the going-about-the-day world it's impossible to notice our bondage. In the world of reflection it's impossible to deny it.

Down here in our walking-around self, we can only *think* that Ronald, that rascal, is blameless for forgetting to close the door. We get mad at him anyway because anger cannot be *thought* out of existence. Down here where we do life we do not and cannot live entirely according to our reflections, however idealistic. The attempt to do that results in the well-known inner emaciation common in ascetics and fanatics—in all those whose inner experience has not yet ripened into more than idealism. Trying to stop blaming because we think we should merely creates a wall of inner repression so that the anger and intolerance that prevent forgiveness—and largeness—become invisible.

However much our reflective thinking reminds us that no one is responsible for anything, our approval-disapproval of our own actions and the actions of others is an impossible-to-dispense-with feeling-state. This is why mankind has philosophically, morally, and habitually defended the notion of free will. It just seems to be how things are, and if it's all an illusion, well then, it's a necessary one, so kindly do not trouble me with too much thinking.

As we consider the I-do-this feeling and our consequent I-did-that memory, it might be useful to acknowledge the immediate, in some, and inevitable, in most, impatient irritability at being told we are in bondage despite our freedom-feeling. Absurd! Have I not always done what I wanted? Can I not continue to do what I want?

No doubt. But you cannot choose to want what you want.

Here lies one of the great perplexities of existence, that only a small noticing reveals our bondage to desire (though it has taken centuries for our minds to clear sufficiently to recognize that, and some, reading this, will no doubt remain confounded), and yet this noticing is still powerless to alter the mesmerizing effect of the freedom-feeling that accompanies every moment of doing. We are pulled through time by the desire-ring installed in our nose in every moment of consciousness and follow these desires under the concealment we call choice. The feeling of choice, the freedom-feeling that accompanies our acting, is an illusion both irresistible and essential for natural living. This freedom-feeling, then, is the phenomenon we must examine to understand human nature.

Freedom-feeling results from the experience that, as we come to the fork of choice, we are not grounded in the intellect, the reflecting pool of mentation which alone is able to mirror experience and comprehend our bondage, but instead we are confronted with chocolate or vanilla, and let's see, hummm, chocolate! *The taking of chocolate is an act of doing we call will, and acts of doing-willing happen always without reflection.* Reflection occurs after or before action. (While he is bound in thinking, Achilles can't even beat a turtle in a foot race.) Only as we reflect, can the question come: Oh self, why chocolate? I like it. Did you choose to like it? Ah. (To keep our thoughts in order, it's worth mentioning here that even reflection is an act of will, since it is a doing powered by desire, so that always, importantly and confoundingly, we are bound in the prison of will, which is, after all, the desires that continually propel and inhabit us.)

Though the massively overlapped and shaded desires of the ego make self-considering fraught, it is still possible to employ intellect, intuition, and memory to notice desire's working. But only after the act. I turn my head. I lift my arm. Only afterward can I reflect that it was desire that impelled me. *The awareness of my enthrallment to desire is never simultaneous with the act of will.* Somehow, in the act of desire called will, notice is forbidden by the very structure of consciousness. Even if I move my hand very slowly across the space before me, concentrating on the desire that continues to impel the hand, at any moment I can stop the motion and am utterly unaware when the arrival of the stop-motion desire will arise. Or if I decide in advance to stop the motion when the hand lines up with a window pane, I am still unaware how the window-pane-stopping decision arose.

All this means what we already know—thinking about willing is an after-the-act or before-the-act phenomenon. This does not negate the value of impulse control, but merely notes that the desires that arise to control other desires in impulse control are themselves part of our comprehensive desire bondage—and, like all desires, not chosen or chooseable. Reflection about which desire to act on—the thoughtful weighing of desire—is useful, but is itself a desire-imposed (hence bound) state. Further, even if we hesitate before acting by thinking, hummm, should I pull the trigger, at the moment of trigger-pulling reflection has packed its bags and vacated the premises. Yet thinking has its place and a place of no small importance. Without thinking, we would pull many triggers, get fat, and crash cars. Still, the thinking that prevents trigger-pulling is itself inspired by desire.

The what-is-it of will has occupied philosophers and legal scholars for centuries—and yet remains stubbornly mysterious because of the freedom-feeling and consequent implacable notions of responsibility. To fully understand the functioning of consciousness in the act of choice we must examine even more thoroughly the junction of consciousness and unconsciousness.

The blanket thief

That the ego cannot notice its bondage to desire—and that in these pages we have noticed that bondage—is a clue to the nature of egotism. How do such notice and unnotice operate—and cooperate?

The unnotice, as discussed, is natural and essential for the smooth operation of willing. The home of notice is reflection, the stepping-back mentation inherent in consciousness. We sometimes call this stepping-back-and-noticing function intellect, but its richer, deeper, and more immediate power is the power of intuition, the meaning-getting power beneath and behind all thought. In the act of will, which is the see-the-world-and-do aspect of desire, we have no above-and-looking-down point of view until intellect and intuition step away in reflection. (This separation between thinking and doing is why we can't master the golf swing by reading a book.)

For human beings, of course, thinking is essential. The division in human consciousness between doing and thinking about doing can be usefully, if always vaguely, understood as the division that gives human beings their ego-forming power. We might imagine that tigers, because they don't have much of the overlooking power of mind, don't have a lot of ego—and for that reason don't get a lot of blame. Dogs, though, have a bit more separation between their front desire-self and their steering back mind which is why *bad dog!* isn't as absurd as *bad tiger!* and definitely not as misguided as *bad mosquito!* The discordance of *bad person* is what we're considering.

It is the separation of the doing-willing part of our being from our thinking-about-doing part that creates our notion of personal responsibility—and law.

"You didn't have to do that," says the judge. The smallest thinking can fairly reply, "Yes, I did."

Close-noticed thinking leaves blame in tangles:

Look, Judge, I took his blanket because if I didn't I would have froze to death.

Judge: *Well, that's just what made him freeze to death.*

I know, judge, but it was him or me, and I had to go with me.

Judge: *Well, the law has to go with him.*

But why, judge, since he was keeping the blanket from me, which means that he was going with himself instead of me, which was just what I was doing. We were both me-firsting, and I just me-firsted luckier. Bottom line, he was laying there blanket-taking while I was freezing. If I hadn't robbed him, and it was me that froze, would you arrest him for murder? Plus, judge, he won that blanket from me in a hand of poker, and you can say it was my fault for playing, but he was playing too, so he's just as guilty as me about that. If he hadn't been in the game and won, I wouldn't have had to rob his blanket. It's not my fault for being unlucky in poker by losing and having to rob him any more than it's his fault for being lucky and dying by winning. You gonna hang me, judge?

Judge: *Hummm.*

These perplexities only persist because the hawk of blame is restless for a place to settle in the tangled thicket of willing, and in that thicket, blame has no legitimate perch. It's not that clear-thinking judges must refuse to pass sentence. It's that anyone that can think clearly, and judges too, after close-noticing the bondage inherent in every action, cannot justify blame.

Yet blame is so natural to our emotional center that repressing it ties the ego in knots. And anyway, what to do about criminals? When a villain is waiting in line on judgment day, can he raise his hand and say, Oh God, since I had no choice in anything, what's all this judgment business? For a God disposed to blame this question is a stumper—and is also why the freedom-of-choice notion, however absurd, has been so persistent in culture and law. The insight that no one is guilty because everyone is compelled produces a shattering reappraisal for individuals and for societies. That's why, in the Abrahamic religions—Judaism, Christianity, and Islam—God has always been conceived as a being separate from creation. That way he can overwatch with a reproving eye. And if it makes sense that God can judge us, it makes sense that we can judge each other.

Blame doesn't make sense though, ontologically, psychologically, or spiritually. The freedom-of-choice doctrine not only separates creation from God, it produces the oddity of the Abrahamic religions and allows us to proclaim love as the highest value while simultaneously sanctioning its opposite. All this because of our failure to grapple honestly with our no-freedom fix.

Before proceeding, let's pause to answer those who sanction blame by pointing out that human beings often and normally experience a here-and-there pulse of misgiving during bad actions—our reflective self trying to get a word in while, for instance, we pillage the village. This overwatching conscience is what judges point to as everyone's shared accuser. Indeed, in law, the slightest forethought can alter murder from second degree to first (depending, as we unhappily know, on the mood/caprice of the prosecutor). The answer to this embrace of conscience is that even conscientious forethought, and also regret, is dependent on unchosen desire. Does anyone conscientiously consider their actions without wanting to? It is wanting-to that compels both action and conscience, and wanting-to is imposed, not chosen. This observation doesn't obviate conscience or character as useless, it merely grants their bondage in desire.

Well, damn—when a wrongdoer stands up in court to explain that he didn't have a choice (his upbringing, poverty, bad parenting, too many Twinkies, defective mind, or the blanket thief's unluck in poker) can he legitimately hope to hesitate the gavel of judges? Will the close-noticing of the unfreedom of choice freeze gavels entirely? If no one is guilty, can villains celebrate?

Absolutely. But in prison. Gavels must fall. A right-thinking judge understands every criminal's helpless bondage. A wide-thinking judge sentences him anyway—both for his sake and for the sake of others. If a man beats his wife, he can be taught to count to ten. If he beats his wife when he reaches eleven, he can be jailed. Societies and psyches and tigers too order themselves through consequences. But clear-thinking societies and psyches cannot order themselves through blame. Recognizing our bondage through reflection does not free us from that bondage, nor does it free us from the narrow response of blame. But it does point, and emphatically point, to an inner condition beyond blame.

Have we then, through thinking, somehow justified the advice of Jesus to turn the other cheek and to endlessly forgive? If we have, will we find this thinking as unnatural to our inner nature as his admonition was? So far at least, most of us have agreed with Jesus in spirit but comfortably ignored him in practice. The cry of the French revolution was liberty, equality, fraternity. Fraternity failed, and the natural war between liberty and equality is fought ever more ferociously today, and world-wide, between conservatives and progressives.

The problem is this: if no one, at least ontologically, is responsible for anything since doing-willing is inflicted on them from within by unchosen desire, and worse, if recognition of that bondage is impossible at the moment of doing-willing, and later only through the mereness of reflective thought, how are we as societies and psyches to address this insight? How, as societies and psyches, can we respond usefully and fulsomely to our morality-dissolving, ontologically-imposed bondage?

Humility, the redeemer of everything

After exposing such a mighty dilemma—the unfreedom of freedom—how to deal honestly with it? Through close-noticing, we have broken from a thicket of thought into the open meadow of simplicity and clear seeing. There we have found the structures of knowing—sameness and recognition—and the embryonic forces of love and humility that shape our moment-by-moment experience of the world. It is these two, humility and love, that can equip us with an understanding that gathers in one armful the squirming, rascally, and unhappily vague ideas and isms that have beset us throughout history—and leave them at the forest's edge. We will see that to understand love and humility is to understand the structure of the mind—and to understand the universe.

We have mentioned that love and humility in their most rudimentary forms have to do with acceptance and letting-be. In their deepest form they are: I-see-life-issuing-not-from-me-but-through-me from the unknown and vast Where-of-all-being. And I trust. This state hides in the tangle of living in near perfect camouflage. It must be approached tentatively, respectfully, patiently. And alas—and daunting to the truth-seeker—the warrant to its presence is exquisitely tangled in the thicket of desire.

This recap (and mild complaint): we have noted desire and meaning as the two primitive-most elements of consciousness. We have noted the existence of the consciousness-unconsciousness junction where the ego sits as ignorant suzerain. We have discovered the working of sameness which points to wholeness, the final sameness. We have noted the working of recognition and the embryo of love in meaning and desire. We have discovered the sizing of desire in our discussion of magnanimity.

As we appreciate these elements of existence, it becomes more and more evident how limping, pasted on, and massively supposed are the two explanatory systems of physicalism and neo-Darwinism. Though their omissions and errors are natural to developing mind, and though their defense is natural to the effort and eminence of their promoters, their failures as true maps of the complexity and depth of being have become provokingly apparent. Their offering is like a stream that gleams as it springs forth but vanishes in the desert of its own supposing. A better supposing recognizes the existence of the Darwinianly useless state of humility and begins to wonder if that state is after more than mammoths.

To reach and reside in humility is not merely a mental stepping back, a removal of notice from the front-self-wanting of ego, but is instead a deepening of front-self wanting to a larger wanting. That's why detachment is not merely, ah, I see myself wanting. That's useful, but it's a state better named *awareness*. Detachment is, I move from wanting small because I have begun to want large. Detachment is not a change in our meaning-station. It is a change in our desire-station. It is a change of heart.

It's useful again to note that humility is not, just as desire is not, in our keeping. This is why modesty, humility's counterfeit, is so often thrown forward by our front-self will. We intuitively feel the value of humility as a release from the prison of egotism, but our effort to produce it creates only modesty. Our will, that credit-taking and blame-asserting force of egotism, and humility, that gracious force of deeper desire, are both formations of desire—and thus, like all desire, compelled and not chosen. That fact is for some disconcerting—until we come to understand that everything is compelled, that nothing whatever is in our keeping. Only the state of humility begins to comprehend this. It appears in the basements of mind in a manner most natural—and utterly beyond choosing. It grows like a mushroom in the moist soil of need.

As earlier noted, the two events that make us up, seeing and wanting, nest each in the palm of the other. That we can only want what we see is clear enough, but to hold that we can only see what we want means that wanting creates a shield or veil that obscures seeing, a smudged lens through which seeing must notice and by which notice is bound.

The objection naturally comes—but surely I see plenty I do not want? But it is not these surface wantings that proscribe our seeing—this food, that person—but instead our dispositional wanting, the general tenure and attitude of our mind-station. The phrase *dispositional wanting* points to something interestingly psychological in the structure of our being, that there is, besides the more evident (conscious and noticeable) wanting that flows continually through us in time, also a background (unconscious) wanting that structures our psyche. Just as we understood that hidden in the wholeness-sameness of any bit of idea-meaning is an unconscious penumbra of the meaning-parts that uphold it, so too hidden in any conscious desire is the unconscious penumbra of the dispositional station from which it emerges and that gives it ground and sanction. This dispositional penumbra, because it lies in the unconscious (outside experience), has taken centuries to clearly suppose, but its supposition is as natural as supposing that the tree does not disappear when I look away. A further supposing is that this under-the-surface dispositional penumbra itself is made up of desire-bits and that each of these desire-bits are likewise composed of penumbra-bits of desire. (A turtles-all-the-way-down structure, which, as we will discover, leads to the marvelous mutuality of human intelligence.)

It is only by recognizing the existence of this background unconscious wanting—that is, by making it more conscious—that the widening and deepening that is humility can be experienced. The unconsciousness of this background wanting is the reason humility is so elusive—and introspection often so vague. In essence, the unconsciousness of our background, dispositional wanting creates all the trouble of living. After all, given that desire has sizes, if anyone were at any moment conscious of the complete range of his or her desires, higher and lower together, is it conceivable that he or she would prefer rage to love, condemnation to kindness, selfishness to generosity? The work of introspection is the revealment of the body of desire hidden in the unconscious, and the emergence of these desires happens only in the inner welcome of humility. Since everything that emerges into consciousness emerges only through desire (we see what we want) what desire in the inner world can provide that welcome? What desire is largest and best to have? And how to get it?

If we knew that we could solve the hardest problem, the problem of what to do all day.

The plagiarism of pride and the highest desire

To comprehend the nature of the desire that produces humility, it is useful to consider again humility's opposite, pride, an absurd and fascinating mind-station that manifests confidence and ignorance simultaneously.

Consider: if you ask a champion athlete of what she is proud, she might hesitate and think well, it can't be my body, since I didn't make that, and I guess not my skill either since that was gifted too, so I guess, hummm, all I can be proud of is the effort and dedication it took to develop my craft. But clearly athletes don't stand on the podium beaming with pride in their character. And even if a rare one did, might not some jealous philosopher tap her shoulder to remind her that her ambition to excel was likewise a gift and not created by herself, that her long hours of effort resulted from desire she herself did not create, so that even pride in her character has to be discarded. Only the briefest thinking exposes every instance of pride as a subtle fraud, a kind of plagiarism.

Athletes are generally not philosophical, of course, and though some touch their heart and point upward after they make a three pointer or touchdown, even these are sensible enough to beam as the exhilaration of accomplishment has its natural way with them. Yet the naturalness of pride does not sanction it as an estimable aspect of personality. After all, anger and greed are natural too. (It does, however, indicate that pride has an inevitable place in human development—and a use.)

The desire that produces humility is the largest desire. It is a desire that, like love, hides in embryonic form in every desire. It is named *longing*. It is sometimes named (misnamed) discontent, angst, sometimes even depression. It is the underlayment of the rackety noise of all front-self wanting. It is the always-there-in-the-background appreciation that this pizza, that girl, those diamonds, are only stopgaps in the tide of discontent that continually threatens to engulf us. It is longing that drives us to that lonely field at night, that impels us to sort irritably through the junkyard of our lives for something that will quiet our restlessness. In essence, every desire is a form of longing. If it is not merely an eccentricity of evolution, but is instead an essential structure of existence, we have found a clue and a directional arrow that points to the nature of existence.

So that: we come naturally to think that existence has at least something to do with living fully and deeply. After all, when we query the jury of humanity—what's best, everyone, to catch mammoths and make babies or to live fully and deeply—the hands that go up for babies are raised mostly to provoke. Everyone wants to live fully and deeply (whatever that might mean). Which is why everyone likes humility. These pages are a careful spiral around that truth. And spirals have a bottom.

To see how longing works, we must consider the nature of existence itself. This is the uttermost task of all thought—and, alas, for thought, a futile one. When longing raises its head from the trough of ordinary life, it finds itself marooned in a desert of ignorance. This is because thought is merely reflection, and it is the thing reflected we are trying to get at. But we have at least used the tool of reflective introspection to examine the nature of intelligence and found there illuminating structures of being—meaning, desire, sameness, recognition, and love. Now let us spread our armful of thought on the meadow of wonder and consider: what sort of beingness can best explain what we have so far gathered? As contemporary philosophy might put it, what inference leads to the best explanation?

The Conjecture

A google is the number ten to the hundredth power, and a googolplex is the number ten to the google power. A googolplex, let it be known, is a number so vast that it cannot be written out since the paper that would take would overflow the universe. "Oh c'mon!" says the man-on-the-street. "No number is that large!"

The man-on-the-street's problem is our problem now—incredulity is not a thought-derived state. It is a desire state, a reluctance based not on careful thinking or wonder but instead based on emotional aversion. The aversion many educated people have today for thoughts of anything transcendental results from, one, they don't experience it, and two, if there is a transcendental being, how come he doesn't help out more, and three, and besides, all belief is usually mostly hopeful—and mostly bad—thinking, and transcendental-thinking is even worse since it suppresses, simplifies, and starts wars. And four, if we needed one, believers in the so-called transcendent too often permit the suspension of doubt so they can indulge impermissible certainties. Yet, as mentioned, oddly, and most humanly, in these educated scoffers, it is a similar indulgence in impermissible belief-certainties that creates the sanction of atheism, a belief-certainty that results from holding physicalism as the basis of truth. Again, the only friend of good thinking is wonder.

What sort of world then can we conjecture to account for the clues and hints so far assembled? The conjecture would have to explain our mysterious conscious and unconscious intelligence, the bump-into universe resplendent with natural law, the wondrous physicality of metabolism, the structures of recognition and sameness, desire's sizes, humility, and the marvelous mind-reading across space known as empathy. In short, it would have to account for everything.

Now, like the mechanic who gropes beneath the engine, suspecting some bolt somewhere is holding that plate in place, we too must grope and suspect. We must first consider whether such a bolt exists, then consider its location, then whether or not it will come loose. What bolt, if loosened, frees the binding plate of life's mysteries?

After we overpass the limping explanations of physicalism, a conjecture begins to form: *what if all existence is manifested by a silent, subtle, really big intelligence that produces, permeates, and* is *all that exists*?

This is a massive supposition, with massive consequences, but its massiveness is obliged by the problem it confronts. It not only has the welcome property of explaining everything—solving even, as we shall see, the mind-body problem— no other conjecture can gather into its arms the full complexity of existence. In short, no other conjecture makes sense.

While the common name for that intelligence is *God,* these pages would happily avoid that name since, alas, the term *God* has been so long submerged in doctrine and culture, to many it has become almost repellent. To usefully employ it we must strip it of its sludge, a process that demands patience and honest intelligence.

By the term *God,* do we mean, as the olden religions seem to have it, that friendly invisible fellow walking always by our side? Because if so friendly, why not visible? An explanation sometimes offered for the hiddenness of God is that life is a test of some kind, which we can fail utterly and forever. But since we have shown that so-called freedom of will is illusory, then if it's a test, the test is rigged, since whether we pass or fail is out of our keeping. That old-fashioned sort of God, the one produced by centuries of superstition, fear, and tribalism, will clearly not do.

But if some sort might, what sort will? Can we sketch out, through the hints so far gathered, what might be the intent and motive behind creation? And if we can somehow sense the structure and plan of being, is there a way we can use that plan? Can we, for instance, begin to feel the breath of divinity on our cheek and become more and more happy and more and more purposeful? If there is God, is there also a somehow-available deep sweetness we can experience? Because if all we have is thought—even if all we have is what is commonly called faith—we are still stranded in agonizing aridity.

Thinking about the existence of God is a bit like encountering a sealed black box and trying to discern its contents by tapping it here, then there, shaking it, probing with instruments and monitors. If we can never get inside the black box of God, can never immerse ourselves in its interior, what is the point? Because even if there is God, humanity is justifiably fed up with merely thinking him. Though we call our maps of existence by the name of truth, Truth capitalized is better understood as the thing maps are maps of. Capital *t* Truth lies forever beyond the maps that describe it. In this meaning-haunted existence we are embedded in, whatever it may be, what we do not experience we can only suppose.

If God never emerges from that black box, he's no help in our moments of midnight loneliness. We remain spectators in a cosmic game. Beneath us, a vast unconsciousness produces meaning-that-peers-out. Before us, we are embedded in both the within-world and the bump-into world and are always, as we suppose are cows and crickets, relentlessly pinioned in onrushing meaning and uprushing desire. We are, as it were, lived by whatever-is-living-us.

Every culture and era has supposed God (or gods) many times, and their supposing, when integrated into their society and culture, has produced hope and inspiration as well as superstition and suppression. The gift of science was the overthrow of the latter, its penalty the destruction of the former. Most scientists today are atheists because they insist that measurable evidence is the only legitimate guide of good thinking. Yet they are human, and thus are all too avid to adventure beyond the periphery of evidence and plant the flag of atheistic certainty in the shadowland where the last explanation lurches into silence. In that land, as these pages have shown, only conjecture is sanctioned and only wonder, the friend of humility, can wander.

So how would a theory of infinite intelligence as the basis of reality meet and satisfy our so-far-gathered clues? For one thing, it would make short work of the ancient realism-idealism issue of philosophy, since everything existing would be both real and ideal simultaneously. The world would be material, since however much bump-into stuff is a figment of infinite intelligence's imagination, it does in fact exist, at least as imagination of some sort and continually exhibits bump-into-stuff's impassive reliability. It would also be idea of some sort, since all that exists would exist solely as meaning in infinite intelligence. We would have then, bump-into-stuff as imagination actively and continually imagined by infinite intelligence and also mind, that-which-receives-and-thinks-meaning, created and continually ised by infinite intelligence, and behind both of these the supporting and sustaining existence of infinite intelligence itself.

As this discussion continues, we will see how this infinite intelligence supposition solves the mystery of empathy and accounts for meaning-getting-and-holding, desire, sameness, recognition, love, and humility. And metabolism too! In short, it explains everything. And no other supposition can.

While this conjecture remains fairly mile-high—we don't see infinite intelligence in action at our kitchen table—supposing it offers an integral, good-sense solution to life's issues, whether scientific, social, philosophical, or political. Still, perhaps disappointingly, the supposition of infinite intelligence as the basis of existence does not mean that the idea is the bosom friend of religion. Religions, at least in their man-on-the-street parts, are threaded through with dull and desire-bound thinking and while they may have, at bottom, an ancient friendship with a notion of infinite intelligence, most have wandered so far from their base they are often useless, at least in their externalities, as companions in thought. It may be that for those who can cut through the thickets of religion's error and rediscover that ancient friendship, they are beneficial, since, however misguided, they are for many—or at least their founders are—able to emit an aura of warmth and good companionship. Though this aura can be useful in the inner world, for most of us, cutting through religion's errors leaves a harvest of historical blunder strewn in the fields of thought.

It's interesting to consider that this meaning-thing that is making the world must be remarkably big, so big that even to call it infinite is to belittle its size. That's because the term infinite seems to mean something, at least mathematically, and thus to suggest that we have somehow captured infinity in a word. But when we peer, as deep field telescopes now peer, into a drinking-straw-size piece of sky we see gleaming through that portal thousands of nebulas and billions of stars. Not even the word *infinite* can capture or suggest or in any way mean that vastness to us (a vastness entirely unknown in the religion-producing past). Its size is both heartening and disheartening. It heartens because it suggests that whatever this infinite intelligence is, it is mighty indeed, and we are held perfectly in a great and intelligent palm. It disheartens because how can this creator of a ninety-three billion light years sized universe have any notice—or interest—or time—for us? Even if we grant that the conjecture of infinite intelligence settles the most perplexing issues of philosophy, and even if a circumspect metaphysical theory can be developed from such a conjecture, isn't that merely another form of atheism? Infinite intelligence is one thing. A benign infinite intelligence is entirely another. After all, if God is good, how come tidal waves and war? The ancient and most plaguing question appears: why all this suffering?

Atheists and theists might well be united in support of the supposition that infinite intelligence is behind everything, since both might easily agree that, whatever the nature of existence, it makes good metaphysical sense to conjecture that existence is intelligence, and that intelligence is the first-in-line element of being. Where theists and atheists must part company is in their consideration of the nature of this intelligence, whether this mighty destroyer of children and villains in the same flood has any regard for our welfare, whether it is utterly indifferent, or worse, whether it manifests the caprice of favor or condemnation in response to our beliefs or behavior. In this regard, the difference between atheists and theists is not about whether God exists, but about whether he cares, and, if he does, how he cares. We may have noticed him, but does he notice us back, and kindly? The God of atheists might well be the universe itself, however intelligent, however produced and determined by the force of love, spinning along eternally and indifferently. Whether the good God of theistic belief can be salvaged from this thinking must at this point remain in question.

Good God?

The children-and-villains-in-the-same-flood problem, as well as the nature of evil problem, must be dealt with clearly and honestly to construct a God-is-good conjecture. The question is whether the components of existence of which we are presently aware, or can become aware, are sufficient to sanction the supposition, however wishful and loneliness-inspired, that God, even a God conceived merely as a form of intelligence, is lovingly overlooking creation. Clearly, the conjecture that intelligence and the sameness inherent in love are the isnesses of God's being cannot be the determining factor in our thinking, since those conceptions are easily comfortable to both atheists and theists. It is conceivable that, though God is the isness within all, everything that exists, you and I and every electron, however produced by the oneness of God's love, are the momentary stuff of his caprice and pass away into nothing.

Let's see whether some of the structures of existence we have uncovered can offer insight into the nature of God. We have noted that desires come in sizes, and that larger desires (which are not the merely mentalized urging of ethical systems), as they manifest, displace and subsume smaller desires, greed giving way to generosity, lust to benevolence, anger to equanimity. This giving way, releasement, and acceptance create the inner station we call humility. We have seen that hidden in this giving way is sameness, the element of being essential to recognition. We have seen that as humility develops, the ability to perceive sameness increases, desire deepens, and meaning widens. And love, that always-in-attendance power, becomes recognizable as the binding glue of all experiencing.

We are trying to notice in the existence of humility (the structure of being that most intelligently experiences existence) any hint about the goodness of God, to inquire whether God has only lighted the match of being and then drifted back to sleep—or perhaps even watches with unattractive relish the pained cavorting of his creatures. Perhaps the question is partially answered in noting that the sameness inherent in knowing and desire is known by the name of love, which, by its unifying power, draws us toward the source of that meaning-being, which is God. But the complaint remains—if God is suzerain over all being, all powerful and all creating, why this travail? We have seen that our bondage to desire is complete, so how can any God that drives us through a gauntlet of pain be good? The essential question persists: if God is good, why isn't life more fun? In the East, they say that creation is God's Lila, his play, but honestly, if he's so nice, how come he doesn't play a game we all like?

We have come at least in this thinking to a conjecture that God as intelligence makes sense of the problems presented by physicalism and its ally, neo-Darwinism, since those systems have not yet noticed the ground of being beneath their feet—intelligence itself. This thinking has made that notice, but still confronts the issue of whether the intelligence supposed is benevolent—and the insistent corollary of that issue: what should we do all day?

About suffering: it would be unsatisfyingly simple to assert that it is only through pain that we come to know and need God, a claim that implies, at least superficially, that he is somehow an austere, unrelenting, and sometimes wrathful master. The old religions have it that we create our own destiny by our choices, that we get what we deserve, but here we have shown that no one chooses his choices, but instead our disposition is a system that operates us with the puppet strings of desire. We are plunked down in the middle of this theater without in the least having bought a ticket. As the play unfolds, God may be suffering along with us, but couldn't he have designed more comfortable seats?

Before we get to the why of pain, we must first understand its what. Pain is thwarted desire. It is what-we-do-not-want. The match burns. You didn't get the job. Or the boyfriend. A child dies. As soon as desire appears in consciousness, which is the instant consciousness appears, satisfaction appears, and pain—unsatisfaction—appears as well. And fear, and greed, and anger, and jealousy. We have seen that in desire, and in knowing too, there is a laddering, a one-thing-larger-than-another desire-valuing based on the swallowing power of sameness inherent in existence. Kindness swallows cruelty, humility swallows pride, remorse swallows guilt, and not because of an imposed morality but because the desire that swallows is larger and more satisfying than the desire swallowed. The phrase *more satisfying* hides an important secret—that as consciousness widens, shedding small desire for larger, it finds in those larger desires a *depth of delight* unappreciated by small desire. This is the natural laddering of the desire world in which we continually struggle, the one-thing-after-another forsaking and expanding we name maturity and growth and inner development. The ascension of the inner ladder of desiring is the essence not only of mental health but of spirituality, here understood not as the mereness of belief in God or conformity to a religious system, but as a recognition of the structure of existence—and an aspiration to employ that knowing in action.

Do these thoughts answer the question of suffering? Can they excuse God's cruelty? This much at least we can now see—that we are driven by pain to larger desire and in that larger desire is more delight. Yet how can God answer, in his court or ours, the accusation that he is pitiless? How can a good God permit not only suffering, but worse, the suffering of the innocent?

The answer that offers itself is twofold.

The first answer to the accusation that God is cruel is that nowhere in the universe is there a court to hear the case. The God-as-everything idea, which we are testing and which is common to the esoteric parts of all religions, means that the accuser and the accused are one being. If all is manifested by God, the out-there world and the in-here world too, we are not only *from* God, we are *of* God. Whatever happens to us is done, however unconsciously, by us. To accuse God is to ignore this structure of being. No doubt that ignoring is part of the trick of the consciousness-unconsciousness polarity, but complaint about that condition is absurd since we, as God (since God is both parts), are complaining to ourselves. We are like a man playing poker with himself. Both his winnings and losses end in the same pocket, his own.

Yet even if true this is cold comfort, since it's nothing but thought. It may help us comprehend that bitterness toward God is misplaced, but when our child dies, the pain is more real than faith. Faith and belief can seldom reach the baffled place where outrage lives. Even if our real self is God, and even if from that point of view, which is secretly ours, there is no issue whatever of the injustice of suffering, yet still, down here where suffering happens, things hurt. Hurting may be part of the structure of the universe, and even if God is hurting with us and through us and in us, all that is dry consolation. In the everyday dimness in which our journey begins, resentment for this invisible being that we unconsciously are, however unjustifiable, is inevitable—and completely natural.

The other explanation for suffering in the it's-all-God hypothesis is that from God's point of view, which is ours in hiding, there is no suffering. All suffering is a form of delight that steers us/God toward the creating-isness of the in-here and out-there that is God. When desire and knowing arose and stationed themselves in time, suffering rose simultaneously as the not-wanted of the laddered path, all held and understood by the sameness of love in the being of God. Again, however true, a bit of fairly cold comfort.

How then to make these truths warm? This is the always-burning question, the question continual and insistent not only in our moments of suffering, but in our moments of boredom, restlessness, and obsession. If it is not the oldest question it is at least the most important: how can we, despite the travail and uncertainty of life, be happy? Though we may have spotted, from the mile-high view of this thinking, a sensible truth-map that explains suffering, how to transmute that map into everyday cheer?

To answer that, we must lay bare not only the source of acute suffering, but also the source of the habitual discontent that inhabits us. For those experiencing a train of successes this discontent may seem unimportant, part of the easily endured spaces between exhilarations, but for most, and especially for those becoming sensitive to the inner world, it can become the chief form of suffering—how to dispel the emptiness, indifference, and despair of existence itself? This despair was the fashionable complaint of the existentialists of the twentieth century. They recommended courage, a sort of that's-life-deal-with-it endurance. They had thought their way free from the hypocrisies of religion and myth, and if they were then compelled to enter the desert of meaninglessness, well then, forward bravely! The forward-bravely exhortation is the compelled cry of atheism, and of physicalism and neo-Darwinism too, and has at least the subtle comfort of heroism.

This thinking wonders if that desert is truly empty and has begun to suspect, by an examination of the ingredients of consciousness, that it is not.

How then to descend from these mile-high supposings into the thicket of being where we grapple with the day? If it is true that God as infinite intelligence is in us, and we are in God, what sort of fellow is he? How to make the good-God hypothesis valuable in the everyday—despite the world's misery and the haunting, taunting obstinacy of injustice? To attempt that, we need to complete our inquiry into the mechanism of consciousness. We need to more fully vivisect the inner being.

The world so far

And we are part way there already. We have noted our elemental being as desire and meaning, have noted the ego as that masterful, invisible butler of desire, have recognized our strandedness at the intersection of consciousness and unconsciousness, and have recognized the sizing of desire that produces magnanimity and humility (and every other virtue). Further, we have concluded, by an examination of numerous clues, that importantly include empathy, that a sensible conclusion is that some vast, perhaps infinite (whatever that may mean), intelligence is producing existence.

Yet, so what? Even if, as the religions proclaim, God is always with us, perhaps he is with us only as an audience, and we are, oh well, marooned on the desert island of existence. Our honest and justifiably emphatic question is: if God is interested, what's the evidence? This dilemma has always been confronted by the preachers of the world by venerating the standing of belief, which usually, mostly, and lamentably means, believe us, not your eyes.

Annoyance with preachers convulses most religions from time to time and reminds us now to deliver a hearty kick to all of them (the religions, not the preachers), not because they are not well-meant (at times they are) or because they are entirely unintelligent (at times they are), but because they appear before us infested with human wishfulness, pride, mountains of bad thinking, and considerable suppression and violence. Yet in their core, particularly in their founders, we catch the scent of something heartening, uplifting, cheer-making, and discontent-dispelling. If we could only have that without the trappings (that subjugate women, make a fetish of ritual, submerge inequality, and sanction self-righteousness). To learn whether we can, we must descend from our mile-high thinking and notice our going-about-the-day.

We wake, there's somebody asleep beside us (or not, and missed), we need to urinate, a baby's crying, we're hungry, we need to hurry because someone's waiting. We may occasionally find a gleaming new plan or ideology, but plans and ideologies always tatter, and the next morning the baby's crying again, and it's still hurry hurry. We need some untatterable plan to enthuse us but also to calm us, a plan that can lift our spirit and keep it lifted, or at least have a provision for relifting it. What we don't want and cannot trust is some idea, however hopeful, pasted on from the outside. What we want is something emergent from and natural to ourselves, some force perfectly comfortable, intimate, and well-knowable by the immediacy of intuitive recognition.

Where's home?

We understand and can sense that in the state of humility we are inhabited by larger desires that see farther and rest deeper within us, and we know too that the path to this humility lies in the releasement of the small desires that claim our attention and further, that this one-by-one releasement creates an inner ladder of ascent. We're not sure about what we might be ascending toward, but it makes sense from this thinking to suspect it is somehow God as infinite intelligence, that this God-being is the sameness-making power within consciousness that produces knowing and desire, and that we can rightly call this power love, understood as the attraction within sameness for itself. The terms *God* and *love* as used here, we remind ourselves, must be well-scrubbed of cloying religious sentiment and have arisen within us solely through fountains of notice, wonder, and conjecture. The existence of God as infinite intelligence makes sense as the power which accounts for the marvel of intelligence and its structures. Love as the ontological force of sameness makes sense as a desire power essential to the functioning of being. It's natural that our suffering and discontent has made so much of these two in the past, and natural too that that sense-making has been distorted by wishing.

Still, though thinking about the ingredients of consciousness has led us to conjecture God's possibility, it is not by good thinking alone that we can free ourselves and experience our depths, which, if this supposing is true, is this very infinite intelligence. We can free ourselves only by the enlivening power of experience. At this point, it's worth remarking to the somber atheist, who may be listening with arms folded and brow creased, that we have arrived here on a tide of thought and not on a river of wishing. Indeed, at this point in this thinking, we may gently inquire whether it is the atheist's own wishing (or reputation) that keeps his arms folded.

The question before us is this: if humility is a state of insight best productive of delight, joy, and happiness, and if humility results from the natural process of replacing small desire with larger, and if this replacing reduces egotism, opens the inner world and calms, widens, and deepens, and if it makes conjectural sense to suppose that all this activity is manifested by the isness of infinite intelligence through the power of love, what is good to do all day? And if the answer is that we can at least get a bit of calm before we snap out of existence—the answer of the current crop of meditation-recommending atheists—well, damn. That's equivalent to the DJ announcing, folks, a thermonuclear missile is on the way, but it's not here yet, so enjoy the music. Such a declaration can be either extolled as brave or reproved as a limp exhortation of hopelessness, but, more importantly, it obfuscates a central experience in the developing psyche, namely longing. Is the longing natural to developing consciousness as it searches through the aridity of existence merely one more senseless pain to endure before the lights go out forever? Or is it a directional arrow that points toward an important Something?

The court of experience

This thinking has noticed structures of existence that point fairly toward infinite intelligence as the basis of all being, and also noticed that longing arises naturally from the inexorable emptiness of existence. Thus we are brought at last to the greatest and final court, the court of experience. Here two questions come: first, are we meant to get Somewhere? And second, if we are, then how?

Careful thinking from evidence (science) has no answer to these questions and with good reason—it is proscribed by its assumption to consider only the so-called physical and so has nothing to think about (no evidence) and can form no questions. The unconscious, from which all being continually erupts, is invisible, unmeasurable, likely immeasurable, and supposition about it is possible only through the within of introspection. Though some scientists plant the flag of atheism in this vast unknown, their certainty can be excused as an efflorescence of egotism—and kindly ignored. They have yet to walk barefoot in the inner being, noticing the freedom-unfreedom illusion, noticing the working of love in sameness, the liberation of humility, and the enchantment of empathy, all insights that lead to this fair conjecture—a vast intelligence not only produced *but is producing existence.*

The question before us now, after the common-sense conjecture of the existence of such an intelligence, is how might this intelligence be comported toward the entities it creates and sustains? What, if anything, is the program of such an intelligence, and what might its involvement with its creation be?

It's tempting at this point to consult the world literature of mankind's relationship with what has hitherto been called God.

But that would entail a study too vast for a human lifetime, and anyway, what could such a study accomplish? There are two kinds of truth, recall. One is the mapping kind that the intellect offers. The other is the experiencing kind, the moment-by-moment impressions that arise as we do life. Thinking can pry the first sort of truth at least partly into the light, but the second sort of truth, the going-about-the-day experiencing kind, is where discontent lives. And that sort of truth, and that discontent, is mostly and unhappily immune to thinking.

Thought experiment: you enter the consultation chamber of a perfect psychologist who in an hour, or a year, details for you, accurately and entirely, your conscious and unconscious desire-disposition. You pay his fee and off you go. Are you changed? Do you meet the people on the street and your family and friends with suddenly sublime intelligence and empathy? You don't and for good reason—the psychologist has delivered only thought, and thought is reflection and not the thing reflected. The thing reflected, your disposition, must be experienced to become susceptible to change. The only force in the universe that creates this susceptibility is humility, which is not only a seeing inside, but a living inside. *The key that opens the door of humility is the large desire of longing.*

Ah, but this problem: the dispositional ego and its desires are submerged in the hidden intelligence we call the unconscious and are available only through introspection. But isn't introspection itself a form of thought, of reflection? And reflection, as noted in the above thought experiment, possesses no pry bar to change us. True. But introspective noticing, when it is the servant of longing, produces confirming and consoling insight so that the longing that guides us has the assurance that its path is sensible. We can comfortably hold that what introspection sees is the base-most stuff of being, the first-in-line experiencing of the world that we are embedded in. Introspective close-noticing lights the roots of our isness and scatters the roaches of generalization. Through introspection, the scent of this thing-that-is-making-the-world becomes available.

Still, the spiritual literature of the earth is not barren, and in it, across different cultures and traditions, we notice gleams of common insight. The properties of large desire have, throughout history, been the concern of so-called saints, prophets, and mystical thinkers. Though they were ignorant of the physical universe with its atoms and galaxies and though ideas of the unconscious, if not unknown, were unspoken, we find resonance in their testimony. While much religiosity is crusted over with punditry and complacent naivety, the reports of the inner explorers of every culture coincide with what these pages have discovered introspectively—namely, that life issues not from us but through us, and that humility sees and experiences that issuing. As we rap the black box of God for clues, we will, so say these adventurers, begin to sense at first the faintest stirring of ever-present divinity and eventually its resonant silence. That silence, we are told, imparts the essence of humility as well as the comfort and guidance we sought in that lonely midnight field.

The difficulty of hearing such a pronouncement for the modern mind is that, however repackaged and rediscovered in these pages, it has the odor of ancient, commonplace, and failed sanctimony. It points to a door that for many refuses to open and thus, for many, offers only the grim comfort of doctrine. Modernity's disgust with doctrine was inevitable. It was produced not only by the assaults of science, but also by the twentieth century's most-massive wars which exposed idealism as a frail and tinsel guide. The subsequent electronification of the earth has spread disillusionment far and wide, and hatred, anger, and contempt have become pandemic in every culture.

Today, above all, we require experience, some dependable way to enter into the depth we have begun to suspect is within us. Thus enter yoga, meditation, gurus of every stripe, herbs, astrology, mediums, psychics, a variety of drugs, remote viewing, near death experience research, reincarnation research, and on and on, all in an effort to penetrate the implacable veil between our ego and our unconscious. But alas, humility, the gradual coming-to-experience the isness within and beneath us, can be learned but not taught. It cannot be produced by drugs. It cannot be created even by meditation. It is produced by restricting the fountain of small desire and increasing the flow of the great desire called longing. How then is such a process begun and sustained? And to what does it lead? And can Infinite Intelligence (capitalized hereafter to signal its identity with God) help?

Doubt

As we make our approach in the inner geography we must confront and somehow pass the formidable fortress of doubt. Consider: two starving philosophers discover a date palm in the desert and suspect it may be a mirage. The first, made hopeless by the desert's trickery, refuses to eat. The second, a more adventurous fellow, is likewise confounded and munches a date while he considers the problem.

Doubt is natural, and its repression is an affront to honesty. But it is no stopping place. It is merely consciousness becoming aware that certainty is a property only of self-enclosed thought systems. I am certain that four is twice two because as fourness arises in consciousness, so too, and simultaneously, does its essence as double twoness. The reason Achilles can't catch the tortoise is that reflection exists in a different realm than experience. That's also the reason he never loses. As we move forward in the inner world, at first catching only the wisps and tails of insight, we must, as we do every day with our friends, at work, with our family, at the breakfast table, as we grow sleepy in the evening, as we rise refreshed, always and continually we must—*press-on-regardless*. Call this attitude faith if you like, but it's not the trinket faith of an unexamined life or a faith scooped together from the suppositions of ancient texts, however august with authority. It is a faith based on the experience of the wholesome regularity of the within, on the notice that small desire can slow and that large desire can rise.

The nature of compasses

It is said that when Laozi was leaving China in his seventies, a border guard spoke to him: "Sir, will you leave us bereft of your wisdom?" And so Laozi delayed long enough to compose the 5000 characters of the *Tao-te Ching*, a wandering full-of-insight exposition of existence. Though Laozi did not provide a detailed system of behavior, as did his contemporary Confucius, the *Tao-te Ching* has been beloved for centuries since its sunlike rays of thought somehow have the power to pierce through the clouds of surface confusion. One particularly cogent insight is Laozi's mention that water, the cradle of all life, as science puts it, is an apt symbol for the nature of the highest consciousness, in that water finds the lowest place and stills. This stilling, this letting-be, is the essence of humility, in which we see not merely the quiescence of desire but more, an awareness of our consciousness held, as it were, in the palm of being, since as we unfocus on small desire, we find that we are continually supported in a vast cradle of isness. And can more and more begin to *experience* that isness as benevolence and unimaginable intelligence.

We have seen that as we begin the search, we must enter the realm of desire itself, of our own consciousness, a fluid, shifting, unmeasurable maze of being available only by way of introspection, the inner being's sole flashlight. This search is a kind of map-making, a gradual accumulation of insight from which we hope to draw the contours of existence. The chief tool of this search is honesty, a willful integrity that makes no claims, eschews desired outcomes, and is content as it wanders to let-be-what-is. This, after all, is how we make all maps—we don't draw peninsulas that don't exist because we think they should, or because the mullah, the Bible, or Father Jones said... It needn't trouble us that the contours of the inner world are amorphous, since even the most meticulous physical science must fold its hands and sit resignedly as its own explanations vaporize in the outer atmospheres of thinking.

Though maps have their use, and though it is longing itself that produces them, it is also maps and their differences that produce the division in theologies, between the Sunnis and Shias, between Protestants and Catholics, between Taoists and Confucians, between Hindus and Muslims. Though maps provide intelligent expectation, helpful order, and an undercurrent of support, and so can be a bulwark to press-on-regardless faith, if they are to be useful and not an encumbrance, they must be held lightly in the palm, like a compass, and as we follow the arrow of their direction, *we must keep our attention not on the arrow but on the oncoming toward which the arrow points.*

A map, sort of

The map proposed in these pages is that the universe is manifested and supported by a mighty intelligence, a speculation arrived at by examining some of the properties of consciousness—empathy, meaning, recognition through sameness, humility, and love. Though we normally allude to this intelligence by the term God, it's clear that that term is so fingerprinted with competing systems as to be almost a barrier to wonder. The notion of God immediately brings on board the unexamined sentimentality of doctrine, a history of splintering contention, and the presumption of priests, garbed in the pompous sacred. The welter of doctrine means that today's truth-seeker must either ply through volumes of books and conversations or else abandon circumspection and plunk his or her effort down on some likely somewhere. All too often the search remains barren, and the seeker either remains stubbornly in place, in denied despair, or must trudge off to yet another somewhere, another book, thinker, leader, guide, or guru. The search can seem endless. Nevertheless, every seeker's faithful companion is the ache within that drives, lures, and even encourages. Seekers are like Kafka's hunger artist, who, as he dies of starvation, at last reveals the secret of his talent for fasting: "I could not find the food I liked." Hunger is a lifeline and a ladder and is, in fact, our old friend, desire, that persistent inner force we repress, battle, condemn, exalt, and misconstrue. It is likely the force that began the universe. It is longing.

As we begin, it must be recognized that this map, as is the case with every map, is only a go-that-way pointing. Maps stand outside the thing they describe. They are part of the holding power of mind, not the getting. Their message to the getting power of consciousness is simply and always: go that way, you'll recognize it.

How then to elaborate such a map, to draw no unreal peninsulas and leave no real ones undrawn? A famous story from the East reports that a sage, to help a king understand God, brought an elephant to some blind men and asked them to describe it. One said it was like a rope (the tail), another like a wall (the flank), another like a column (the leg), another like a pipe (the trunk). God was like that, the sage said—everyone experiences from a point of view. We can extend that tale by reflecting that even the sage didn't know the entirety of the elephant, since he himself was not directly experiencing elephantness, as was, say, the elephant, and more, that even the elephant, though experiencing as much fullness of elephantness as possible, could in no way account for or appreciate his own being, since, after all, elephants are mostly thinking about their next meal. The elephant simply was *that*, as we are our own *that*, peering from the peek-a-boo curtain of consciousness into the whirling complexity of creation. The sage had a good point though. We can see only from the fastness of our point of view. This is not a dilemma to be solved, but a condition to be acknowledged.

The map sensibly supposed in these pages is that some sort of intelligence not only manifested all existence but is continually manifesting it, peering out from each piece of its being into the universe it creates. The window it peers from is intelligence, a kind of lens through which it sees. Behind or beneath that intelligence, and constructing it, is a vast unconscious intelligence, an unseeable-by-consciousness something that supports and constitutes the isness of everything, so that it makes sense to suppose the existence of a universal mind composed of both conscious and unconscious parts. This universal mind is intelligence itself and is the source of the mysterious meaning that erupts from each of us every moment. This intelligence is also the celebrated fine tuning of the cosmological constants made so much of by physicists—the existence of which provokes some of them, entirely to avoid the anathema of affirming divinity, into imagining a multitude of universes with different constants, ours being a life-supporting lucky one. The world means to us, and it is that meaning itself which points beyond itself to Meaning, capitalized here to note its station as the structure beneath and inherent in all meaning. It is isness. It is meaning-getting-and-holding. It is the astonishment of existence. When meaning-getting-and-holding and desire at last begin to cooperate, these two begin more and more to experience the Isness that created them both, the Universal Mind behind everything. Their natural and inevitable response to recognizing that Isness is humility, a deepening honesty that sees not only the multitudinous population of the Isness, but more and more sees and senses the Isness itself.

This map is not disruptive of science, but instead offers science an infinite field of exploration. It accounts first and most primordially for intelligence itself, that meaning *is* (solving the hard problem), that existence is resplendent with rationality, and that this unexplainable rationality accounts for the customary world of space, time, cause, effect, and law in which we are embedded. Further, it accounts for our ability to notice rationality by the rationality within us, which is to say, by the intelligence peering from beneath the hooded eye of our consciousness. Being begins to sense and see itself by becoming more clearly conscious.

This map of existence is able to account for the mystery of empathy, explaining how we see and experience the within of others, and can also account for the maddening complexity of metabolism and life processes. It can gather the fossil record, molecular biology, and evolutionary thinking into a coherent and unifying conjecture. It clarifies valuing, blame, error, delusion, and can construct a workable system of social cooperation. Most importantly, it provides a day by day meaning and importance to every experience of our lives. It provides a reason for living.

A few details

Ah, but these mile-high maps! Many readers perusing the last pages, or even the entire text so far, might scoff and dismiss, since those readers might have a disposition held and developed by a different supposing. And supposing, after all, is all we get, at least as we begin. Every explanation sputters, and maps are only pointers. They require fleshing out to become useful and not more of the gaudy pomp of hopeful thinking. But this: as we begin to draw our map's peninsulas and corollaries, we know at least that we have arrived here not by theological supposition, but by introspectively examining being.

Those who scoff because they are without experience of this so-called God-intelligence are in good company. Those who are held by some alternative belief are in good company.

If the map of these pages is accurate, all of us are in quite good company.

So far we have made sense of meaning and desire by positing that we must be embedded in a universal mind that peers from each portion of its own being into its own being. Though that simple formula overcomes the impasses inevitable to a purely physicalist approach, in order to make sense of the wherefore and whither of such an existence we have to invest this mile-high map with details. All religion is an attempt at this detail-making, and each falls into its own particular confusion, prey to its own particular assumptions. Thus, at least in its exoteric parts, no religion has reached an extensive and useful subtlety. The subtlety needed must deal with suffering, choice, immortality, and all the daily perils and tribulations of life. It must be a full and accurate map. It must be true and tell us truly what existence is. And whether, given the misery surrounding us, it has a purpose. Because if life ends at death, for many of us it's a big why-bother—and for all of us it's a why-so-much-bother?

Many are the souls and minds who have attempted to think their way into and out of this issue, and the history of thought and theology is scattered with their efforts. Too often their thinking descended from the heights to be drowned in the knock-about world, emerging as rites, rituals, and morality. Thus Vedanta sanctioned caste, Christianity produced intolerance, and Islam made war. But unless God were to station himself on every street corner with a placard, this is inevitable. The tide of desire flowing though mankind was produced by a slow animal evolution which rewards power (the insight of Darwin and Nietzsche). Any doctrine or theology which presumes to instruct humanity too often finds itself ground into a paste palatable to this appetite. Theology, allied to its era's society, governing power, and spiritus mundi, could not untie the Gordian knot of all philosophy and religion, the reconciliation of love and blame, and so devolved to become the wagging finger of admonition. This was inevitable and thus unlamentable. Whether such an outcome will remain inevitable for mankind is a question only time can answer. Here at least we will untie that knot.

Two cartographers

Many are the figures in history that have described a universe coincident with the close-noticing of these pages, but the two most modern and complete are Aurobindo Ghose and Merwan Irani, known to the world as Meher Baba.

Aurobindo was a Bengali educated in England, was fluent in seven languages, and wrote more than 30 dense volumes of his discoveries in the inner world, not only spiritual philosophy but also poetry, plays, and voluminous essays. The scholar will find his magnum opus, *The Life Divine,* a profound metaphysical undertaking, and the seeker his *The Synthesis of Yoga* a useful setting-forth of the nature of the inner world. Additionally, his four volumes of *Letters on Yoga* provide a rich mine of insight, with sections such as: *The Parts of Being and the Planes of Consciousness, The Transformation of the Vital, The Evolutionary Process and the Supermind*. He died in 1950, and all his works are now available online. (See sriaurobindoashram.org)

Meher Baba asserted that he was, and is heralded by many as, the divine incarnation, an Avatar of God himself. He stopped speaking in 1925 and lived until 1969 without breaking his silence. He left the world several books, some only being published long after his passing. Hundreds of books and a 5000-page biography have been written about him, his life, and his message. (See avatarmeherbabatrust.org. One book, which he referred to as the new Bible for humanity, has yet to be found.) But he also said this: *I have come not to teach but to awaken.*

About Meher Baba's I-am-God declaration: such a claim creates an interesting problem. It falls inevitably into the consciousness of the world as the repellent boast of either a madman or a self-deluded fraud. For many, it's equivalent to someone announcing at a cocktail party that he is the smartest person who ever lived. Anyone who said, "Really? Tell me more," would be pitied. The passage of time, of course, tends to soften this response, and those who have claimed enlightenment in the past—Jesus, Rama, Krishna, Buddha, Zoroaster, Mohammed—are today heralded as the saviors of mankind. But if God does incarnate on earth from time to time, it is likely he would want people to know, and so, in a sense, he's in a fix—how to assert divinity into the jealous egotism of the world without being thought an egotist yourself?

The briefest review of Meher Baba's actual life and the lives of those who surrounded him is assuring. He was a whirlwind of selfless activity, inspired devotion in powerful men and women, and the purity of his love commonly left visitors in tears. In the end, there is no authority to consult except one's own inner response. Meher Baba once remarked to his devotees that from their mouth to the ear of others may be their duty, but from the ear to the heart is his duty. He is the one, he said, whose past is revered, whose future is anticipated with fervor, and whose present is ignored. The course of the Avatar's advent, he said, was like the course of the sun—at its rising and setting it is considered most beautiful, but while it is directly overhead, providing light and heat, it is ignored.

In a desert of mirages, when a stranger points over the horizon to water, whether we walk in that direction will depend on which is greater, our doubt or our thirst. It makes sense, of course, to ask for the stranger's credentials, and for those interested, Meher Baba's biography, written by one of his close ones, is freely available online (see lordmeher.org). Still, his real credential is not available in any book. That issues from the inner world.

Here we do not urge a conclusion. The clarity of his thought, at least, makes perfect sense of what these pages have so far discovered.

Since the views of Aurobindo and Meher Baba are largely coincident, we will offer Meher Baba's own declaration, contained in his *The Discourses,* as the basis of their thinking.

Meher Baba's explanation of the universe:

The Journey of the Soul to the Oversoul

Atma, or the soul, is in reality identical with Paramatma, or the Oversoul—which is one, infinite, and eternal. The soul is in fact beyond the gross, subtle, and mental worlds. But it experiences itself as being limited owing to its identification with the sharir (sthul sharir, or gross body); the pran (sukshma sharir, or subtle body, which is the vehicle of desires and vital forces); and the manas (karan sharir, or mental body, which is the seat of the mind). The soul in its transcendental state is one—formless, eternal, and infinite—and yet identifies itself with the phenomenal world of forms, which are many and finite and destructible. This is Maya, or cosmic Illusion.

The phenomenal world of finite objects is utterly illusory and false. It has three states: the gross, the subtle, and the mental. Although all three of these states of the world are false, they represent different degrees of falseness. Thus the gross world is farthest from Truth (God), the subtle world is nearer Truth, and the mental world is nearest to Truth. All three states of the world owe their existence to cosmic Illusion, which the soul has to transcend before it realizes the Truth.

The sole purpose of creation is for the soul to enjoy the infinite state of the Oversoul consciously. Although the soul eternally exists in and with the Oversoul in an inviolable unity, it cannot be conscious of this unity independently of creation, which is within the limitations of time. It must therefore evolve consciousness before it can realize its true status and nature as being identical with the infinite Oversoul, which is one without a second. The evolution of consciousness requires the duality of subject and object—the center of consciousness and the environment (that is, the world of forms).

How does the soul get caught up in Illusion? How did the formless, infinite, and eternal Soul come to experience itself as having form and as being finite and destructible? How did Purusha, or the supreme Spirit, come to think of itself as prakriti, or the world of nature? In other words, what is the cause of the cosmic Illusion in which the individualized soul finds itself? To realize the true status of the Oversoul—which is one, indivisible, real, and infinite—the soul needs consciousness. The soul does get consciousness; however, this consciousness is not of God but of the universe, not of the Oversoul but of its shadow, not of the One but of many, not of the Infinite but of the finite, not of the Eternal but of the transitory. Thus the soul, instead of realizing the Oversoul, gets involved in cosmic Illusion; and hence, though really infinite, it comes to experience itself as finite. In other words, when the soul develops consciousness, it does not become conscious of its own true nature but of the phenomenal world, which is its own shadow.

In order to become conscious of the phenomenal world, the soul must assume some form as its medium for experiencing the world; and the degree and kind of consciousness are determined by the nature of the form used as the medium. The soul first becomes conscious of the gross world of consciousness through a gross form. The consciousness of the gross world that it has in the beginning is of the most partial and rudimentary type. Correspondingly, the soul assumes the most undeveloped form, that of stone.

The driving force of evolution consists in the momentum consciousness receives owing to the conservation of the impressions (sanskaras) left by diverse desires or conditions. Thus the sanskaras cultivated in a particular form have to be worked out and fulfilled through the evolution of a higher form and a correspondingly more developed consciousness of the gross world. The soul, therefore, has to assume higher and higher forms (like metal, vegetable, worm, fish, bird, and animal) until at last it assumes a human form, in which it has fully developed consciousness—in all the aspects of knowing, feeling, and willing—of the gross world.

The manner in which sanskaras result in the evolution of consciousness, and the corresponding forms, has a useful analogue in ordinary experience. If a man has the desire to act the part of a king on the stage, he can only experience it by actually putting on the garb of a king and going on the stage. This is true of aspirations and desires; they can only be worked out and fulfilled by bringing about an actual change in the entire situation, as well as the medium, through which the situation may be adequately experienced. The parallel is very helpful in understanding the driving force of evolution, which is not mechanical but purposive.

The sanskaras are not only responsible for the evolution of the form (body) and the kind of consciousness connected with it, but they are also responsible for the riveting of consciousness to the phenomenal world. They make emancipation of consciousness (that is, the withdrawal of consciousness from the phenomenal world to the soul itself) impossible at the subhuman stage and difficult at the human level. Since consciousness clings to the previous sanskaras and experience of the phenomenal world is conditioned by the use of an adequate form (body) as a medium, the soul at every stage of evolution comes to identify itself with the form. Thus the soul, which in reality is infinite and formless, experiences itself as finite and thinks of itself as being stone, metal, vegetable, worm, fish, bird, or animal, according to the degree of the development of consciousness. Finally, while experiencing the gross world through the human form, the soul thinks that it is a human being.

The soul has fully developed and complete consciousness in the first human form, and therefore there is no need for any further evolution of the gross form (body). The evolution of forms thus comes to an end with the attainment of the human form. To experience the sanskaras cultivated in the human form, the soul has to reincarnate again and again in human forms. The innumerable human forms through which the soul has to pass are determined by the law of karma, or the nature of its previous sanskaras (whether of virtue or vice, happiness or misery). During these lives the soul, which is eternal, identifies itself with the gross body, which is destructible.

While developing full consciousness of the gross world, the soul simultaneously develops the subtle and mental bodies. But as long as its consciousness is confined to the gross world alone, it cannot use these bodies consciously in wakefulness. It becomes conscious of these bodies and the bodies' corresponding worlds only when its full consciousness turns inward, that is, toward itself. When the soul is conscious of the subtle world through the subtle body, it identifies itself with the subtle body; and when it is conscious of the mental world through the mental body, it identifies itself with the mental body, just as it identifies itself with the gross body when it is conscious of the gross world through the gross body.

The homeward journey of the soul consists in freeing itself from the illusion of being identical with its bodies—gross, subtle, and mental. When the attention of the soul turns toward Self-knowledge and Self-realization, there is a gradual loosening and disappearance of the sanskaras that keep consciousness turned toward the phenomenal world. Disappearance of the sanskaras proceeds side by side with piercing through the veil of cosmic Illusion, and the soul not only begins to transcend the different states of the phenomenal world but also to know itself as different from its bodies. The spiritual path begins when the soul tries to find itself and turns its full consciousness toward Truth (God).

At the first stage the soul becomes totally unconscious of its gross body and of the gross world, and experiences the subtle world through the medium of its subtle body, with which it identifies itself. In the second stage the soul is totally unconscious of its gross and subtle bodies, and also of the gross and subtle worlds, and experiences the mental world through the medium of its mental body, with which it now identifies itself. At this stage the soul may be said to be face to face with God, or the Oversoul, which it recognizes as infinite. But though it recognizes the infinity of the Oversoul, which it objectifies, it looks upon itself as being finite because of its identification with the mental body, or mind.

Thus we have the paradox that the soul, which in reality is infinite, sees its infinite state but still continues to regard itself as finite; because while seeing its infinite state, it looks upon itself as the mind. It imagines itself to be the mind and looks upon the Oversoul as the object of the mind. Further, it not only longs to be one with the objectified Oversoul but also tries hard to fulfill that longing.

In the third stage the full consciousness of the soul is drawn still further inward toward itself, and it ceases to identify itself even with the mental body. Thus in the third and last stage, which is the goal, the soul ceases to identify itself with any of the three bodies that it had to develop for evolving full consciousness. Now it not only knows itself to be formless and beyond all the bodies and worlds but also realizes with full consciousness its own unity with the Oversoul, which is one, indivisible, real, and infinite. In this realization of the Truth it enjoys infinite bliss, peace, power, and knowledge, which are characteristics of the Oversoul.

In the beginning, because the soul has not yet evolved full consciousness, it is unconscious of its identity with the Oversoul. Hence, though intrinsically inseparable from the Oversoul, the soul cannot realize its own identity with it or experience infinite peace, bliss, power, and knowledge. Even after the evolution of full consciousness, it cannot realize the state of the Oversoul—although it is at all times in and with the Oversoul—because its consciousness is confined to the phenomenal world, owing to the sanskaras connected with the evolution of consciousness. Even on the path, the soul is not conscious of itself but is conscious only of the gross, subtle, and mental worlds, which are its own illusory shadows.

At the end of the path, however, the soul frees itself from all sanskaras and desires connected with the gross, subtle, and mental worlds. It then becomes possible for it to free itself from the illusion of being finite, which came into existence owing to its identification with the gross, subtle, and mental bodies. At this stage the soul completely transcends the phenomenal world and becomes Self-conscious and Self-realized. To attain this goal, the soul must retain its full consciousness and at the same time know itself to be different from the sharir (gross body); the pran (subtle body, which is the vehicle of desires and vital forces); and the manas (mental body, which is the seat of the mind) —and also know itself as being beyond the gross, subtle, and mental worlds.

The soul has to emancipate itself gradually from the illusion of being finite by liberating itself from the bondage of sanskaras and knowing itself to be different from its bodies—gross, subtle, and mental. It thus annihilates the false ego (that is, the illusion that "I am the gross body," "I am the subtle body," or "I am the mental body"). While the soul thus frees itself from its illusion, it still retains full consciousness, which now results in Self-knowledge and realization of the Truth. Escaping through the cosmic Illusion and realizing with full consciousness its identity with the infinite Oversoul is the goal of the long journey of the soul.

What this means for us, plus panpsychism

For those of us without a complete experience of the soul, which is all of us, the above description must be gathered tentatively into our thoughts. But this at least—the thinking in this book began with close-noticing two fundaments of existence, meaning-getting-and-holding and desire. From there it moved to a consideration of the compulsory nature of desire, to a discussion of physicalism, neo-Darwinism, ego, consciousness and unconsciousness, humility, recognition, acceptance, sameness, blame, empathy, and even metabolism. All these discussions left us stranded in mystery, and, as we shall see, in the work of Meher Baba and Aurobindo, these mysteries are illuminated by positing the existence of the three worlds, the gross, the subtle, and the mental. (Aurobindo generally refers to the subtle world, which Meher Baba describes as the "vehicle of desires and vital forces," as the vital world.) When we add three additional ideas—reincarnation, the assertion that consciousness exists in all beings (stones, for instance), and that there exists a single divine intelligence that has imprisoned itself in creation—while there are many puzzles yet to solve, the structure of the universe begins to make a far more complete sense than any religion has yet proposed. (Note that Meher Baba uses the word *stone* as a placeholder for all most rudimentary forms, electrons included.)

Are these ideas the unfounded conjectures of hopeful religionists? A peremptory rejection has no more validity than a peremptory acceptance. Careful consideration is required to see whether this view of creation has explanatory power.

One place to begin thinking is to consider the assertion that all existence contains consciousness and intelligence. Modern philosophy has considered this view in the various philosophies known as panpsychism, the view that all material being, from electrons to plants to human beings, possesses consciousness and intelligence. The often-cited difficulty of this view is what has come to be known as the combination problem. How does electron intelligence combine to produce stone intelligence? How can insect intelligence be conceived as a jumble of plant minds? Still, panpsychism does circumvent the hard problem of consciousness by asserting that intelligence always was, or at least began, at the first instant of creation. The universe is somehow made of intelligence.

A sort of panpsychism is coincident with the view of Meher Baba, Aurobindo, and also with the ancient texts of Vedanta contained in the Upanishads: the universe manifested from the unknowable being of divinity, referred to in Meher Baba's sketch as the Purusha, or spirit. The so-called combination problem is not a problem at all in this view, since the three bodies of each being, the physical, subtle, and mental, develop in complexity over time through accumulated experience. Electron intelligences do not combine to form greater intelligences, but instead, the nearly unconscious soul-intelligence begins the evolution of intelligence by identifying with an electron. After sufficient experience it drops that form and identifies with the next higher form, and in that way develops a wider, fuller, and richer lens through which to see being. That lens is its three evolving bodies through which the soul, which is Infinite Intelligence, is peering. Two of these bodies (the subtle and mental) are not material, and though we may eventually discover they have some measurable, or at least logically supposeable, form, we can at least presently hold that they are made of intelligence, and that they receive, and are compounded of, impressions of meaning.

The argument for the existence of the subtle and mental bodies is not an argument for the supernatural, because the functioning of these bodies is just as natural as the functioning of the physical world, and in fact underpins the physical world.

No doubt supposing a divine intent hidden in existence invites speculation about the nature and interests of this intent, but it does not automatically invite or sanction the crude, wishful, and often power-seeking speculations of the olden religions. This view of creation as a vast arena of developing intelligence, joined beneath by the oneness of infinite mind, invites scientists and theologians to sit at the same table, not across from each other as antagonists, but at a table made round by common supposition and wonder.

Intelligence development, and its consequent greater and greater consciousness, is thus a form of learning, and learning, as we have come to understand from psychology, is a form of pattern development, one thought pattern lying beneath another to create understanding (standing-under), the way a chess champion recognizes pattern on a chess board with the immediacy of developed intuition. How this compounding is done is mysterious and unavailable to conscious perception (and is the study of Gestalt psychology), but that it is done is apparent in the knowledge required to draw a picture, make a layup, speak a language, or enable the Arctic tern to fly 90,000 kilometers without GPS.

A new Genesis

So how did things start, and why, and what is everything? A good place to begin is to consider whether everything in the universe is intelligent, or are some things, as it were, dead, that is, without consciousness or unconsciousness? Consider: when the universe manifested 13.8 billion years ago (the Big Bang), and Purusha, as the embodied but nearly unconscious soul, began experiencing and developing its three bodies, what did it look from and into? If everything at that point was Purusha, the bodiless intelligence of God, what did Purusha see in order to have the first impression that began the whole long layering process of consciousness/intelligence evolution?

From Meher Baba's *God Speaks*: *The infinite original whim that surged in God and the consequent infinite urge-to-know Himself made manifest in God the infinite triple attributes of Creator, Preserver and Dissolver, with all the paraphernalia of the Nothingness of the latent Nothing.*

The Nothing referred to here is the creation itself, which, says Meher Baba, is the product of God's infinite imagination. That's why when the innumerable just-manifested souls first opened their almost unconscious eyes onto the world there was plenty to experience—even though in Reality, the creation they experience is Nothing. And, since that Nothing was God-made, it was itself marvelously full of intelligence, or, as a physicist might put it, of stunningly precise cosmological constants. That Nothing offered the just-conscious soul something-to-see and can be rightly thought of as the gift of God's being.

Clearly, considering the bump-into stuff of the world, and our thoughts and feelings too, as Nothing can be at first off-putting, since after all, there everything is, right out in front and inside of us, day after day. But the idea of creation's Nothingness becomes more sensible when we wonder what this infinite imaginer of everything might actually be. When we finally unite with that Imaginer, with that Something which existed before creation existed, which created and continues to create creation, it makes sense to suppose that the here and now that we experience might seem, well, like Nothing.

All this is why there is no deadness anywhere. Everything is 100 percent perky with Infinite Intelligence. Which means that the Genesis account in the Bible got it slightly wrong—God didn't rest on the seventh day. God is continually making the world, now and now and now.

A little reflection grasps that if the universe is the eternal busyness of God's manifestation, the something-seen and the something-seeing as well, then we are not only embedded in the being of God, we are ourselves made of God-stuff—but as yet unconscious of that. Within each of us, and within everything that exists, is the initially groggy but eventually robust force of God's urge to know himself consciously. That urge is the longing we have previously identified as the force that draws us to that lonely field at night. It is the hunger which lies beneath all hunger. It is why you are reading this.

Meher Baba said that God manifests in human form every 700 to 1400 years in order to cleanse and straighten the accumulated sanskaric knots of creation, aiding the development of both evolution and involution. These Avatars, as they are known in our recorded history, were, from first to last: Zoroaster in Persia, Rama in India, Krishna in India, Buddha in India, Jesus in Palestine, Mohammed in Arabia, and Meher Baba in India. (Why so many in India? According to Meher Baba, it's closest to the Om point, the origin of the universe's manifestation.)

It's fascinating to note that the first published conception of the universe as originating from a tiny point, later referred to by one of its sarcastic opponents as the *Big Bang*, was written in 1927 by a Belgian priest named Georges Lemaître. After a decades-long discussion among scientists, and much experimental work, the steady state theory of the cosmos—held even by Einstein—gave way to the big bang conception. Yet two years before this public wrangling began in the world's universities, in a small village in Maharashtra, India, in 1925, Meher Baba first wrote his description of the beginning of the cosmos as originating from the Om point, the gross emanation of Infinite Intelligence that expanded and became the cosmos.

It's easy to see that the religions that develop in the wake of Avataric advents find it impossible to bear the charge of this truth. The core of every religion and spiritual tradition is an aspiration toward love and fellow feeling, but each has devolved, despite a now-and-then current of high-mindedness from a here-and-there saint, into strife, ritual, and blood. If now comes a new manifestation of divinity, one which, said Meher Baba, will be the greatest in our known history, how will it be absorbed into the current collective mind? In considering Meher Baba's explanation of the universe, an explanation which invites all scientific, spiritual, and philosophical thinking, we can glimpse a portion of that development. Let's see how these ideas work out in everyday knock-about life.

Everyday, damnit

Even if we somehow become convinced that the universe is a divine manifestation and that we are ourselves secretly God peering murkily into existence, the pipes still freeze, the landlord is unsympathetic, the one we love doesn't love us back—plus, damnit, we're impatient, irritable, and self-pitying. What to do? There are plenty of paths and practices, and all have their devotees and limitations, and there are plenty of writers and guides, some of which may have even glimpsed a portion of the invisible elephant of God.

Even though the best written guide today can be found in Meher Baba's *The Discourses* (a sort of manual of spirituality), it's not through the armchair of thought that we can find release. It's through living a life. And we all have that.

If Meher Baba and Aurobindo are right, we are never disconnected from God, because in fact we are That, albeit an unconscious That, which is why there is a breadcrumb trail leading home always somewhere ready-to-hand. Unexpectedly, that breadcrumb trail is desire itself, the force that wakes us, that escorts us through the day, and that puts us to bed at night. Desire is God's own urge to know himself consciously.

What a battering this poor fellow desire has taken over the centuries, accused of all viciousness, branded as the enemy of virtue, and hunted to emaciation and near extinction with the slings and arrows of morality. No doubt desire needs a good beating from time to time, but far more does it deserve understanding, companionship, and guidance. If our cartographers are right, as desire lets slip from its hands the ignorance that has baffled and smothered it, it will find that the greatest, most natural, and deepest desire is the longing to be one with our own inner Self that not only made the world but is continually making it.

The Avatar

The station of the Avatar cannot be explained without first explaining the structure of the universe.

The following discussion is from *God Speaks.*

At first there was no universe at all. God existed in what Meher Baba calls the Beyond-Beyond state, which he characterized as the original infinite divine vacuum with everything that would eventually be manifest existing only in latency. Of course, the term *latency,* which seems to make at least some sort of sense, is hazardous, since the Beyond-Beyond state of God is beyond human understanding. Interestingly, in the Beyond-Beyond there is neither consciousness nor unconsciousness. That does at least make sense, since both of those are mental windows that contain something, and in that most original state before creation there was no something.

In this original state, God experienced the *lahar,* or *whim,* the urge to know himself. In essence, God asked *who am I*? And the universe appeared. But in a fascinating and illumining way.

The lahar provoked the Beyond-Beyond to produce two new and distinct states of God, which Meher Baba calls the Beyond states. One of these states was entirely unconscious. This was the state of God that began experiencing the universe—as atoms and animals and finally us. The other state was infinitely conscious—but only conscious of God and utterly unconscious of the universe.

This division of God into two states created an urge-desire-longing in the unconscious God-state, composed of numberless bubble souls, to realize the conscious God-state. Thus starts the long journey of form-taking as the soul develops fuller and fuller consciousness. This form-taking is the life after life evolution that develops the soul's subtle and mental lenses. The bubble soul's journey begins when it appears in creation and ends when it becomes conscious of itself as God.

An interesting by-the-way: just before the Truth dawns, as the soul is on the verge of God-consciousness, Meher Baba relates that the soul experiences the infinite divine vacuum, which is the nirvana that Buddha referred to. An instant later, the soul achieves oneness with God and experiences God's infinite power, knowledge, and bliss. (In other words, Buddha stopped explaining at nirvana, which gave rise to the so-called godlessness of Buddhism.) Another interesting feature is that when the soul becomes conscious of itself as God it usually loses consciousness of creation and abides entirely in the infinite bliss of God-consciousness.

Except in a special case—which gives rise to a third God-state, a state vastly important to humankind.

In this third state, the soul not only becomes God-conscious, possessed of infinite power, knowledge, and bliss, but *also regains consciousness of the creation* that has provided the ladder of its long assent. This creation-consciousness creates an entirely new station of God, the Perfect Master or Man-God, as well as the Avatar, the God-Man.

When a soul gains God-realization, its relation to the creation it has transcended can vary in three ways. One, it can become unconscious of creation. Two, it can remain conscious of creation but have no duty (these souls are known as *Majzoobs).* Three, it can remain conscious of creation and occupy the station of a God-realized Master. There are always five of these Perfect Masters, also called Sadgurus, and every 700 to 1400 years they precipitate the Avatar into creation. This happens only on earth, which Meher Baba said is the only planet where Masters occur and where souls are realized.

All Masters have an identical state of being, but the Avatar is unique in that he has the function of reorienting the earth's consciousness by ushering the world into a new birth of understanding. Perfect Masters, though usually locally known and admired, sometimes even famous (Sai Baba, for instance, is heralded throughout India and beyond), are generally not world figures. The Avatar is, since his advent is for all humanity. The Avatar is the Self in all, God conscious of himself and of the universe and also of himself as every journeying soul. It is the always-withness of the Christ station.

Thus, each of us is stationed in time, peering through a growing sanskaric accumulation that develops intelligence but obscures unity. But the self is in reality the Self, and it is the Self that does both the creating and the experiencing. Our unconscious contains not merely our own more immediate and apprehensible unconsciousness (our hidden desires and inclinations), but also our unconsciousness of the Self, which is everything that exists. Our small-self unconscious we might call our personal unconscious, our sanskaric shadow-sheathe, and it is that unconscious that prevents us from experiencing the infinite consciousness of God.

With this understanding in tow, it's interesting and informative to consider the journey of the first soul through creation. It was this soul's realization that gave rise to the third state of God, the consciousness of creation and God together. That first soul had things somewhat easier than we do. Back then there was not this gigantic buzz and clutter of infinite culture, tribal enmity, complicated thought systems—in short, the helter-skelter accumulation of living-and-thinking that we must now pierce through to see the eternal simplicity of Being.

As the first soul neared the end of its long evolution and involution, it began to notice that it was not the source of noticing, but instead something was noticing through him, so that he was a had-to-be part of a vast noticing noticer. At that point it would make sense that he, as he more and more fully noticed the noticer, finally ceased entirely to notice himself, who had never actually noticed anything anyway but had always been an imaginary vehicle for the noticing. And thus the first soul became conscious that he himself was the noticer, and more, was not only the noticer, but was himself the Creator of the noticed, the imagination, the universe.

This first soul became infinitely conscious not only of God but also of creation, creating the Master station of being, and when he looked behind him he noticed the next soul in line, ready to notice everything as he himself had, except that now the everything that the second soul had to notice is not only what the first soul noticed, but the second soul, poor fellow, had to additionally notice the infinite consciousness of the first soul, which is now infinitely and consciously noticing-and-creating the universe.

There is, in short, for this second soul (but not for the first soul) an infinite consciousness in creation which he, the second soul, must now notice. But no problem, since that first soul is exactly and precisely identical to the second soul, which the second soul senses and feels as he is welcomed, not as a guest and separate being but as the same being, by the infinitely conscious first soul. So that God, after passing through all his material disguises, comes home again and again and again.

In other words, this third-state-of-God first-soul consciousness that each succeeding soul must encounter is nothing but the hidden consciousness/intelligence of each and every soul, now clouded over with atom life, stone life, metal life, plant life, worm life, fish life, bird life, animal life, and human life, and is named by Meher Baba the *Avatar*. The Avatar is the God within all, the universal mind, and its identicalness to our own inner being is why the approach to this being is through love. Love, as discovered earlier in these pages, is the force beneath sameness that makes all recognition possible and which points to a final sameness. Which is God.

Ah, well. That sigh issues because even if all this is true, it doesn't solve the problem of life-living. It's only a map and has the built-in trouble with all maps—they are not the place itself.

The Path

The headache of all religions is that they separate the hurly-burly of ordinary living from the sacred. But if the above version of the world is true, then everything is sacred, because nothing is outside the Being of all beings. And if everything's sacred, then nothing is sacred in that old way of using that term. The old way of the sacred is the way of separation—we're doing sacred stuff over here, but over there they aren't. But deeply, deeply, too deeply for notice, everyone is doing sacred stuff or no one is. It's not that some things aren't better to do than other things, it's that the term *sacred* imposes the ontological error of separation. But wait—criminals and rascals are also doing sacred stuff? We'll eventually figure out how to think about that.

To make fullest sense of this subject we must examine the elements of experience, what Meher Baba calls sanskaras, a Sanskrit word from the Upanishads. It's a general catch-all term for all the stuff of existence—the meaning-bundles of sense impressions, thoughts, feelings, moods, acts. Every moment of consciousness/intelligence is produced by and produces more sanskaras, which are, in essence, the scars of experience that create our inner being. In short, sanskaras are compounds of meaning and desire, our familiar first-in-line elements of being.

Desire compels us through this interminable chain of sanskaric accumulation and spending, and, because a lot of our living is unconscious, the process of this spending and accumulation down here in the knock-about world is vastly vague. It is the mysterious working of existence, the production and emanation of the infinite being as it makes the world. Still, however vague, this working leaves a breadcrumb trail we can catch the scent of. And follow.

In spiritual texts this trail is called the Path. No doubt in some sense we are all on the path, because once you're in the universe you can't get out except by the door to love. But the capital *P* Path is distinguished from normal living in that it begins on what Meher Baba calls the first subtle plane. In all, there are seven main planes in the inner world (the word *main* is used because there are lots of sections in those main planes): three subtle planes, then the fourth plane, a transition between the subtle world and the next one, called the mental, with two planes, the fifth and sixth, and finally the seventh, the plane of God-realization. Interesting, certainly, but all this naming and particularization, however confirming, is a bit premature for most of us. Still, good to know for the time when you have to pack your bags. Saint Francis might have appreciated knowing where he was headed. All that can be described with some now-useful effect is how to get to the Path.

It is desire as longing which leads to the Path, and desire as the I-want-stuff of living that obscures it. Aurobindo refers to the psychic area which houses these smaller desires as the lower vital, a reservoir of hostility, jealousy, vanity, all the little me-centered power impulses natural to our development from animals (which we have all been). When I am struck, there arises within me a lower vital impulse to strike back, and this impulse can be resisted only by the appearance of a higher, wider impulse. (Larger desire eats smaller desire.)

Too often, of course, the larger impulse doesn't come or comes too feebly to interfere, except with guilt, at our returning a good wallop for the wallop received. But when we are able to resist—and resist not merely with a moral-ethical-mentalized finger-wag of disapproval—this better resistance is produced by a stepping back. Why do we step back? Because we want to, because we have contacted a larger desire world.

This is the territory of character and of conscience, and, perhaps surprisingly, of faith. Here's how that works. At first, we experience every moment of our existence as an inner assault of the lower vital, of those animal sanskaras (Meher Baba's term) that express and create greed, lust, and anger. Eventually and inevitably new forces in us emerge. Something in us widens and slows and develops (the emergence of what Aurobindo called the higher vital). Now, as those intoxicating lower impulses arise, they appear in a new and developing sobriety that resists them. At first this resistance may be aided by the external urging of ethical admonition, but soon enough, as the fruits of the resistance of larger desire (calm, patience, kindliness) become evident in our lives, ethics is abandoned as unneeded, as an external and too-crude force. In *The Discourses*, Meher Baba describes creative control as the *adjustment of behavior in the light of perceived value*s. Non-creative control, then, must be the adjustment of behavior in the light of external rules which can instruct but are not yet fully experienced—useful for the masses but superfluous, and even misleading, for those immersed in the inner adventure.

Of course, as we develop, not every moment of lower vital desiring is countered by a higher vital impulse—which accounts for the three-steps-forward-two-steps-back nature of inner development. And which points up the usefulness of faith, a sort of handhold in the murk and chaos of living. We may not have at every moment the awareness of our higher nature to offer resistance, but at least we can have an inner determination, however fragile, that is based on authentic intuition. This sort of faith we may call faith in the larger self within us that is linked to the largest Self within all. From *The Discourses: True faith is grounded in the deeper experiences of the spirit and the unerring deliverances of purified intuition. It is not to be regarded as the antithesis of critical reason but as the unfailing guide of critical reason. When critical reason is implemented by a deep and living faith, based on pure intuition, its functioning becomes creative, fruitful and significant instead of barren, ineffective and meaningless.*

Though often obscure, we eventually begin to feel this larger self with its larger desires more and more emergent within us. In a sense, faith in our larger self is identical with faith in God and also with faith in the universe, because, after all, the Infinite Self which is making everything is one and is, in fact, us. Which, by the way, is the solution to the what-is-good-to-do-all-day problem: do things that make you bigger. This is not an external commandment. It's a condition of existence. It's how Being operates and what, sooner or later, everyone must do and will do.

Here's the interesting, beautiful, and frustrating truth already discovered in these pages: love is the fruit of longing, and like longing, it cannot be produced by will. Love can be properly described as the gift of God. No doubt our determination can prepare a place that aids in love's appearance, but the experience of love itself arrives from a place beneath and inaccessible to will. It comes through a need that produces a deep indomitable sincerity.

Another issue is that as we shed the lower vital lens of being, that indefatigable counterfeiter, the ego, obligingly produces plenty of higher vital imitations that it hopes will pass muster with our front self. That way the lower vital can go about its business. But this merely produces the "spiritual" ego. In ourselves, we often protect this sort of egotism by terming it *righteousness*. In others, we call it *self-righteousness.*

Religion attempts to catch hold of egotism with its *all are sinners* refrain. But the only authority to name egotism out loud issues from the surrender of humility, and humility cannot blame. Accusation and blame succeed only in making God two, the God part and the bad part. The scolding fellow at the pulpit has a real dilemma. His haplessness brings to mind the farmer trying to instruct the tourist how to get to Chicago: "Well, you go down the road about a mile and…no, wait, you turn off at… well, let's see…you head on out…no, wait, you go...well, I'll be damned—you can't get there from here."

Theologies and religion come from a different place in the psyche than love does, a cruel fact inwardly felt by every preacher and imam in the aridity of the pulpit. Christ could speak authentically of love because he was love, and so he had the authority to name what was not love. But what is a loveless priest to do? The fall-back position is blame, since that at least seems to point in the right direction. But like the bewildered farmer, you can't get to love from blame. Blame and all its scriptural support are cold fires and cannot warm the hands of need. No doubt blame has been for centuries a best-we-can-do offering, but scripture lies, and must remain, outside the heart where longing lives.

Another admission

At this point, it's good to acknowledge and plainly grant the trouble with this explanation—like all explanation, it presents itself at the wrong port, where the custom officer can permit entry but is not empowered to grant assimilation. Things of the mind, thought things (this book too), sit grumpily on top of the dark knotting of ego, that invisible disposition fed by desire, memory, resentment, self-pity, pride, envy, selfishness, and so on. Thought's inability to penetrate this moody self-barrier is what makes change so hard for a person, a nation, and an era. Thought is like a beach ball kicked merrily back and forth by the swirling legs of ego, a pastime which ego, that shadow servant of desire within each of us, celebrates, since that thought-game provides the something-to-do-that-seems-important-for-eighty-years but doesn't threaten change because it cannot penetrate the depths, cannot lever into light our crafty invisible selfness. If it could, the earth would have become a utopia years ago. After all, everyone loves love best. Except for our shadow self, which likes its own way. Its own way are its desires, which, as noted earlier, are actual things and possess a stubborn thingness. They cannot be tricked, advised, compelled, or guilted into compliance with even the shiniest of shiny methods, yogas, cults, explanations, religions, or doctrines. We produce change in ourselves only if we want to.

When we want to, it may not be easy, but it's doable. When we don't, it's impossible.

Still, though we can't get to love by thought, thought has its place. Higher thoughts, called ideals, can at least act as bait, luring the fish of the self up from its dark wonderment to a lighter world where its higher feelings and desires can have the scaffolding of at least some sort of explanation. Too often, of course, the planks of ideals are hammered into the decrepit edifice of a power structure (a national religion or philosophy) where they rot into effectuality. In temples, mosques, and churches, everyone sits, however uncomfortably, on their wallet. We pass the peace but seldom the money.

Therefore: even if the best, most inclusive, explanations so far are Meher Baba's and Aurobindo's, how to proceed? How to keep this shadowy self-fish from returning to its comfortable dark? How to get on the Path?

The four aids

In *The Synthesis of Yoga* Aurobindo mentions four aids in this process. The first is knowledge, which is insight, in-sight, the meaning that arises in each of us every moment and in which we are continually embedded. It is meaning itself, one of our faithful ontological companions. The second is effort, the work produced by the restless desire for God. The third is the master, not a physical master, but the overwatching presence of the internal master, the universal mind, which he later refers to as the supermind. This master is eventually experienceable but is most elusive and goes mostly unnoticed. And the fourth aid is time, our being incarnate here in this workhouse of existence.

A note about effort and the longing that produces it: each of us, insofar as we are here, and you, insofar as you are reading this, have a claim. Still, it is true that no one makes an effort in the within without the restlessness of longing, and true too that longing cannot be created or willed into existence. Longing emerges as the final desire from the bewilderment of existence. Ages ago, too long for memory, time saddled each one of us like a mare and drives us still through vexatious multitudes of tribulation, which are his celebration, until at last we cry enough. Until at last we sense within the final hunger. The strength of that hunger depends on how long a soul has been here, and that depends on when that soul was first manifested into the cosmos. Likely, if you're reading this book, you've been around a while. Also likely, if you're reading this book, you'll be around a while longer. (It's doubtful that anyone on the sixth plane browses the thoughts-about-existence section of the bookstore but, sixth planer, if you're reading, most welcome.)

Aurobindo, instead of remarking that the second aid was our longing for God, which then produces our effort, said the second aid was effort. He was, after all, the guide of many yearning souls, and by substituting effort for longing he was encouraging them to get off their duffs, O spiritual seekers, and be busy with your salvation. He well knew, though, as all introspective thought knows, that we can't want God by decision, in the same way we can't love by decision. In the beginning, we don't so much want God as we want relief. At least until we *catch the scent*. Then something new happens, as the following poem expresses. (In what follows, unattributed poems are the author's.)

Thus Comes the Soul

Thus comes the soul,
To part the reeds at earth's shore,
Seeking in the water a deep drink of experience,
For in his dark heart he hears
The deep water's own dark heart calling,
And he comes.
He is an ancient traveler,
And has worn the shoes of time too long.
He burns for something finally good,
For something finally worth life's rude unstopping shock,
Worth the sorrow of dignity made mean,
Worn out by emptiness,
Worth the swindles of pleasure that jangle
Pretty nothingness in the face of discontent,
Worth loud-talking anger
That struts in the palm of love,
Worth the knotted grip of unpayable guilt and living remorse unpaid,
Worth doubt, fear, hatred, and all bringers of desire and loss.
Thus he comes,
To part the reeds
And know himself,
And be free.

Getting to God, part one

Getting to God is seemingly so vast a subject and complicated an undertaking that many conclude the only way forward is to find some written-down practice or flesh-and-blood guide to learn what sort of clothes to wear, diet to eat, routine to follow, mantra to chant, meditation to employ. This feverish desire for authority is a natural result of our being embedded in this knock-about world of only good-enough knowledge. It's also the reason every religion has a too-ferocious advocacy of its practices and rituals. Yet amid all this spiritual detritus a simple answer, and practice, gleams. We can find it in the best-selling poet on the planet, Jalāl ad-Dīn Muhammad Balkhī, called Rumi.

Rumi lived some 800 years ago at a time when cities had big walls because that was the only way to protect life and wealth, when there was not much in the way of books or plumbing, and the world beyond your own language was mostly known by traveler's hearsay. Rumi was, said Meher Baba, a Perfect Master, one who had reached the end of his travels, become one with God, and had a duty to stay awhile. He had a faithful companion who wrote down his poetic utterances in a book now called the *Mathnawi*. Many writers have used that book as inspiration for loose translations, or renderings, as they are called. Here are a few lines from one by Daniel Liebert:

The way of Moses is hopelessness and need,
And it is the only way to God.
From when you were an infant, when has hopelessness ever failed you?
Hunger makes stale bread more delicious than halvah.
Discomfort is spiritual indigestion.
A mouse is a nibbler.
God gives mind in proportion to need.
Without need, He gives nothing.

Then how to get need? Jesus addressed this issue with the utterance, *Ask and you shall be answered*. A reply might be, but I ask all the time and get nothing, which is why I need church, a puja room, incense, and candles, and why this troublesome family is my main problem. The central question remains—if need is the way to God, why doesn't everyone do it? And importantly, can we learn to do it?

And so we come again, and most naturally come, to the second of the primitives that structure the universe—desire. But not desire for gold or women (the main things to watch out for, said Perfect Master, Ramakrishna—for women, of course, read *lust*). Instead we come, and inevitably come, to the desire for God, which is the hidden desire within all desire, the desire for the Being behind everything, in everything, and above and below everything. The inner work is to make that desire more and more conscious, since, as Rumi says, without the desire for That, *God gives nothing*.

And importantly this: don't worry about having that desire. However disguised your wanting may be, however misdirected, the very fact that you want anything means that, however secretly, you want God, who is the last want, the big want, the end of want. If you're miserable, you want to be happy, which means you want God. If you're happy, you're afraid of losing happiness, which means you want God. This simple good sense is hidden in every moment of existence, and, if Meher Baba and Aurobindo are right, it is gradually making its way into the consciousness of the planet.

So how does this busy-body little self which imposes its little-self will on everything turn and get intelligently interested in absorbing and being absorbed by the big Self—and do it without being diverted by sacred robes and the self-important pronouncements of the talk-talkers?

By the way—talk-talkers? Of course. After all, it's natural for the greatest court, God's, to assemble multitudes of favor-vying courtiers, and natural too that their talking be loud and long. Searching *spirituality* on the internet invites an endless offering of earnest opinion. And this book? No doubt, it too emits the stink of opinion, and for that your humiliated author rubs his nose at your feet. But he is soon up again, pointing and insisting, really, friends, it's *over there*. Go and see. (It is not, note, *come and see.* Everyone goes alone.)

Where then is this over there? It is the within, the dark, amorphous terrain of thought, feeling, mood, vitality—and depression, pain, sorrow, loss—that produces the marvelously intelligent shadow self that conceals the infinitely intelligent real Self. It's a drawing back from absorption in the movie of your life to notice, why, I'm in my own movie. As Aurobindo put it in *The Synthesis of Yoga: A most effective way of purification is for the mental Purusha to draw back, to stand as the passive witness and observe and know himself and the workings of Nature in the lower, the normal being.* Does this sound like the popular doctrine of mindfulness? Partly. But mindfulness alone is a gruel too thin for the appetite of longing.

The work is to notice our self and to continue to notice, to notice each moment, more and more to notice, more and more to draw back and move within and begin, slowly but inevitably, to notice the Noticer.

Getting to God, part two

Meher Baba asserts that intelligence/consciousness is developed by the accumulation of sanskaras, or impressions. From the very first impression, when God's thinking first encountered God's imagination, to the state of human consciousness where consciousness is, says Meher Baba, fully developed, we are led by desire to pile on layers and layers of impressions, and this gigantic, unimaginably complex layering is the who we identify with. This who, this me atop and presiding over this accumulation of impressions, resists our steering because this ego-who has a plan of its own, which plan is to express every last one of its accumulated desires. As we begin our inner adventure, we discover a scampering, busy, nimble—and utterly invisible—little me-self intent on outflanking every imposition of discipline and high-minded aspiration. To call it crafty is to underestimate its tireless intelligence. It knows us and our devices of self-discipline better than we can ever know them because it sits comfortably by their side in the dark of our own disposition, more intimate to our nature than our futile topside consciousness can ever be. Yet oddly, and importantly, this me-self is not our enemy, but is instead a most valuable and essential friend, since only by its tireless industry have we been able to gain the fullness of our present consciousness. No doubt it goes too far, no doubt it is little concerned with honesty and has no sympathy for our emptiness and angst. Still, it is the faithful servant which wakes us in the morning, chugs us through the day, and puts us to bed at night. It even welcomes our efforting at spirituality, since that too is desire and grist for its churning mill of self-expression. Only not too much, thank you, since spiritual efforting has a sometimes tendency to interfere with ice cream and sex.

So how to finally catch hold of it? How finally to get enough grip on our slippery disposition so that we can begin to somewhat steer the careening vehicle of our lives? Many seek out what are popularly called spiritual practices, that is, systems of sitting for meditation, chanting, fasting, attending retreats, and so on. These efforts markedly contrast with the everyday life of egotism, and that contrast has value, like discovering the sea after years lost in the jungle. But too often egotism remains stubbornly in place and in fact often builds a nicely modest hut by the shore where it resides in contented "spirituality." Kabir—a poet beloved in India, and, said Meher Baba, a Perfect Master—captures this dilemma in this Robert Bly rendering:

Friend, please tell me what I can do about this mud world
I keep spinning out of myself!
I gave up expensive clothes, and bought a robe.
But I noticed one day the cloth was well-woven,
So I bought some burlap, but I still
Throw it elegantly over my left shoulder.
I stopped being a sexual elephant,
And now I discover that I'm angry a lot.
I finally gave up anger, and now I notice
That I am greedy all day.
I worked hard at dissolving the greed,
And now I am proud of myself.
When the mind wants to break its link with the world,
It still holds on to one thing.
Kabir says: Listen, my friend,
There are very few that find the path!

The unrelenting chameleon of the ego cannot be hushed or harshed out of existence. But when you become conscious of longing, it's time to relax. You have caught the scent. The rest is unfoldment. And quite interesting.

Eventually this scent-catching produces the experience of what Aurobindo calls the *psychic being,* the soul within. Its residence is center-chest, like the emotional heart which produces our sentiment, tears, and anguish, but it is not that heart itself, but somewhere beneath it. Wordsworth alludes to it in his phrase *thoughts that lie too deep for tears,* and Shelley in his lines, *The desire of the moth for the star,/Of the night for the morrow,/ The yearning for something afar/From the sphere of our sorrow,* but really to describe it further, or attempt to precisely delineate its texture, location, and phenomenal being is to commit a fraud of exactitude. It eludes description in the same way that the taste of a tomato does, but is also just as lively and existent. To dismiss it as *mystical* has no more validity than dismissing the taste of a tomato. But, you reply, I can taste a tomato! And you can taste the psychic being, even if you haven't yet.

This some-can, some-can't dilemma is the cross that humanity—and each of us—must bear as consciousness evolves, then involves. The elusiveness of the sense of the divine in experience has produced the fantastic speculations of the hopeful, the authoritative pronouncements of talk-talkers, and the public enthrallment with mediums, gurus, and psychics. It has led to reliance on church authority. It has led to the disgusted denials of atheists.

Are we tempted to complain that God makes it too hard, too subtle, too vague? Why not make billboards magically appear on highways: *Think of God, folks! Get that psychic being going!* After all, what would a few billboards cost this infinite imaginer of everything? Magic billboards could certainly cure atheism. Maybe even silence the talk-talkers. But billboards wouldn't expand our hearts. They wouldn't deepen us and make us ready for the presence of the Self. In fact, they would probably make us feel so bad we would tear them down, which was Dostoyevsky's insight in "The Grand Inquisitor" section of *The Brothers Karamazov*. If Jesus came back, said Dostoyevsky, we would kill him, just as we killed him two thousand years ago. To catch God, we need a huge mitt, the way a baseball catcher uses a huge mitt to catch a knuckleball. The divine knuckleball is so elusive we need a mitt the size of God himself, which is the soul, and the way to that is through what Aurobindo calls the psychic being.

Aurobindo, because he used the word *yoga*, might be thought of as one of those teachers that prescribed lots of meditation, maybe fasting, maybe chanting. He didn't. The term *yoga* means union, and that was his essential message. God is within all. Some get to him this way, some that, but, as it is said in the East, though the paths to God are as many as the souls of mankind, all paths are one. The process for all is the same—the gradual slowing and deepening of the desire-disposition. Aurobindo was, said Meher Baba, not only a saint of the sixth plane, but one who had climbed the inner ladder unaided by any external guide. Plus, he was a genius that could remember the first word on page 108 of the book he had just finished. In his later years, he isolated himself and for ten years wrote twelve hours a day. It is reported that when he died, Meher Baba gave him realization. On earth, he was not an incarnation of God, but his writings make the inner ladder wonderfully clear. Below is a bit of that concerning the transition in the self produced by contacting the psychic being.

From his *Letters on Yoga I*, page 94:

> *When one leaves the outer consciousness and goes inside, it is here that one enters—some or most entering into the inner vital first, others into the inner mental or inner physical; the emotional vital is the most direct road, for the seat of the psychic is just behind the emotional in the heart center. It is absolutely necessary for our purpose that one should become conscious in these inner regions, for if they are not awake, then the psychic being has no proper and sufficient instrumentation for its activities; it has then only the*

outer mind, outer vital and body for its means and these are too small and narrow and obscure.

Page 97:

When one realizes the psychic being…this brings the sense of union with the Divine and dependence upon it and sole consecration to the Divine alone and the power to change the nature and discover the true mental, the true vital, the true physical being in oneself.

The "I" or the little ego is constituted by Nature and is at once a mental, vital and physical formation meant to aid in centralizing and individualizing the outer consciousness and action. When the true being is discovered, the utility of the ego is over and this formation has to disappear—the true being is felt in its place.

Page 84-85:

For this transition, if it is to be at the same time a transformation, there is only one way, one path. First, there must be a conversion inwards, a going within to find the inmost psychic being and bring it out to the front, disclosing at the same time the inner mind, inner vital, inner physical parts of the nature. Next, there must be an ascension, a series of conversions upwards and a turning down to convert the lower parts. When one has made the inward conversion, one psychicises the whole lower nature so as to make it ready for the divine change. Going upwards, one passes beyond the human mind and at each stage of the ascent there is a conversion into a new consciousness and an infusion of this new consciousness into the whole of the nature. Thus rising beyond intellect through illuminated higher mind to the intuitive consciousness, we begin to look at everything not from the intellect range or through intellect as an instrument, but from a greater intuitive height and through an intuitivized will, feeling, emotion, sensation, and physical contact. So, proceeding from intuition to a greater overmind height, there is a new conversion and we look at and experience everything from the overmind consciousness and through a mind, heart, vital, and body surcharged with the overmind thought, sight, will, feeling, sensation, play of force, and contact.

From Letters on Yoga II, page 55: *A simple, straight, and sincere call and aspiration from the heart is the one important thing...*

The above passages make one thing clear: the process of getting to God is not as trivial as believing something. And it's not about meditation or prayer either, though those two have their place. Mostly, and naturally, it's about aspiration. It's about getting tired of emptiness. It's about going within into the at-first dark of inner emptiness, and prevailing there until in that darkness you begin to make out the shape and nature of your being—and the Being beneath it. For that we must understand the use of three of Aurobindo's aids, knowledge, effort, and time.

Knowledge, the meaning that surrounds us every moment, is available only through honesty, and honesty is possible only through need, a desire for truth so utter that it is able to burn the dross of our suppositions and most prized opinions. Effort too depends on need, and while it may from time-to-time lead to sessions of prayer and meditation, its most characteristic effect is a new and more and more continual concentration on the inner being, on its operation, its excuses, subterfuges, ignorance, and its sometimes knee-weakening exultation. And all this takes time.

The following poem expresses the knock-about happenstance of the search (in the forest of the inner being). The last line assures that even the poet is without authority in this press-on-regardless world.

The Forest

A forest starts behind your house.
Eventually you'll want to wander there.
Go when you must,
In the daylight or the night.
There time is unimportant,
And the only light is shadow.
The eyes of beasts will follow you from thickets,
But so what?
You have as much right there as they do.
So then it's dappled clearings, misty starlight,
This and that.
The paraphernalia of knowing.
Notice what you can.
The forest is immense.
No one can notice much.
Eventually you'll find a creek,
And deeper wonder starts.
See the way the water moves.
Everyone goes upstream,
And so will you.
Eventually the earth inclines,
And you're deeply breathing.
The water's clear and cold
And mumbling something true.
Notice what you can.
No one can notice much.
Eventually wild thirst begins,
And you'll get so tired of dryness,
You'll tear out all your chest bones
To let the water in.
If you can,
Kindly let me know what happens next.

The fourth aid

As mentioned, there are plenty of talk-talkers at the spiritual court, an expected and natural outcome of the station where all begin, in egotism. The talk-talking courtier system is made even more complicated and hard to parse since the courtiers are courtiers of an entirely invisible world where flair of personality and pithy commentary can seduce the naive. And each of us, as we begin, is that. How then can the message and being of the Self be recognized and become useful to humanity? And more, if Meher Baba was truly the Avatar, of what use is he, a person once alive, but now passed away?

Thus we come to Aurobindo's fourth aid, the master. This subject must be opened carefully, since investigating it involves all the rich delicacy of existence itself. We have seen that in this knock-about world knowledge is inevitably only good-enough and all are compelled to live a press-on-regardless life. Reason is useful in parsing and sorting knowledge, but for the stuff of knowledge itself we must resort to the immediacy of intuition, which is at best vague and at worst wrong. Recognizing this state can produce both anxiety and exultation, anxiety because we come to see there is nothing to trust but the ever-elusive within, exultation because we are no longer burdened and bound by forms of thought imposed from without. It's worth noting that the word *without* here means not only those forms imposed by the thoughts and explanations of others, but even those thoughts and forms produced by our own mind but outside the core of our uttermost Self, where lies our uttermost need. Coming to this junction within is the beginning, perhaps not of the Path, but of the path to the Path. This state is a kind of wonderment, a rejection of formula, even formulas most prized, most based on texts previously useful and valuable, even the Bible, the Koran, the Upanishads, even the books of Meher Baba. (An interesting by-note—many, if not most, of Meher Baba's own mandali did not read his books. They did not need to. They had no need of reflected light, since they had the Source among them and within them.)

It is by abandoning everything fixed and certain, by throwing ourselves wholeheartedly into the inner releasement of our longing, that we begin at last to understand those texts, to stand under them, as it were, and see the illumination within them. And only then, as this releasement deepens, can we begin to feel the outline, indefinite at first but growing ever more clear, of the inner world. And eventually of the master.

Which is best conceived as the *inner* master.

The stairway

In his book *The Everything and the Nothing,* Meher Baba offers a three-part progression: *Love is a gift from God to man, obedience is a gift from master to man, and surrender is a gift from man to master.*

This simple formula conceals the essence of all spirituality and helps clarify the relationship of the soul to the inner master.

Love is a gift from God to man. The word *gift* in that statement seems to imply that love is given through divine whim—let's see, thinks God, maybe today I'll give this one some love, but not that one. But that would imply a capricious God who, when confronted with two identical souls, chooses one and not the other. Caprice would make God, as are we, the pawn of desire, not its creator. Instead, the word *gift* can only mean that the source of love is God himself and that his always-withness is poised to respond when our longing ripens. Love, in other words, is not gained by our decision or our will, but appears within as a response to need. Love descends, dawns, or appears when the longing for Truth reaches some mysterious inner crescendo.

Here it's important to recognize and note that thereafter longing and love are inseparable companions. And also that love's frequent disappearance is as natural as its reappearance. Its back-and-forthing within us sharpens our longing and makes that longing an ever more resilient and trusted ally, and ever more precious. Longing is, in fact, our most faithful and important friend. It is the core desire on which all spiritual seeking depends. It is desire itself, not the desire for things, but the ever-more-agonizing desire for the Being of all beings—and it is inevitable and eventual in everyone's development. Love begins to appear, however tenuously and evanescently, when the deepening anguish within us provokes a response from the Being of all beings—and that response is felt love.

The term *love*, no doubt, has been confined to positive feeling for centuries, and so it's good here to mention its nature again. Love is the secret force that pervades all existence, the unitary intelligence within all things. To hold that love is present only between friends or lovers or at the culmination of the universe—in saints or in God-realization—is to forget that each moment of existence is an active ongoing creation that issues from God's unity, and that that unity, that oneness, is itself the active force of love holding things together. The habit of sentimentalizing love places it on the shelf of admired but distant objects. It is instead the unifying glue that binds all creation. All existence is nothing but the complex working, and inevitable freeing, of love. Love is the ontological unity of the Being that is making the world and accounts for the action of sameness and largeness in our psyches. Whether our love is for a named being (Jesus, Meher Baba, Mohammed) or whether it remains anonymous and is for a nameless God, or is even a generalized love of life, love is always for the Being beneath being. That's why even so-called atheists, if they love life and their fellow man, are lovers of God. They just haven't come to terms with it yet. In a sense which is true and useful to acknowledge, all love goes from here below to some place beyond creation where God as the Being-of-All-Being sits in infinite oneness.

Still, it is easier for love to focus when it is directed toward the Avatar or a Perfect Master, since those souls, besides being one with the source of all love, have a name and image. Devotion to them, whether they are embodied or disembodied, is simplest. This is particularly true of the most recent Avatar, since that embodiment of Truth is most closely connected to the spiritus mundi of the age. (The linkyness of the God-Man will be explored in a later section.)

This important side note: in *The Discourses*, we occasionally find statements like this: *"The Master may sometimes give instructions with the intent of preparing his disciple for a higher mode of life."* Such pronouncements give the impression that a seeker, if he knows what's good for him, had better seek out a living Perfect Master and get some verbal guidance. This emphasis in *The Discourses* was natural since when those essays were written (in the 1930s by his mandali from notes he dictated) Meher Baba was in the body. Yet we also read this in *The Discourses*: *The relationship between the Master and the disciple is often carried on from one life to another for several reincarnations. Those who have been connected with a Master in past lives are drawn to him by an unconscious magnetism, not knowing why they are thus drawn.* Any relationship with a Perfect Master (and this includes relationship with the Avatar), whether direct through embodied relationship or disembodied through the inner being, is a relationship of love, and that state is utterly inner, resulting from the recognition of the Master's egoless purity. In both types of relationship, whether direct or indirect, the felt osmosis of love is identical. In either case, the faith required and the resultant guidance is from the inner master, the God within, the Self in all. And the eternal and always available Perfect Master, said Meher Baba, is the God-Man. *You and I are not we but one,* he said. He said, *I never come. I never go.*

The second term of Meher Baba's triad: *obedience is a gift from master to man.* Immediately we recognize an oddity. We might suppose that there is a reversal here, that the gift of obedience is better conceived as a gift from man to master, since after all, isn't it we who decide to obey, and thus we who should be given credit for offering the gift of our obedience? But in this second piece of the triad is hidden all the limitation of morality and all the uselessness of proselytizing.

To understand this second section we must understand more fully what is meant, and can only be meant, by the term *master*.

The master is, in essence and in short, the sense, vague and elusive initially, but growing more and more distinct as longing deepens, of an internal presence within, a presence whose guidance is not in words but in silent and loving assurance. The appearance and continuance of this inner master is so maddeningly gradual that the impatient aspirant often craves visions, miracles, experiences, and an external guide. Yet visions, experiences, and guides, though sometimes supportive, can not only become a focus of egotism, but are outside the presence in the now of this inner master. Even external masters, unless they are perfect, are outside this presence. And are themselves dependent on this inner master. In a sense that is important and true, the use of all external guides is to point and say, *it's over there. Which is always in here.*

There is a story told by Perfect Master Farid al-Din Attar in *Muslim Saints and Mystics*. Rabia, a saint, was in her kitchen one night preparing supper and found herself in need of an onion. Just then a crow flew over and dropped an onion from its beak into her pan. She lifted the onion from the pan, considered it, then tossed it into the street. She remarked, "I am not sure whether or not this is some trick." Rabia distrusted the external, however tempting, however seemingly a response from the Unseen to her physical need. (In her next life, she became Babajan, the old lady Perfect Master of Pune whose kiss awakened Meher Baba.)

Kirpal Singh, a saint with a world-wide following, recognized Meher Baba as the Avatar, and once asked Baba if he gave his disciples experiences, since he, Kirpal, found it useful in luring them from illusion. Baba, in preparation for Kirpal's visit, had had a sign posted behind his chair: *One who knows everything displaces nothing.* To Kirpal's question, Baba shrugged and said he knew nothing of experiences, but if Kirpal was interested in such things he could visit the room of Kaikobad, one of Baba's men, who was said to have experiences. Kaikobad, who had been given by Baba the task of repeating Baba's name 100,000 times each day, revealed to Kirpal his frequent experience of a million suns flaming in his consciousness. Yet Baba shrugged and remarked that he gave no experiences—and also gave no importance to them. Instead, he gave God. Throughout his advent, this was his continual refrain.

Extraordinary experiences are possible. Visions may come. Even what are called miracles may appear. But the central and most supportive experience is the gradual, more and more continual, and most natural emergence of the inner master (which Aurobindo called the psychic being).

The growing presence of the inner master is why obedience is *his* gift to us, not ours to him. Obedience is the natural response to the Master's *appearance in the within.* Without that appearance, obedience can only be formal allegiance to an ideal. But when the warming fire of love is lighted in the heart, the source of that love gradually appears as the inner master. The aspirant then wants only that this fire be kept burning, and so he carefully tends it, feeds it the branches and twigs of contrary desire, feeds it doubt, impatience, resentment, envy, and on and on until more and more he himself, the silo of doubt, fear, anger, and contrary desire, is gradually consumed.

The appearance of the inner master makes obedience possible, since without that manifestation obedience is yoked only to the guidance of the external in the form of morality, authority, or scripture (called *shariat* or *sharia* in the East). This external guidance is useful, even necessary, in the earlier periods of our development, just as parental guidance is useful in shaping the child. But the continual reliance on the external guidance of this culture or that, this guru or that, this doctrine or that, cannot pierce the heart, and more, leads to conflict (and contempt, fanaticism, and violence) as these guidances clash. External guidance, like law, is essential for a society but tasteless for a seeker.

The subtle emergence of the ever-more-clear inner master is an ontological fact of the inner life, described in texts ancient and modern. This delicate force has sometimes been demoted to the force of conscience, and while there is truth here—the inner master is no doubt the true conscience—too often we have linked conscience to external doctrine and thus devalued it. True conscience has nothing to do with the externalization of right and wrong. True conscience deals with good and bad. (Everyone knows that an act can be wrong and good or right and bad.) Between right and wrong and good and bad is a vast and essential-to-understand difference. Understanding that difference is impossible, though, without contact with and trust in the inner master, the true conscience within each of us. Understanding that difference reorganizes thinking about spirituality, God, and life itself.

Meher Baba demanded strict obedience from his close ones—his brooms, as he sometimes called them—yet he also said that if one of his orders conflicted with their conscience, they must choose their conscience. This is because even he, whom they took to be the incarnation of God Himself, the Krishna, the Jesus, the Buddha to whom they had surrendered, stood outside the inmost guidance of their true master, their deepest conscience, the inner master. No doubt through his external agency, through the kicks and kisses of his instruction, the inner master within each of them took firmer and firmer shape, but Meher Baba himself was merely the physical embodiment of that master. His often-repeated instruction to them was: *Try to see me as I really am.* (These mandali—122 of them in total—were, as might be expected of those close to the Avatar, on their last few births, and so their need for truth was ripe.)

Fourteen hours before he dropped his body, at ten at night, he called one of these close ones to his bedside, fixed him with an intense gaze, and gestured in Hindi, *Yad Rakh* (remember this), then gestured in his unique silent language, *I am not this body*. He called this disciple again an hour later and repeated, *Remember, I am not this body*. An hour later, at midnight, he called him yet again and repeated that instruction. Then began the mysterious spasms that ushered him from life. In essence, his last message to humanity was: *I am beyond externality, even the externality of my own form. I am within*.

A few complications—and surrender

Before we come to the last part of Meher Baba's triad—*surrender is a gift from man to master*—let's consider the Avatar's physicality and both its use and challenge for humanity.

We have noted that the external form of the Avatar is only the physical manifestation of the Self. Still, according to Meher Baba, the Avatar's physicality is required for divinity to give things a straightening and fresh orientation. This he called his inner work. Though he said he was about this work continually, he also spent months in isolation to accomplish it.

It's also true that, since we are confined in a blur of seeming where all knowing is only good-enough, the Avatar's physical manifestation is likely required to get our attention—without offending naturalness by manifesting billboards. Even with bodily manifestation, it seems the Avatar must sometimes, as he did when he was Jesus, resort to miracles to get us interested. Eventually, as the Avataric form draws the world's attention, it becomes a focal point for devotion. But though that form is useful for the beginner and even the advanced, and essential for the many, it can become associated with doctrine and so be misunderstood as part of some external system of religion or morality. But the inner master is not the idea of God but instead the force-presence of divinity that has always been a secret inhabitant in our within. As inner experience develops, we come to see that God is like a cloud. From a distance, a cloud seems substantial. As we approach, it seems more like breath.

When the divine form is disentangled from externality its identity as the inner master becomes comprehensible. Failure to perform this disentanglement can not only support the spiritual ego, that front-self posturance that nurtures a secret pride in its right-seeming understanding, but can also deceive the seeker into thinking that acceptance of or belief in an external form is the required "spirituality." In this way, the form of the divine, the God-as-person, can sometimes stand as obstruction to the emergence of the inner master, the guide common and essential to all inner seeking.

In addition, the external form of the Master can create perverse stresses in the psyche. When we see the Master in human form, our old habits of interpersonal relations involving modesty, tact, and respect—as well as anger, resentment, and guilt—create in us a welter of confusion and self-repression, so that the Avatar, seen merely as the best of persons, can become a kind of parental figure.

These reactions, usually inevitable, are temporary and disappear when the inner master begins to manifest within and love softens the boundary between the shadow self and the Self. Which is how the last part of the triad becomes possible: *surrender is a gift from man to master.*

For the inner master to take his place as the supreme guide, the journeying soul must receive the gift of love and then the gift of obedience that more and more develops as the inner master appears. This is a deepening, a recognition that it is only the emergence of the inner master that makes authentic obedience possible. That recognition creates and sustains an inner relentment—and vast contentment—that is the essence of surrender. In this state there is no question of pride since there is no ownership. Likewise, there is no suggestion of guilt, since responsibility lies beneath and beyond. Thus, one of the clues that led us to this understanding, remorse, is abandoned. But its sister clue, humility, remains, since the state of surrender is the essence of humility.

Contact with the Master is contact with the soul of all Being, and does not depend on external contact. In fact, external contact with a living Master, the destiny of only a few, to be useful and significant in a disciple's life—whether in the presence of a Perfect Master or not—must be felt internally.

For the seeker whose longing has come to fruition, the inner master emits the scent of divinity and becomes our deepest conscience. As this purity and clarity develop, creative control, the replacement of the lower by the higher, becomes more and more clear, simple, and automatic. The inner life is no longer a matter of faith but of experience, and we more and more feel life issuing not from us but through us. The impressions received from the inner master have the unique power of dislodging the lower elements of our being by the potency of divinized sanskaras (or as Aurobindo would put it, by the supramental influence of the psychic being). The response to this state is gratitude, love, and self-forgetfulness produced by Self-remembrance. The receiving of these impressions is called grace. The portal through which they pass is longing. This is not religious life, somehow separate from normal life. It is our deepest normality. It is truth imparted by the Truth.

Meher Baba: *Deny your false self and your Real-Self asserts itself. Ask for nothing and you get everything. Renounce everything to such an extent that you eventually renounce even renunciation.*

Higher desire unseats, dissolves the ground beneath, unfoots—in short sublimates—lower desire, and lower desire's energy is released, forsaken, abandoned, relented. The power that drives this work is the vigilance of longing. This is the process of involution, and it is, in a sense, the ordinary process of all maturity. In spiritual work, though, it is done more and more consciously.

From a rendering by Robert Bly: *Kabir says this: When the Guest is being searched for, it is the intensity of the longing for the Guest that does all the work.*

In *The Discourses*, in the chapter entitled, *The Ways of the Masters,* Meher Baba writes: *The aspirant has to walk his own way. The contribution of the Master consists in confirming and consolidating the previously acquired intuitions and perceptions of the aspirant, and in precipitating his consciousness into the next stage...*

The first emergence of the inner master may be said to be the emergence of true conscience, the deep conscience natural to the Self. This emergence is often painfully slow and replete with stops and starts. It develops from its origin as insatiable discontent to become a fuller and fuller and evermore indisputable force of soul—and ends in a response of love for the awakening Self which our longing has roused from slumber. The confirmation and consolidation described above by Meher Baba is an entirely inner and felt-for experience, and, however faint, evanescent, sometimes even doubtable, this force-presence becomes more and more clear as experience deepens and clarifies.

Most importantly, the inner master is not only an unerring yardstick that confirms and consolidates our experience in the inner world, but is also the felt presence of sustaining love. The love within all love is the love of the Great Sameness for itself. As our longing draws us inward, that Sameness rises to meet us and, with the omniscient skill of a perfect psychic surgeon, dissolves the knots of desire that obstruct our seeing. This Being is the only one always and perfectly in attendance at the operation, which is our daily life, now and now and now.

This is the work of the Christ, the Spirit, the Friend, the Guest, the Avatar, the psychic being, the soul, the inner master. However the aspirant comes to the search—through whatever external guide, guru, doctrine, or practice—the Guide is the same for all.

From one of Coleman Barks' renderings of Rumi:

Who looks out with my eyes? What is the soul?
I cannot stop asking.
If I could taste one sip of an answer,
I could break out of this prison for drunks.

I didn't come here of my own accord, and I can't leave that way.
Whoever brought me here will have to take me home.

The state of surrender can become so complete as to appear preternatural. The Perfect Master Ramdas (1608–1682) had a favorite disciple named Kaylan who it is said provoked jealousy in some of the other disciples. One day in the bright, sun-lighted ashram hall, Ramdas said, "Why is it so dark in here? Cannot someone light a lamp?" The others watched in amazement as Kalyan rose and began to grope his way toward the lamps. His Master had remarked that the room was dark, and so Kalyan had become unable to see. Since we have not experienced such surrender, we might, like Ramdas's other disciples, consider such a state extraordinary to the point of madness. Yet the logic within it is irresistible. Kalyan had become so completely identified, through surrender, with the inner master residing within him that he unreflexively saw the world more and more through his master's eyes. His identity with Ramdas, the outer form of the inner being with whom he was merging, was so complete that whatever the first said was realized in the experience of the second.

The following tale from *Muslim Saints and Mystics* illustrates surrender from a different viewpoint and delightfully reveals that even among the advanced the snake of egotism can insinuate:

One day Hasan of Basra, Malek-e Dinar, and Shaqiq Balkhi went to visit Rabe'a on her sickbed.

"He is not truthful in his claim," Hasan began, "who does not bear with fortitude the lash of his Lord."

"These words stink of egotism," Rabe'a commented.

"He is not truthful in his claim," Shaqiq tried, "who is not grateful for the lash of his Lord."

"We need something better than that," Rabe'a observed.

"He is not truthful in his claim," Malek-e Dinar offered, "who does not take delight in the lash of his Lord."

"We need something better than that," Rabe'a repeated.

"Then you say," they urged.

"He is not truthful in his claim," Rabe'a pronounced, "who does not forget the lash in contemplation of his Master."

When we hear such stories something within us cocks an ear in delight. Partly it is because longing is marvelously tuned to detect and reject imposture, but more, it is because we sense in Rabia's embrace of self-forgetting the release we crave.

The vast vague workhouse of the spirit

Before we address the workshop of day-to-day spiritual effort, let's consider why there are so many, various, and fiercely defended alternatives. It comes simply down to the most exasperatingly opinioned dilemma of the inner world: whence authority? The whence-authority issue has schismed every religion. The Shias wanted Mohammed's relatives to lead them. The Sunnis wanted the imams. The Catholics wanted the churchmen. The Protestants rejected them as corrupt. These divisions occur because as consciousness tries to develop a notion of divinity, it confronts an outer world ablaze with conflicting thought and an inner world with no clear where-to-stand. But that's simply the unremitting human predicament—we are imprisoned like ancient insects in the even more ancient amber of ignorance, which, however divinely ordained, makes it hard to see.

The invisibility of the inner world, which is the essence of ignorance, is one reason it's hard to see clearly. Another is our inner resistance, which is just as invisible—and immune to will—as our ignorance. The adage *God can heal a broken heart but you have to give him all the pieces* is apt here. What prevents that giving is not only ignorance of what to give, but also the hard-to-see-through mask of hypocrisy—which is the only fault, said Meher Baba, that God is helpless to forgive. The reason for that unforgiveness is phenomenologically simple. The inner master appears only when honesty and urgency produce inner nakedness. It is only that nakedness, that innocence, that can confront those earlier-mentioned seven modes of egotism—greed, lust, anger, pride, selfishness, jealousy, and hatred. And who among us, particularly when they are trying on their spiritual clothes, wants to see that in the mirror? And so: the obliging mask of hypocrisy to the rescue. Meher Baba once asked his mandali what he, the one who was everything and in everyone, could possibly want. After all, if he was God, as they took him to be, he already possessed everything. Various wrong answers were offered until finally he answered the question himself. The only thing he wanted, he said, was their imperfections.

As Jesus said, it's easy to see the faults of others, hard to see our own. That's because the context of our seeing, our unconscious world-shaping disposition, the lens through which we see, is our fault—not fault as in something that we are responsible for, but fault in the sense of an imperfection in a diamond. When longing deepens we see more deeply from the diamond and more clearly, and that developing clarity sees oneness.

Developing this inner sight is an inch-by-inch, moment-by-moment, year-by-year undoing of the sanskaric tangle of a dark disposition. According to Meher Baba, there is a best way to do that and some other not-so-best-but-still-sort-of-effective ways.

First, the sort-of-effective ways. These come under the heading of what has been popularized today in the West, and worldwide, as mindfulness. Mindfulness is paying attention to the inner world and recognizing and refusing expression of the lower desires that press up continually from the shadow self. We commonly think of this sort of effort as self-control, and even self-denial, and it is in general a commonsense attitude for living. We call it mindfulness when it becomes a more formalized process, meaning that it has a more and more conscious place in our minds so that we become more aware of our desires and thoughts and are gradually able to consider, withhold, and refuse response. And eventually no longer feel as bound. This new awareness is like drawing the face back from the window-lens of desire to become aware of desire's stagecraft and romp in the theater of mind. Yet only when mindfulness is supported by longing can it prevail and endure. Without longing, mindfulness is a flame without oxygen and eventually expires.

The Discourses contain four chapters on the function and removal of sanskaras, and several more on meditation, all of which may be thought of as Meher Baba's discussion of mindfulness. He describes the nature of external renunciation (helpful but preliminary) and internal renunciation (more effective but not final), and the hazards associated with these practices. The hazards are that in preventing the expression of sanskaras (solitude and fasting), in loosening the seat of sanskaras (penance), and in all the no-no impulses that are the essence of inner renunciation, the seeker can form new sanskaras of attachment to these practices and possibly even a "spiritualized" ego. Another hazard is that this process can be dry and not immediately rewarding.

Aurobindo offers a constructive insight about mindfulness. He notes that as progress in the inner world develops, the aspirant becomes aware of an inner doubling. One part of his nature is the puppet-of-impulses front self. The other is the growing calm of the deeper self that has begun to express new and larger desires. That new self begins more and more to experience the front self as bound, secondary, and separate.

From Aurobindo, *The Life Divine*, page 551:

> *...we have to go into our inner being and learn to live in it and from it; the outer mind and life and body must become for us only an antechamber. All that we are on the outside is indeed conditioned by what is within, occult, in our inner depths and recesses; it is thence that come the secret initiatives, the self-effective formations; our inspirations, our intuitions, our life-motives, our mind's preferences, our will's selections are actuated from there...*

In this developing mindfulness, there are reversals, of course. Time and again the aspirant makes flailing starts and stops, feels the backlash of self-accusation, and sometimes welcomes the release of indulgence. These are common to all and almost inevitable, since the movement within is from small desire, which has power and grip, to larger desire, which is initially wavering, vague, and unfooted in the psyche. But the haste, impatience, aridity, posturing, and confusion of the effort is a deposit in the spiritual vault. From that, longing grows—and grows wiser. The journeying soul, said Meher Baba, is a mischievous chicken that must eat everything before finally consuming itself.

As the process of mindfulness continues, familiarity with the inner world grows and produces a more assured confidence. Confidence that has not penetrated the false front of the ego is frail and wavering and reeks of bravado, but with the deepening of inner awareness confidence is not only more natural, but—and important for our watching and doubting mind—more sober and more true. In an important sense, all human action is expressed through the agency of confidence, however beleaguered and confounded by pride, inner conflict, and misgiving. Confidence is founded on the secret but natural letting-be of humility, which is, in essence, the love that enables intelligence to receive the sense inherent in the world. Confidence is the always-required province of our miraculous power of meaning-getting-and-holding. (Neurosis and psychosis can be understood as loss of confidence in the reliability of life.)

Yet the methods of mindfulness are only sort-of-effective. They are definitely useful, especially as we begin the process, since they are something-we-can-do, but as Meher Baba often pointed out, the ego can easily attach itself to these new practices. There is a better practice, a practice for which mindfulness is a preparation.

In September 1968, a few months before he dropped his body on January 31, 1969, Meher Baba gave his mandali yet another discourse on this best and easiest path to God. As self-denial goes to war with the front self, that struggle is vitiated by the aspirant's tendency to become attached to denial itself. Meher Baba continually emphasized the path of love, and that day in Mandali Hall said:

> *There is no end to denial and counter-denial, and even the strongest will and stoutest heart will break down on this path. But self-forgetfulness can be practiced by everyone, and its way is easy and delightful and safe, because it is always under the tender regard of the Master.*
>
> (From *The Ancient One,* a book from Meher Baba's spokesman, Eruch Jessawala)

What then is self-forgetfulness? Recall Rabe'a's advice to her companions: *He is not truthful in his claim, who does not forget the lash in contemplation of his Master.* It is only through growing humility that self-forgetfulness becomes possible. The quickest way to God is the way of love and self-effacement, which is why the watch-phrase of Meher Baba, imprinted on his emblem, was: *Mastery in Servitude.* In a later section, we will more completely examine the nature of self-forgetfulness, but this at least is clear: we forget the self by remembering the Self.

The lenses of intelligence

As earlier noted, both Aurobindo and Meher Baba reveal that our inner being is composed of three bodies, the gross, the subtle, and the mental. Each of these bodies is a lens of experience and focuses the mysterious intelligence that we are, an intelligence which, we have conjectured, is the infinite intelligence of God. Further, these bodies are connected so that they overlap, intersect, merge, and flow together into our unitary beingness to create a mind structure at least as complicated as the currents of water in a stream. All of these bodies are developed and constituted by what Meher Baba called sanskaras, or impressions, and this development began ages ago when we first landed in creation to begin our identification with electrons, stones, metals, worms, plants, fish, birds, animals, and human beings.

We don't know, and Meher Baba did not fully disclose, the details of the universe's operation. Still, in books and verbal testimony, he left clues and directional hints, and those clues, when combined with our intuition, can be a good-enough pointing in the knock-about world so that we can be usefully about our business.

After reaching the human state, Meher Baba says intelligence is complete and able to grasp the infinitude of creation. But it can't, since it is compelled to look through the lens of its sanskaras. Meher Baba discloses in *God Speaks* the gradual development of the three bodies, revealing that the plant, for instance, has only a rudimentary subtle and mental body, and that animals have more developed inner bodies (which he called instinct). These bodies develop as the soul proceeds through the stages of evolution. In human beings the inner bodies are fully developed.

These bodies are not intelligence itself. They are the lenses through which intelligence sees. Intelligence itself is the most primordial, basal isness of mind, the power, essence, and whatever-it-is stuff of meaning. As mentioned, it is beyond understanding because it cannot be stood under and seen from any power beneath it, since it is the beneath-most seeing-power that stands under everything. It is the stuff of all being. It is the stuff of God's noticing.

That's why the discussion of the bodies through which life develops is not a discussion of the essence of intelligence itself, but rather a discussion of the refracting lens through which it sees. Whatever intelligence is, it is that-which-makes-meaning, and is why meaning-getting-and-holding is a sensible first ontological primitive. Meher Baba reveals that God himself *is* this intelligence looking out through an ever-ripening lens of sanskaras.

Though intelligence itself must remain elusive until we are realized, sanskaras can be at least tentatively considered: they are the bits of meaning and desire through which intelligence sees as it evolves and which somehow create the lens of mind. Some of these meaning-bits we call sensations, some we call intuitions, some concepts, and so on. Every meaning bit—a sound, a thought, a mood—appears in a surround of meaning so that we are embedded in a vast context of meaning that rises, falls away, leaves imprints of memory, inspires ideas, is forgotten. The intimate arms of our life-context are a vast layering of sensation, intuition, and idea, a layering that can become available to intelligence when the flashlight of consciousness turns toward it.

The exploration of this contextual layering is the province of psychology, philosophy, language theorists, mystics—and seekers. Though theories about its nature and mechanism abound and conflict, those whose introspection has been deepened by longing find more and more agreement in the simple notion that: a fathomless Something is making and seeing the world through us.

Since Plato and the Upanishads, much thought has been given to how this lens of mind might develop and function. Understanding the mind and its interaction with the world is tantamount to understanding existence—and is the supreme prize of all thinking. This is a notoriously difficult undertaking where introspection and depth of insight count more than learning. This thinking does not propose to wander much in the wilderness of inner context, but advertises the adventure.

It's worth emphasizing again that lifting the psyche into thought requires the grounding and guidance of a mind power beyond and beneath intellect, which is only the holding part of intelligence. It needs the power of intuition, the getting part of intelligence, the experiencer-seer that alone can *be-with-meaning* as it arises, naked and without the clothing of concept. Great scientists, as great artists, are produced not by the holding power of intellect, but by the power beneath intellect that gives intellect its foundation and range, the getting power of intuition. Even geniuses need something to think about. A genius who knows only half the alphabet still cannot make as many words as a fool who knows them all. Einstein commented that he thought in imaginative images and only with great effort could he translate those impressions into mathematics. Great thought is not abstract thought, not a pulling away from being through intellection, but an immersion in being, a close-noticing, a seeing (ancient thinkers, after all, were called seers). Even intuition has limits, of course, since it too is merely a power of thought, however immediate and naked of concept. Even a sixth plane saint like Aurobindo, who testified that he saw Brahman erupting into manifestation at each moment, does not experience the oneness that is continually making existence, since even the sixth plane mind experiences itself as one thing and God as another.

The origin of ego

It's interesting to consider how, at that first moment of creation, the infinite intelligence of God was duped into thinking itself separate from the creation it created. In the book *Meher Baba's Tiffin Lectures*, a manuscript from 1926-27, Meher Baba offers a revealing, five-tiered layering of the psyche. Its inmost layer he termed *ego.* After that come intellect, mind, the subtle world, and finally the gross world. That the ego layer comes first reveals one of the deepest secrets of existence. We customarily think of the ego as that proud, jealous fellow within each of us, and in Meher Baba's *The Discourses* it is that too, but it first appears as an ontological station produced by the lahar, which precipitated the first-most desire to know and be. The ego structure of being enables the soul, the Infinite Intelligence that is God, to peer, at first dimly as an electron but finally most widely as a human being, into existence through the agency of its sanskaras, or experiences, and *identify* itself with what it sees. The ego layer of the psyche appears simultaneously with the very first sanskara as the receiving station of experience. In short, ego is a pivotal structure of intelligence and produces our experience of existence by identifying with the stuff it experiences.

But what's this *identifying* business? The word derives from the Latin *idem*—meaning *same,* to experience identity with. The power to identify, then, is a primordial attribute and power of the soul. We can get an idea of what it means to *identify* with something when we think of our own bodies, which at first somehow seem to be us but after a moment's reflection are clearly better understood as a sort of vehicle of our selves. (When we score a goal in soccer, we feel proud of ourselves, not our bodies.) The soul feels its identity, mistakenly, with the stuff of the cosmos, starting with electrons and moving to stone, metal, plants, and so on. It is the odd, inevitable, utterly marvelous, and falsifying power of the soul.

When we consider the numberless bubble souls that appear in the infinite ocean of God at the first instance of creation, the question naturally comes: what do they experience? If the universe at that moment is nothing but a multitude of bubble souls, are we to suppose they stare uncomprehendingly at one another and shrug? But that's inconceivable, since how could they even notice one another if none of them yet had a body, or media, that could be experienced by neighboring souls?

That's why as these intelligent bubble souls manifested in the infinite ocean, simultaneously there manifested the something-they-could-identify-with stuff of the cosmos, which stuff at that first moment was the electron, the first-most particle of the gross world. So that: as the bubble soul manifested and identified itself as an electron, it experienced, most dimly, a bunch of surrounding electrons. And where did all these electrons come from? Were they just lying around in spacetime when bubble souls appeared? No, says Meher Baba, they appeared simultaneously with the bubble souls as the something-to-see-and-identify-with. They are—as is all the outside and inside stuff of our being, and indeed as are all the structures and ingredients of the cosmos—the stuff of existence that the creator creates. They are the gift of God, the gift that precipitates the long journey to Self-noticing. (In *Infinite Intelligence,* Meher Baba names this maker-holder-ender feature of God *Ishwar*, the creator, preserver, and destroyer (what Vedanta calls Brahma, Vishnu, and Mahesh).

The next layer of the psyche, said Meher Baba, is the intellect. Just as Meher Baba's idea of ego in the Tiffin lectures is best conceived as an ontological station and not as our personal me-centered ego, the intellect in Meher Baba's sense is best conceived not as our idea-juggling reason, but instead as an ontological structure of being. It is sense itself. It is meaning.

It is the logos. It is the infinitely fine cosmological constants of the universe.

(The last three elements of the Tiffin lecture's delineation—the mind, the subtle world, and the gross world—are more evident to understanding.)

It's worth noting that Aurobindo in *The Life Divine* and elsewhere continually made reference to *knowledge by identity* as the underlying and foundational structure of all knowing, and we recall again our discussion of the notion of sameness as the power beneath all recognition and knowledge. (That business of recognizing a coffee cup as just another coffee cup.) The great sameness, the thing everything is finally like, is the Self, and its nature is the perfect seamlessness of oneness, which is love, which is the final sameness.

Thus, we have traveled from our earliest insight, that meaning and desire are the most primordial features of our intelligence, to a wider, deeper, more complete view of the cosmos and found those two waiting patiently there for our arrival. We can now add the sense of self, and the deeper Self within that self, as their companion. So that: the essential, initiating, and basal-most structure of being is the identity-making power of ego, the self-thing we seem to be and the Self-thing we actually are. The Self has imprisoned itself in the self, and its first and last urge is to escape.

Desire, then, is not just one of the many features of our psyche, but is its essential power and charge, the driving force of interest, need, and curiosity that began when God woke from the Beyond-Beyond state by asking the universe-initiating question: *who am I?* This asking, the lahar, produced the foundational desire that precipitated existence. Desire, though utterly ignorant—after all, it first considered itself an electron—is the force which drives everything, the urge within God himself to become more and more conscious. In its purest form, all desire is longing, which is our base-most and highest desire. It is the desire not only to know fully but also to *be* fully. It is desire for oneness with the Self, which is love.

Oh Brother Seeker

Oh brother seeker,
Come a little closer to this fire of love.
Don't think of what you've left behind.
While you're with us,
The desert beasts within will cool
Their patient bellies on the sand.
Come closer!
I have seen or dreamed your face before,
those eyes, that cheek...
Such beauty quiets thought.
And then the secret's taught—
You're nothing but a mirror identical to me.
Oh God, what a beauty I must be!

The misfortunate iceberg of egotism—and belief

Somewhat more elaborate ontological explanations of creation's structure are available in the books and statements of Meher Baba. There we find mention of the heaven and hell states, which are temporary, the number of planets with human life, 18,000, and the number of human lives it takes to reach God, 8,400,000. But the elaboration there still leaves many questions unanswered. After all, the work for each of us is not to become intellectually competent in describing the architecture of the universe but to become fully conscious of God, the one producing our existence and everything else. The next few sections will begin to come to grips with how that might best be done.

This invisible, elusive, whatever-it-is entity we call the ego (meant here as that customary little-self fellow, not the ontological station) can be usefully imagined as a kind of energy-ball, floating ahead, behind, above, and around us. This energy-ball is our prison, our nature, our desire-disposition, our poking-about intelligence. The term *whatever-it-is* is commandingly appropriate because to grasp its essence is to grasp the initiating mystery of all meaning and desire. The ego energy-ball sits happily ignorant in the court of this uttermost mystery and commands, flails, lies, boasts, weeps, and longs its way through one life after another. It has a higher range of feeling-understanding and a lower range and these contraries are maddeningly merged as the stuff of our lives.

Though our imprisonment in disposition makes living and knowing unreliable, emptiness and longing lure us forward so that inch-by-inch through the day and mile-by-mile through the life a body of character begins to form. And beneath and behind character, inevitably and certainly, grows contact with the soul. All this takes time and the slow-growing clarity of patience. This is why Meher Baba and Aurobindo both emphasized equanimity as a crucial attribute of the aspirant. Equanimity (the word derives from the word equality) is the more and more notice of sameness. Sameness-notice gradually creates detachment, which is a release from smallness and the embrace of a deepening largeness. Through equanimity, the psyche becomes more and more able to measure and sort the impulses that arise in it. It grows in character, which is reserve, which is a sobriety that refuses unthinking assent. Equanimity is, in fact, the manifestation of obedience, the second part of Meher Baba's earlier-mentioned triad of love, obedience, and surrender. Equanimity has noticed something true and full-making, something large and high and bright, and goes, sometimes happily, sometimes disconsolately, about its work of creative control. Its distress is the weary pace. Its reward is the deepening contact.

The complaint of the ego mind against this vast, slow, impartial development is, of course, completely natural, since after all, the ego sees only the top half of existence, the conscious half, which is not even half but proportioned more like an iceberg. The other part of the ego-disposition, the dark part, resides beneath the surface of mind in the vastness of the unconscious where lies the patient, ever-present and ever-influencing sanskaric accumulation of many incarnations. These sanskaras are hard to get at, but their force is irresistible and undeniable. They cannot be imagined away, repressed away, complained away, or ignored. They are the deep *who* within each of us. To reduce the bondage of sanskaras, seekers must develop patience and resilience. As contact deepens, they find, said Meher Baba, that hopelessness and helplessness are their most dependable allies. Hope is, after all, a not-being-present, and helplessness is the essence of humility, surrender, reliance, and withness.

That's why belief alone, though it has its use in bridging chasms of doubt, disappointment, and discouragement, is a too-flaccid force. The prize is experience. Belief is only a cantilever of hopeful supposition over the void of ignorance, and, besides, has always been, and today especially is, a garment too thin to resist the winds of clear thinking. And science, however mesmerized by its physicalist suppositions, is an unrelenting wind that blows fanciful belief into high relief.

No doubt one of the chief difficulties in the inner approach—and the issue that seems to justify complaint—is that when we or our loved ones suffer it is commonly for completely unknown reasons—tidal waves certainly, but also rudeness, misunderstanding, indifference, delay, accident, violence, and on and on. This happens because of the peculiar nature of creation—that consciousness sits atop a far vaster unconsciousness that grips, guides, and sustains us—but that is utterly dark and contains the shades, tendencies, and debts of many previous lifetimes. Life remains disordered and unpredictable until its deep order is discovered—that somehow everything is held in the palm of Infinite Intelligence. And it is experience alone which confirms that.

Meher Baba: *everyone is an atheist until they experience God.*

The ego as mushroom

The self that blooms within us moment by moment can be usefully compared to a mushroom. Just as a mushroom is the visible and external efflorescence of a vast and hidden substructure of tendrils, so too, our surface self is the efflorescence of the dark tendrilling of our unconscious sanskaric sheath. Our surface self is conscious, and our underneath, shadow self is not, but both are always massively intelligent—composed of sanskaras and ruled by desire. What makes this comparison even more interesting is that just as a mushroom transitions from its underlying mycelium base into its topmost fruiting form, so too, from our own underlying base of unconscious, subconscious, and half-conscious impressions, our deep nature transitions into our topmost personna. The idea of *transition* is important here. As the smaller desires that held sway in our animal evolution are invaded and supplanted by larger desires, life becomes exceedingly complex.

There is a tale from the East that illustrates this dilemma. Drought had devastated the land, and the villagers were starving. Finally, they approached the revered Perfect Master who lived nearby in a forest and pleaded with him to ask God to send rain. The Master said his hands were tied since the drought was God's will. Yet there was one in the village, he said, who could help. Tell us, they pleaded. The Master replied that they must petition the young widow who lived beside the bridge at the end of the lane. The prostitute! they cried. Yes, said the Master. Her prayers alone can reach God's ear. The villagers were stunned but eventually approached the young woman in the hut by the river to plead their case. She frowned, but learning that the Master had advised them, agreed to pray to God on their behalf. The next day the rains began. Eventually the young woman found her way to the hut of the Master and begged him to explain. He sat her beside him and reminded her that one day as she was leaving the market she had encountered a small calf tied to a post. The calf was straining to reach a pile of hay, but the rope was too short. As she passed, the young woman had kicked the pile closer to the calf. This act was entirely selfless, uttered from the depths of inner kindliness, and had flashed through the spheres to the heart of the infinite One, conferring upon her an inscrutable power.

The tale illustrates how the purity of the young woman's act of compassion for the calf, done without pride or expectation, was so free from egotism that it could touch the heart of God. We will let thinkers of the future wrangle about whether such a result is possible or likely, but the tale vividly demonstrates the dilemma of impurity. As the tendrils of our lower sanskaras begin to give way to the largeness rising within us, we find that the purity we yearn for is threaded through with the remnant self of low desire. This blending of high and low is painful, tricky, and confusing, and the operation needed to piece apart the tendrils of high and low requires a master surgeon with complete knowledge and access to this dark knotting. Only one surgeon qualifies, and that's the inner master, the soul, the Self, the psychic being. In short, divine love. Everything else—aphorisms, adages, religion, philosophy, this book—litter the mind's surface as advice.

A last embellishment of this mushroom-mankind analogy is to note that just as the life impulse within the mushroom upthrusts through its mycelia into its topmost fruiting body, so too the life force within our own being upthrusts into the human form. The phrase *life force* here is used to point to the utterly unexplainable, because most primordial, powers of meaning and desire, our faithful ontological primitives. The conjecture of these pages is that God, that unknown Whoever, somehow *is* the meaning and desire stuff we and everything else are made of, and, further, that he diligently, faithfully, and patiently upthrusts into rocks, mushrooms, and mankind, which then become the lens of his deeper and deeper seeing, until finally he sees himself. In Christianity the cross symbolizes not only Christ's crucifixion, but also the burden of purpose-crossed desire this upthrusting must endure as it trends toward its final equality with everything. In Hindu temples, this upthrusting is symbolized in a short stone pillar, the phallic lingam, the root cause and energy of everything, which is God's originating desire to know himself. At the base of each of these symbols is the infinite purity of God. At its apex is the frightful madness of mind this purity must pierce through.

Teleology, so beautiful, so true

Before moving to the beyond-mindfulness way of getting to God, it's worth noting that hidden in Meher Baba's conception of the universe is the ancient doctrine of teleology, the idea that there's a plan and that things happen for a purpose. But Meher Baba's teleology is not quite your grandmother's. Close enough, though, at least in its happy-making assurance.

For Meher Baba's teleology to make sense, we need a more sensible idea of existence than those currently on offer in popular discourse. After all, the reason teleology was discarded by thinkers a few centuries ago is that the olden geographies of religion and even of most philosophy had crumbled into nonsense under the onslaught of science's clear thinking. Then, alas, that thinking succumbed to the absurdity of reductive physicalism.

As we look for a foundational geography of the inner world we sometimes turn to the voluminous writings of the Masters, saints, and mystics that have been discoursing on the subject for millennia. Today their ideas can seem incomplete, since they lack modern scientific knowledge. Still, the current speculation known as panpsychism has begun to labor toward the vision of Aurobindo and Meher Baba. Panpsychism has a variety of philosophical iterations, but in general it posits that consciousness-intelligence is inherent in all material being.

Physicalist scientists mostly react to the ideas of panpsychism with impatience. For them, consciousness-intelligence can only be understood as an epiphenomenon, a sort of accidental, even unnecessary, emergence from material evolution which, some physicalists hold, could function quite happily without generating consciousness at all. They even propose a zombie thought experiment in which everything that happens is conceivable as a physical phenomenon without inner experience attending it. For some, consciousness is not even essential to reality but is instead a sort of hanger-on. By asserting that evolution, and everything else, is simply the bumping about of matter bits, they have limited their thinking by what they can see and measure, and from that limited start they deduce everything they can about existence. Which is not much. They have oddly, maddeningly, and immovably failed to notice that noticing itself is necessary for matter bits to appear. This is the reason that, for them, noticing is the hard problem.

And it is indeed a hard problem, but not for the reason physicalists think. Intelligence is meaning is noticing, the first-in-line, unpenumbraed isness of being. Intelligence is not even merely *qualia,* the experienceable stuff, like color and smell, that some philosophers suggest confounds physicalism. It's not thoughts, it's not emotion, and nor is it merely the logical laws that govern thought, such as non-contradiction, which issues from the even more preliminary law of identity. Intelligence is preliminary to everything, the initiating mystery stuff, the vast, first-in-line isness of meaning in which all being manifests. Everything we are conscious of—matter bits, feelings, dreams—are the objects of intelligence, not the isness of it. Even supposing that intelligence is somehow God—the position of this thinking—doesn't solve the problem of comprehending it. We have noted before (and promise to never note again) that no most-subtle, most-high, most-wide intuition can pry intelligence from its sealed bed of being, since whatever we pry into the light of conscious intelligence is only another object that intelligence sees. Intelligence stands under everything and thus it cannot be understood. But so what? After we suppose that it's divinity behind things, we come to a notion of existence far more complete than physicalism. We've found the first turtle and can begin stacking.

Here's how teleology makes sense. When the oneness of God fractured into the universe, at first the innumerable souls created were only very faintly conscious. As each soul began to gather sanskaras, or impressions, it created a richer and richer lens of seeing. These impressions are an unfathomably layered texture of meaning-getting that receives the ever-flowing meaning of existence. They build and evolve the invisible subtle and mental bodies that accompany us through evolution and involution. As in: an ocelot drops its last ocelot form to reside in the afterlife in complete ocelot satisfaction. But its subtle and mental bodies, though deepened and widened by ocelot experience, still crave even more catness. And so the universe, in kindly anticipation of the ocelot's need for more complete consciousness, conducts the disembodied intelligence-bundle of the ocelot to a jaguar fetus. (Could be a leopard. How these forms evolve and anticipate the soul's needs is clearly a complex algebra of gross-subtle-mental evolution. The author, who has no idea of these details, is keeping things continental.)

That's why evolution, while infinitely complex, is not random, but entirely purposive and in utterly dependable service to the evolving soul. In pre-human evolution, the soul receives its next form according to what its subtle and mental bodies require for their developing consciousness. The sanskaras that propel this pre-human development Meher Baba calls *natural sanskaras*. These sanskaras produce ever more advanced gross forms to accommodate the developing inner bodies which accompany the drop soul as it evolves. In mankind, consciousness is fully developed, but still constricted by a sanskaric lens. The sanskaras that precipitate our next human form he calls *non-natural sanskaras*. The human soul takes life after life, getting and spending non-natural impressions, until the mesmerizing emptiness of existence stirs it to longing, and it goes in search of its depths. This releasing and taking of forms is called reincarnation. Pre-human evolution is a moving-forward into more complete forms. In human life, consciousness is fully developed, and reincarnation becomes a shaking and sorting of experience.

All this naturally compelled form-taking-and-leaving is why the purposiveness of existence does not accommodate—with apologies to all grandmothers—the intervention of a whimsical or judging divinity. Seen from the outside, this conception of creation may seem a grand austerity, but within it hides a beauty far more rich, complete, and sensible than any yet conceived by exoteric religion. Coming to grips with Truth strips away sentiment but reveals within a soul core that responds to growing insight with love and surrender—and develops an experience of God far brighter than sentiment can imagine. Plague, war, heartbreak, and splinters. Then infinite love. What a bargain.

Still, our frequent bitterness toward the God imagined by our front self is inevitable. The Self has fragmented into many selves, and for these separate selves the impartiality of creation can seem cruel. But divine impartiality results from the truth of oneness, and within it is an infinite justice only deepening equanimity can sense. Creation is a ladder, austere at first but more and more perfect-seeming as surrender grows.

No doubt most religions have in their massive bodies at least some suggestion of the complaint-proof inexorableness of God. Paul wrote to the Galatians that God is not mocked, by which he did not mean, as preachers sometimes proclaim, that we shouldn't make fun of God, but that, as Paul said in the following phrase, that *whatsoever a man soweth, that shall he also reap.* In other words, what we do, think, and say creates us. The mantra associated with the first Avatar in our recorded history, Zoroaster, was *good words, good thoughts, good deeds.*

But because of the madness of egotism, we develop the illusion of responsibility, and this responsibility, however illusory, is required for natural living. Bhau Kalchuri, one of Meher Baba's mandali, put it this way in a ghazal: "Since I did not come from this universe, but this universe came from me, there can be no excuse in loving." Yet in these pages we have discovered we are utterly bound in desire we did not create! Still, as it is said in the East, when we find ourselves in God's court, though we well know that God alone is responsible for everything, it behooves us, and most naturally behooves us, to fall on our knees and ask forgiveness. When the oneness of love begins to manifest within, it is entirely natural for questioning to stop as the knees weaken.

The right view

The discussions in the last sections give us a more reasonable, and far more complete, explanation of the cosmos than exoteric religion or physicalism have offered. They are a sensible map, and though maps are not the place itself, they have their use. This is why *right view* in the Buddhi's eightfold path comes first, and, some would say, is the required beginning, and, some would say, the most important element. After all, that's simply how meaning works—we get an idea and use it to guide and interpret experience.

It also means that even if you consider the so-far supposing of these pages good, fulsome, and worthy, *nothing in them is the Truth.* Small *t* truth is accurate mapping, but the Truth is what maps are maps of. The Truth pointed to in these pages is Infinite Intelligence, and the fullest secrets of its being are hidden from thinking until thinking becomes the Being it is considering.

When longing becomes stronger than any previous allegiance or view, the work begins. Maps can be assuring, but are only pointers. Longing lights a fire more precious than any doctrine or viewpoint, and the sole occupation of the soul then is to *protect that fire*. And grow it. Into it are thrown the detritus of all omission and commission, all right and wrong, doctrines, rituals, rites, all the sacred and all the profane. It is a stripping bare and a making naked so that the fire of the inner being, which is the soul, which is the infinite intelligence of love, can emerge and consume us.

Still, the right view has its use, a use which is the scrubbing away of wrong views so that more and more accurate thinking can appear. And thinking, since it is only and always reflection, is only and always supposing. So far in these pages, to account for the marvel of life, we suppose that metabolism must be more than a random bumping about inside cells and instead hides a guidance-force. We suppose that empathy is mind experiencing mind. We suppose that hidden in the marvel of selfness is Selfness. These supposings point to a further supposing that the tripartite systems of Meher Baba and Aurobindo Ghose offer useful explanatory context. The infinite buzzing complexity of the physical world sits atop the infinite buzzing complexity of the subtle world which sits atop the infinite buzzing complexity of the mental world, and all these worlds are continually manifested by Infinite Intelligence. We suppose that each of these bodies develops by accumulating experience life after life and that experience creates our sanskaric sheath, the lenses of our seeing.

This view of the universe describes a long and complicated journey but has this consolation—we are all in eternity. We all get home.

The coming field of inquiry

It's easy to understand that for some this conception of the universe must seem more of the typical pretensions of desperate thinking in need of impossible, even cowardly, consolation. Yet we have come to this conjecture by employing the authority of great souls only as confirmation. We have arrived here mostly by close-noticing, by exposing the cul-de-sac of physicalism, the presumptions of Darwinism, and by recognizing the textures of being that produce humility, sameness, and love. The lively coincidence of these lines of thought led us to the conjecture of Infinite Intelligence beneath and above existence. Now we're just working out the details.

As we probe the fabric and substance of this conception, a world of new exploration opens, and we will have to fit into its structure the current investigations around near-death experience, remote viewing, mediumship, reincarnation, parapsychology, and so on. Science, in its office of honest and careful thinking, will contribute by obtaining ever more data as it is constricted by ever less skepticism. This will take time, since many careers are allied to physicalism-Darwinism. As the grip of these scientific idea-systems loosens, a second siege will begin as science meets the resistance of established theologies and philosophies, where many careers are also bound.

Yet within the supposition of Infinite Intelligence as the maker and sustainer of being is a field of explanation in no way antagonistic to science, religion, or philosophy. In religion, it discards the husk but revitalizes the kernel. In philosophy, it acknowledges morality and atheism as inevitable but preliminary, does not abandon conscience or character, and opens vast new fields of speculation. In science, it seems entirely possible that a notion of the universe as Infinite Intelligence will shed light on the anomalous double slit experiment, clarify quantum entanglement, verify and develop quantum biology, and even confirm faster-than-light communication of information, since, after all, the Being-of-all-being would hardly require ninety-three billion years to glance from one end of the universe to the other.

All three fields will have to leave their citadels and wander together in the meadows of wonder. When they do, they will find their subject is identical and so too can be their investigations. After all, if Infinite Intelligence is behind everything, then we are all, priests, scientists, and thinkers, walking together in the belly of God. And being slowly digested.

It seems likely that in days to come this supposition will be concretized by research so that science and religion will be united. Science may remain more experimental and religion more inspirational but both will have sighted the same elephant. Even psychology, the halfway station between them, will discover that self-acceptance is really Self-acceptance, the gradual sensing, in the within, of the Being of all beings. Small *s* self-acceptance, the overcoming and integration of inner blocks and repressions, can produce workmanlike mental health and even good-humored living, but it is always incomplete and lacks the inspiration and energy of inner contact with Truth. Only when it becomes Self-acceptance, does real health, and real work, begin. Psychology will eventually learn to capitalize the *s* of Self but only when it understands that this capitalization is not the trespass of religion but instead an expansion of its science.

As science refines its suppositions—and instrumentation—it will more and more credit this view and open new fields of exploration. New findings will lead to a reorientation of domestic and international systems of political cooperation and develop new, truer, and fuller justice, economic, and environmental systems. Though the thinkers of the future will make many changes in the world of cultural institutions, the work for seekers will remain an art, a felt-for passage in the interiority of the psyche.

At whatever state of incompletion our institutions and societies might remain, the destiny of each of us is that one by one and gradually, a tenderness comes, a gratitude, a patience, and finally an opening.

The scent of Something

If you ask a guy on the street what life is, his customary reply is some form of religious thought, or scientific thought, or irritable who-cares shrug. If his reply is religious, it's because he's thought as much as he is able or wants to. If it's scientific, it's because he's happy to let those guys do the thinking. If it's who-cares, he mainly wants to get going and keep going without upsetting himself.

But if you ask the guy in the alley what's going on—that's us—he'll say, *no idea, really. You?* Back in the alley, we've elbowed out a bit of light, considered the astonishing fact of meaning-getting-and-holding as well as the force of desire that courses continually through us, considered desire's sizes, considered the junction of unconsciousness and consciousness in that trusty implacable companion, our ego-disposition, and have finally considered the ego's dissolution when love, obedience, and surrender to the inner master begin to rise within us.

We have come to grips with humility, which understands that there is a great Something continually flowing through us. We understand that love feels this Something, that honesty is the resolute seeing that begins to discern this Something, that patience is the slowing of smallness and the awakening of largeness as this Something begins to manifest within us.

This is an ancient proposition and message, and part of the esoterica of every faith, however obscured by time and doctrine. It is also always new, since it comes when its newness is required to scrub away the detritus of incomplete thinking. And the present age, so full of intellection, contention, and violence, needs scrubbing.

Every religion has a unique—and generally confused—answer to how to best live, but what all religions have in common is that the goal of life is to free ourselves in the love of God. In their founders, the Avatars, we find complete purity, and those who find their way to that presence have found religion's core. But alas, the theological offices of religion are absent that purity, and so religion devolves into repression and scolding. This is an absurd result, but also natural. If we cannot abide in love, at least we can hate its opposite. Thus the good in us hates the bad—in ourselves and in others—and in hating we fortify what we meant to destroy.

It's pointless to abuse religion for hypocrisy though. Without inner contact, religion can only be morality, an external, best-we-can-do suppression of the ravenous beast. Besides, morality is at least a form of conscience, and conscience is the faithful companion of the inner search. It is, in fact, the earliest whisper of inner contact. At its beginning, though, it is barren, loud, and wrong. It pursues or leads us down the corridors of mind until at last the ache of need becomes so strong that we turn to abuse our abuser, sometimes even to flaunt our freedom from the dullness of morality by the expression of proud licentiousness. This turning and refusal is common in the arts, since artists have caught the scent of depth, and the inauthenticity of morality embarrasses their intelligence. It is common in thinkers and scientists as well, but for a different reason. They have caught the scent of wideness. Depth, which is of the soul and heart, and wideness, which is of the soul and intellect, are both foreign to external morality, which has little of either. Depth and wideness are not, however, foreign to conscience, which is the gradual seeping forth of the inner voice. But for that, contact with the Self is required, and for contact, longing.

Even as longing begins, of course, there are plenty of stages and stations. Candles, incense, mantras, this and that. Even declarations like Jesus told me to, Baba wants me to, Krishna asked me to. This and that. But as longing sharpens and clarifies, everything else falls away. Longing becomes the marrow of all meaning. And it is utterly silent. Meher Baba said, *Things that are real are given and received in silence.* He said, *Learn to long for the love of God.* He said, *When mind soars in pursuit of the things conceived in space, it pursues emptiness; but when man dives deep within himself, he experiences the fullness of existence.*

How, then, in the aridity and contention of the modern age, can longing begin and endure? How can the rudiments of egotism be most quickly shed? Meditation and mindfulness, as mentioned, have their place but are not themselves forms of longing. They are a preparation, a place-holding, a clearing. When longing begins, when the psychic being begins to open, mindfulness is more and more natural and less and less formal. It is walking-around remembrance. It is welcome and surrender. The remainder is housekeeping.

Good housekeeping

Housekeeping (meaning effort, one of Aurobindo's aids) is required because, as we come under the sway of the inner master, or even before, as our longing flails for grip, our egotism seems to develop a mind of its own. Egotism has been our faithful companion, has attended our every step as human beings, has prepared, nuanced, and deepened our intelligence until at last, dissatisfied and desperate, we turn inward. And find egotism unwilling. And find egotism doggedly addicted to desire. This is natural and inescapable, but the deepening is relentless and has this consolation—the discovery of the within is wonderfully interesting.

In the early stages there is often aridity, a seemingly impenetrable emptiness. Then, sometimes swiftly, but usually slowly, inner experience begins. This may not be experience of the mystical effulgence surrounding us (though sometimes it might be), but it will be an increasing awareness of our understructure. We begin to notice our selves, our ways, and our moods, and in that notice we gradually sense something amazing—the being and seeing that we are *is not from us but through us*. And step by step surrender begins.

Religion sometimes asks us to believe, sometimes to have faith, and there is an interesting difference between those two. Belief is a thought-companion, a kind of mental placard that makes waiting for the opening of the inner world endurable. The penalty of mere belief is that when it is not accurate (not the right view), it obstructs through misguidance. Faith is different. Belief is thought. Faith is force. Faith is a building conviction that makes waiting endurable—and even delightful.

Humankind has developed many techniques for remembrance—prayer, meditation on the various personal and impersonal forms of God, art, chanting, service to others, and so on. In all these, whether explicit or implicit, is the eternal magnetism of love of the Self for the selves into which it has fractured. Love, as shown earlier, is the sameness of being, the sine qua non of all knowing and desiring. Love is the force that creates the attraction of self for Self.

And it is the fastest way to God.

Sanskaras and the fast way

To understand the fastest way to make contact with the Self, it's useful to consider again the nature of sanskaras, the meaning-desire impressions that surge continually forth from the dark of each person's unconscious. Sanskaras are the invisible but potent body of the self, and it is that self and the sanskaras that comprise it that inhibit the Self from manifesting. Renunciation of the sanskaras of smaller desire, a part of mindfulness, is a form of mental control and has its place, particularly in the initial stages of the search when our experience of the Self is often faint and fragile. Yet desires are irrepressible and notoriously seep through self-discipline like water through a leaky dam. Which is why history is rife with the improprieties of gurus and priests.

As mentioned, the no-no of external renunciation eventually leads to the positivity of creative control, the adjustment of behavior in the light of perceived values. Someone speaks sharply to us, and, while feeling in ourselves a sharp reply forming, we feel too the greater value of calm and so do not respond. This is an inner process slightly but significantly different from the more perfunctory assertion of no-no, because in this process we have felt a higher feeling beneath lower feeling and opt for the higher. Thus the higher displaces the lower, and because this is consciously experienced, its practice is not only charming but occurs with an inner sense of releasement and freedom as the energy of lower desire is dislodged and dissipated. In that brief description is summed all the process and consequence of spiritual work. Spiritual work is not repression, and not merely restraint. It is the work of the higher identifying, then resisting, then swallowing the lower.

From Aurobindo, *The Life Divine*, pages 554-555:

> *If the psychic and mental parts in us are strong, the vital comes under mastery and direction to an extent hardly possible to the surface mentality; even the body and the physical energies can be taken up by the inner mind and will and turned into a more plastic instrumentation of the soul, the psychic being.*

He continues with a caution:

> *On the other hand, if the mental and psychic parts are weak and the vital strong and unruly, power is increased by entry into the inner vital, but discrimination and detached vision are deficient; the knowledge, even if increased in force and range, remains turbid and misleading; intelligent self-control may give place to a vast undisciplined impetus or a rigidly disciplined but misguided egoistic action.*

Walking the spiritual path, as they say, is like walking the edge of a sword. The solution is always the same—our deepening need. Meher Baba: *Deny your false self and your Real-Self asserts itself. Ask for nothing and you get everything. Renounce everything to such an extent that you eventually renounce even renunciation.*

Smaller desires may return with fresh determination to get in the game, but the ego eventually develops an easy habit of refusal. Control might well be dutiful refusal in the beginning, but as we more and more make contact with our higher nature, it will become gracious, tinged with the relentment psychology calls self-acceptance, and even produce irony and self-mocking good humor. Eventually, the no-no of self-discipline becomes the yes-yes of love, not merely for others but for our own benighted desire-self that has evolved, bewildered, and driven us for so long on the treadmill of reincarnation.

Inner clarity comes. A new confidence grows, a confidence founded on the natural letting-be of humility that enables intelligence to receive the sense inherent in the world. The opposite of true confidence is the egotism which produces the angst of separation.

The highest confidence results from becoming more and more aware, first of the inner world, and then of the inner master, the sustaining Self who sees creation through you and with whom you are destined to become one.

A by-note: we sometimes think of self-confidence as a fortune of childhood bequeathed by loving and supportive parents, and no doubt a wholesome childhood is helpful in developing the easy back and forth of feeling and thought across the consciousness-unconsciousness divide. A difficult beginning can produce the blocking nexuses of fear and unworthiness—and their compensations of hostility, pride, and contempt. But a healthy childhood is not equivalent to spiritual longing. Many advanced souls take birth in difficult surroundings, and many fortunate children have little longing for truth. It's easily imaginable that a difficult childhood might whet the inner appetite for love, and that a beatific childhood might permit or at least not prevent an uninspired conformity to prevailing values. What is essential for admission to the inner world is not the beginning circumstance of life, but the circumstance of the soul and its desire for freedom.

For all life challenges the remedy is the same. It is longing. Longing produces the courage to see the self and the endurance to see the Self beneath it. Longing produces honesty, honesty produces struggle, struggle produces God.

God's duty to the seeker, who is his unconscious Self, is to offer the scent of divinity and become our deepest conscience. As this purity and inner light grow, creative control becomes more clear, simple, and automatic. The inner life is no longer a matter of faith but of experience. The danger of accepting a badge of pride for spiritual accomplishment diminishes, since we see that all within us flows from this Being—and nothing whatever from ourselves. The impressions received from the inner master have the power of utterly dislodging the lower elements of our being by the potency of divinized sanskaras. The response to this state is gratitude, love, and self-forgetfulness. The self is forgotten when the Self is remembered. The receiving of these impressions is called grace. The portal through which they pass is longing. This is not religious life, somehow separate from normal life. It is our deepest normality. It is truth imparted by Truth.

The Perfect Master Ramakrishna remarked that there were two types of seekers, the baby cat and the baby monkey. The baby monkey explores the world by reaching, groping, noticing, but must cling to its mother of his own will. The baby cat, on the other hand, is held safe and close in its mother's arms and merely mews when in need. It makes sense to consider that each seeker has a baby monkey and baby cat within, the baby monkey (the intellect) probing and questioning, the baby cat (the heart) contented with surrender. Whichever type of baby prevails in a seeker, the central charm of Ramakrishna's symbology is that both types are infants—and in need.

The Highest Road

By now, many of the readers of these pages will have investigated Meher Baba and Aurobindo, and some no doubt will have read with apprehension and even distaste Meher Baba's assertion of divinity. While that acceptance or rejection must remain a private matter, it's worth noting what Meher Baba himself said on the subject of getting to God.

From *Listen, Humanity:*

> *Of all the high roads which take the pilgrim directly to his divine destination, the quickest lies through the God-Man (Christ, Messiah, Avatar). In the God-Man, God reveals Himself in all His glory, with His infinite power, unfathomable knowledge, inexpressible bliss, and eternal existence. The path through the God-Man is available to all those who approach Him in complete surrenderance and unwavering faith.*
>
> *When this is not possible, the other high roads which can eventually win the grace of God are:*
>
> 1. *Loving obedience to and remembrance of the God-Man to the best of one's ability;*
> 2. *Love for God and intense longing to see Him and be united with Him;*
> 3. *Being in constant company with the saints and lovers of God and rendering them whole-hearted service;*
> 4. *Avoiding lust, greed, anger, hatred, and the temptations of power, fame, and faultfinding;*
> 5. *Leaving everyone and everything in complete external renunciation and, in solitude, devoting oneself to fasting, prayer and meditation;*

6. *Carrying on all worldly duties with a pure heart and clean mind and with equal acceptance of success or failure, while remaining detached in the midst of intense activity; and*
7. *Selfless service of humanity, without thought of gain or reward.*

Nothing in the above is contrary to religion or normal conscience, and, if atheists could substitute *universe* for *God*, they too would likely be satisfied.

About grace

We'll consider shortly why the God-Man is the highest road, but first a note about grace, introduced in the above passage. The religious idea of grace as divinity-blessing-the-worthy by a sort of Michelangelo finger-of-God belittles the intelligence and the discoveries in these pages. If love is the very nature of God (the oneness-sameness beneath all existence) and not a kindly, added-on feature of his being, then grace, which is our appreciation and experience of that nature, can be understood in two ways.

One way is by understanding God's selflessness, selflessness here not meaning really-vast-goodness, but instead the absolute absence of self. Selves are wantingnesses, desire-dispositions, and the being that is making everything can only be conceived as wanting nothing since it is and has everything. This selflessness is, of course, incomprehensible, but logically at least must be so utter that it cannot be comprehended as a form of kindness. Kindness has an opposite, cruelty, and the One who is and has all is opposite to nothing, not even the universe, since he is that too. Even the religious conception of God as compassion distorts his selflessness. After all, what sort of compassion sends tidal waves? This is the impersonal aspect of God, austere, implacable, and inevitable, bound by the law he is continually manifesting. In *Infinite Intelligence*, Meher Baba refers to this aspect of God as Ishwar, the creator, sustainer, and dissolver of being. Ishwar—oddly and perhaps startlingly—is unconscious of himself, utterly unaware, impartial, automatic, implacable, disinterested, and inevitable, and is just what is meant by karma. It's the what-we-need. In the case of non-yet-human souls, it's the what-we-need to develop consciousness. In the case of human beings, it's the what-we-need to develop longing. This is the grand teleology of the cosmos, its very purpose, and is the reason Infinite Intelligence troubles itself with creation. No doubt the sanskaric sheath we call karma is a gift of divine love—everything is—but not the love of even the kindest terrestrial mother, but instead the love of the great mother-father of existence, Infinite Intelligence, whose goal is not to bestow niceness on this tribe or that person, but to reveal in himself, who is secretly us, the great niceness of infinite love, the hidden oneness-stuff of his own being. Grace here must be conceived as the perfect and reliable attention of God as Ishwar to the details of creation. This conception of grace may be seen as the perfect duty of God as the continual maker of the trustworthy universe.

The second conception of grace is more in keeping with our customary idea of compassion, but is importantly different from a sentimentalized notion of kindness. This grace is the experienceable grace that results from contact with the inner Self, the personally felt God that waits in concealed but ever-ready vigilance for longing to develop. This grace is a most-subtle, most-delicate inner arising and is a response to the within-readiness of need, to the call of anguished nakedness. It is free in the sense that the entire universe is the free and continual gift of God, but in that freedom God has bound himself to the developing need of the many souls he has become. God's bondage to the seeker's need means that sincere longing is never denied the presence—the grace—it craves.

The two ideas of grace given above can be thought of as the impersonal and the personal, and both could use a further bit of parsing. The impersonal is easiest to grasp—in a sense, it's the universe, the continual isness in which everyone and everything is embedded and sustained, and also it's the whatever-it-is being beneath the universe, the utterly generous manifester of existence. It's the here-you-are offer of being, and likely, even for God, it's plenty of work. When someone does you a favor—God's favor is the cosmos itself—gratitude is the right response, but no gratitude could ever settle our debt to God. After all, the favor of creation is infinite, and the completist gratitude is trifling in comparison. Besides, we might ask, who asked for the favor of existence? (We did, since we are secretly him.)

Still, the gift of the universe, the immense perfection of its working, the fathomless beauty, the faithful reliability—all these, when appreciated, provoke a response of gratitude.

But only after inner deepening stills complaint, and complaint stills with the slow development of the right view of creation. It stills as we gradually begin to sense that all is well. When a saint was asked what the will of God was, she said: *It is the past.* Everything, all the trouble and all the joy, is held in the cupped palm of the Self. As we begin the process of involution, that statement is mostly a guess, but it's a good, sensible, and honest guess, and it leads to more and more inner confirmation. It leads to the second form of grace, the inner master, the Self.

In the following poem, spiders and barking dogs stand for the distractions inevitable in embodiment.

As I Sit This Morning to Think of God

As I sit this morning to think of God,
A spider crawls into my hat,
And somewhere a dog is barking.
No matter—soon Love begins to circle, looking for need.
Sighs pour out like sweetness from a sewer.
I know if I approach, Love's cold and quick away
(I've relearned that a thousand times),
So I set my hunger free and watch it roam.
I've heard that somewhere in this mist there is a doorway.
That makes such perfect sense that doubt is out of place here.
Still hunger hasn't found it yet.
I don't mind.
I'm like a man who's lost his wallet,
Then recalls he left it home,

Then lets it be.
That it's somewhere by has eased the long neck of worry.
In time, I will be home again.
For now I'll keep our bargain of silence,
Though if that doorway doesn't appear in a thousand years,
I might speak up.
I suppose I'm bluffing.
When complaint meets the soul it forgets even its shame,
And in this radiant universe,
I'm happy to be anywhere,
Or anyone.
The morning goes as usual—
Hunger returns unsatisfied,
Love kindly withdraws.
He knows I have business with that spider,
And that mutt is starting to drive me crazy.

The second form of grace is an experience. It is not merely the acceptance of the gift of creation but is also the felt assurance of the growing presence of love within. Its elusive delicacy makes this presence vulnerable to scoffers, especially to the hard-to-please inner scoffer created by doubt, delay, and disappointment. Further, as the above poem suggests, inner contact takes place in the anyhow of barking dogs and spiders, plus rent, measles, injustice, and hurricanes. Though continually elusive and embattled, longing and its development of the growing inner presence of love is not a form of imagination. It is a form of experience and, however cloaked in the garb of any culture's doctrine, it has been recorded many times in the history of thought.

The Avatar and links

Now comes a bit of thinking about how a particular structure of the universe, its linkyness, makes encountering the Avatar useful for the seeker.

As mentioned, the Avatar manifests from time to time to straighten things out, to give the universe a spiritual push. To understand why the universe requires a push and how such a push can be given is to understand the mechanism of being, and that understanding is beyond this thinking, and likely to remain beyond human thinking, since it is a consideration of the infinity of existence. But this at least we are told and what seems evident from history: when the Avatar manifests into the knock-about world, that manifestation somehow forms a valley of impressions down which the waters of aspiration begin to flow. At the bottom, this impressional flowing pools to form the various seas of the world's religions. These seas drown the purity of the Avatar, but those who dive deep can reach that purity regardless of the seas' depth. In the current age, with its vast intellection and world electronification, the voice of the Avatar is hard to hear, and if heard, hard to distinguish from the noise. But its power and influence, said Meher Baba, will be more universal, and the sea of aspiration left behind will be clearer than ever before. And begin a new age of spirituality for the earth. The signs of the coming new age have been sensed already by many seekers.

Recall that all meaning and explanation is held forth in intelligence by the trillion unconscious hands of its beneath meanings (in the giraffe's case, long-neck and Africa). These beneath meanings are the meant thing's links, so that it makes sense to consider all ideas as compounds of their supporting ideas. It also makes sense that the intellect, the holding bit of our mind, often becomes so big-bellied with its held ideas that it can no longer see the ground beneath its feet—or wants to. The invisible penumbra of thought that produces thought's intelligent reach is notoriously vague because hidden beneath every generalization—and all ideas are forms of generalization—is the idea-penumbra of other ideas, and beneath those ideas still yet more idea-penumbra, and on and on so that into the vast unconscious penumbraness of every idea creeps vagueness, mistaking, and the corruption of desire.

No doubt ideas are essential for getting about in the world since they distribute our desire-attention over space and time, but they can be abstracted far from the immediacy of close-noticed intuition. They can become a maze, and it's hard to know if the maze-map they become has much to do with reality. Most ideas and even ideals, because they are compounds of compounds, are corrupted by desire and impotently vague.

This is why when people argue it is not only usually but always about ideas neither of them fully understands. We come to grips with the world through a lens of mind, a lens which is a devilishly complicated layering. This mind-lens charms and beguiles so that we are often left in stricken inner bewilderment. Even when we mount an effort of knowing by reading, thinking, and consulting experts, we end perplexed. Experts always disagree.

All intelligence is a compound of linked meaning-getting-and-holding and desire, a vast web of being that not only manifested 13.8 billion years ago but is continually being manifested by Infinite Intelligence now and now and now. What we know is never known in isolation, but always held forth from the unconscious with the trillion hidden hands of its linked thoughts, so that all knowing is an upthrusting-into-intelligence of undercurrent meanings, the way islands are upthrustings into the ocean's surface and linked below at the common ground of the seafloor.

Consider the word *understanding*. Understanding means to stand under and look up and through to see an idea's origin, then see the origin of that origin, then come at last to the originating isness of the impression that produced the idea, and, further, to see that even that impression is a compound of other impressions and ideas until it seems there is no final where-to-stand in the dancing, dodging fabric of meaning that is mind.

The web of hidden thought beneath every conscious thought provides the invisible trail of meaning that leads us through existence. Words are the symbol-handles of this meaning and allow us to fix meaning in ourselves and to trade meaning (often confusedly) between minds. But unless we penetrate to the meaning beneath words, held only in the immediacy of intuition, the first-in-line getter and experiencer of meaning, our word bondage helplessly circles us back to the stale thinking of the familiar, the already-known.

As mentioned, desire and meaning are intimate twin sisters, but only the elder sister, desire, holds the compass of need, and can thus goad her younger sister into paths of new meaning. Those who are able to think higher and wider thoughts are those whose desires have become higher and wider and who have thus penetrated into the beneath of words and conception. They have abandoned the intoxicating vineyard of thought and have descended into its rich soil where twine the invisible roots of intuition. We step outside the box of our conditioning when, through longing, we begin to understand the prison of words, the mereness of thought, and our isolation from depth.

The soul is led kicking and complaining through the debris of many experiences (and lifetimes), until finally, and with at first maddening slowness, it begins to sense that some force has upheld it in its long journey and upholds it still, that every breath drawn is an upholding, that every thought arriving is an offering, that every emotion felt is a guide.

Rumi, from a Coleman Barks rendering: *For sixty years, I have been forgetful every moment, but not for a second has this flowing toward me stopped or slowed.*

Longing brings a natural not-this, not-this reaction to the objects of experience. Still, in an age of vast intellection such as our own, the cantilevers of belief in some invisible God-presence seem only to extend mere hope over a void far more certain, both to ourselves and to the talk-talkers. After all, the void is what we know from experience.

That's why religious platitudes were inevitable and also partial. Saints could describe the inner world, but the vocabulary of humanity was too undeveloped (witches and devils and an angry God) to contain their insights in doctrine, and when a Master became too informative, like Hallaj or Jesus and many others, they were killed. (It is, of course, possible that many saints refrain from clarity to avoid upsetting the however-limping-at-least-useful prevailing doctrine.)

In our age of high intellection and the careful work of science, it makes sense that Meher Baba, if he is the Avatar, would have brought forth a detailed map of the universe. His writing is that map, rich with detailed intelligence about the inner world, the cosmos, and the Path that leads to God. This is part of the reason that Meher Baba said that surrender to the Avatar is the highest road to God.

But the more important reason has to do with the structure of existence itself. It has to do with its linkyness.

Linkyness is the net of meaning in which we are embedded and is why the high road is through the Avatar. The Avatar is the beginning link and the last link, the universe-generating algorithm that is continually producing the infinite fractal pattern of the cosmos, the great sameness that everything else is like. That's why thinking of the Avatar creates links, and a path, and eventually the Path.

All Avatars are the same being, no doubt, but the merit of recognizing the most recent Avatar is that that Avatar is most closely linked to the developed thinking of the age. Thus, his message and being are most easily assimilated. Eruch Jessawala related that Meher Baba once compared himself to Quaker Oats:

> *What mother is there who would insist on buying the old stock when she could purchase a tin of the fresh new stock? I am the fresh stock. It is all Quaker Oats, and the ingredients are the same. But I am the fresh stock.* (From Jessawala's book, *The Ancient One.)*

Of course, the soul is not seeking mental conviction in this or that Avatar, nor does it want mere possession of even the most accurately mapped view of existence that an Avatar might provide. The soul wants fullest consciousness of the Self—which is itself. The question each soul must ask is whether recognition of the most current Avatar can accelerate that consciousness.

Those who doubt that Meher Baba is that Avatar might usefully consider the Sufi tale of Majnun, who was found by his friend scrawling through the dust of the roadside.

"Good lord, Majnun! What are you doing!"

Majnun said, "I am looking for Laila (his beloved)."

His friend said, "But why look in the dust of the road?"

"I am looking everywhere," replied Majnun, "in hope of finding her somewhere."

Seekers are compelled to look everywhere, and a good, long, and full look into Meher Baba can be rewarding. His life and work are completely available on the internet. (At this writing, see avatarmeherbabatrust.org and lordmeher.org.) Every seeker must make the experiment personally, must determine whether accepting the current Avatar—reading his books, studying his life, visiting his tomb—has the value of linking his or her soul more closely with its source.

No doubt many are the souls that make progress without any knowledge of the Avatar whatsoever. Meher Baba traveled incessantly about India and the near east to contact advanced souls lost on the inner planes—these are the God-intoxicated, called masts (pronounced *musts*)—and many of those contacted did not recognize him as the Avatar. He sat a short or long time with each of them, and, as he described it, reestablished order in their inner being so they could continue to progress. For the sake of his work with them, he instructed his mandali not to reveal his identity. When these souls were discovered (by inquiring from village to village), Meher Baba and his mandali traveled, sometimes for hours through the night on bullock carts (the jounciest ride on earth), to contact them.

Still, many of these masts did recognize him, and this recognition made his work with them more difficult, sometimes impossible. In the book *The Ancient One,* Eruch relates the story of his bringing a mast known as Bhorwala Baba to Mahabaleshwar to meet Meher Baba. Since Meher Baba had instructed Eruch not to reveal his name, Eruch told the mast he was bringing him to see his elder brother. But Bhorwala Baba revealed that he knew Eruch was bringing him to his Master. He added, "Meher Baba has in him the whole universe. He is the master of everyone, and He is within every disciple. He is in this world, and that which is above it and below it. He is in me and in everyone." When they reached Mahabaleshwar, Baba instructed his mandali to serve the mast supper and then sent him back to his village without contacting him.

These journeys are reported most fully in the book *The Wayfarers,* by one of Meher Baba's mandali, an Englishman, Dr. William Donkin.

No doubt, it is easily conceivable that someone awakening to the inner world may remain happily ignorant of even the freshest and most recent Avatar. It is also easily conceivable that someone who is aware of and attracted to the most recent

Avatar may color their thinking with knowledge of him, yet still not have found the longing required for inner contact. Whatever the case, it makes sense that contact with the external form of the Avatar may, at least for some, remove impediments of bad thinking and lead more quickly to inner contact.

As the search begins, no one needs to be—and few are equipped to be—heroic adventurers in the darkness of the inner being. A saying from the East (quoted by Frances Brabazon, one of Meher Baba's mandali, in his epic poem *Stay With God*) is: *Though you be a lion, come in under the shade of this Palm-tree.* That shade, the palm of the inner master, whether conceived as embodied in the Avatar or disembodied as the light within, is felt as love and is the great dissolver-of-bonds. Love creates an easy back-and-forthing across the conscious-unconscious divide. It offers the just-what-you-need, the daily dose of insight and assurance that maintains balance, confidence, creativity, and cheer. Holding the master's hand is an entirely natural way to stroll the meadow of wonder.

However one is able to proceed, whether through the guidance and enlivenment of accepting the current Avatar, or past Avatars, or through other paths—living a wholesome life, rejecting the small in favor of the large, keeping company with advanced souls—all paths converge and the goal is the same for all, reuniting with the Being of all being. The test of your progress is not scored by counting the hours you have learned to meditate each day or the number of books you have read, but by noting your treatment of the next waiter who serves you.

The Avatar's material descent and consequent physical being gives us a glimpse, however external and out-there, of what is called the personal god—and that creates links. Thinking about God as that person creates links. Reading his books creates links. Saying his name or any name of God creates links. Talking to people that knew him, or to people that knew the people that knew him, or visiting the places he traveled to or that represent him—all these activities create links. This is because, in essence, the universe is nothing but links, a texture of impressions contained in Infinite Intelligence, in the God-mind that is making the universe and us, and that God-mind is the Avatar. This is the meaning of Jesus's pronouncement, *No one comes to the father but by me.* The Avatars of past ages—Jesus, Mohammed, Krishna and others—are identical to the last, Meher Baba, the difference being that the links leading to the past Avatars have all too often been clouded and distorted with doctrine, rites, and ritual. But all are the same being.

A continual refrain in Meher Baba's life was that those who came, as he said, into the orbit of his love, should hold onto his *daaman*, the hem of his garment. Holding onto the daaman of the Master begins with the right view and continues with a growing faith that the elusive inner master will take clearer and clearer shape within. Since everything is linked in the meaning-mind of God, the universal mind that is creating everything, it's best that the right view you accept has its foundation in the being of a Perfect Master, one who has finished the journey, so that linkage to that being is linkage to the source.

Fifth and sixth plane saints, those who can see the infinite effulgence of God's being, have their place but only as reflectors and directors. Those on lower planes, or philosophers who intellectualize about consciousness and the inner world (like the author of these pages), can bring you as far as their station, but their linkage goes no higher, and what linkage they possess can be obfuscated by desire and doctrine. A Perfect Master, whether embodied or disembodied, offers the deepest contact. Perfect Masters are continually present in creation as Infinite Intelligence, are one with all Perfect Masters, and can be felt inwardly as love. The eternal Perfect Master is the Avatar, that being who comes and goes and leaves a wake-trail of scent.

Meher Baba said he was that Avatar, the highest of the high. If he's false, it's foolish to consider him.

If he isn't, it's foolish not to.

Acceptance of the most recent Avatar, of course, is understandably rare. The invisible world is dark to most of us and thus easily filled with egotism, fraud, and self-delusion. In an age of tumbled together and hard-to-disentangle intellection, his message and biography can easily be ignored. And most of us start there, in thought, when our life begins to taste like dust. Religion holds out a hand, or philosophy does, and we follow our thinking along those paths until gradually we discover the dust there is merely finer. Our grief builds, as it must, since our growing grief is nothing but our growing sense of separation. This grief can be masked with worldly success, good fortune, and elaborate explanation, but success is never fully successful, fortune never fortunate enough, and explanation tasteless. The grief of living is as natural as it is inevitable because it is a symptom of separation. Even if we somehow come to believe in God through our upbringing or through thought, belief is only a bandage over that wound.

Belief is a beginning, though, since it can lead to faith, and faith is force.

Faith is being stationed in the waiting room of a famous physician, hurting and hoping, perhaps now and then glimpsing a quick white-coated figure moving obscurely in the back rooms, perhaps despairing that your turn will ever come, so that finally, almost as a last resort, you determinedly try to develop patience, then come to see that it is this patience itself that is your cure, because hidden in patience is the power of a growing inner reliance. The room begins to brighten, the faces about you gladden, and perhaps even from time to time you see the physician himself sweep past with a smile, and more and more understand that his treatment is just this waiting, this patience, this surrender. The illness that brought you to him was long in developing, full of layers and nuance, and the cure prescribed is a delicate inner healing that cannot be rushed.

The contentment within discontent

For some—indeed, sometimes for all—the inner journey may seem too slow, too arduous, the inner discontent with a weary life too sharp. This is often apparent in the world's great writers, poets, and artists. These have opened the inner world of higher desire, and many are beset with alcoholism, womanizing (or manizing), irreverence, and, in general, a passion for upsetting the tedium of contemporary morality. Their joy—and use to humanity—is in exposing hypocrisy, the coat of self-repression which not only hides the lower self but also hides the absence of a higher self.

But hypocrisy is inevitable, since when theologies and nations notice that small desire opposes large desire, the readily enforceable solution is to restrain small desire. But if we perform this restraint before larger desire has taken its seat within us, too often restraint becomes repression, and we succeed only in ridding our consciousness of nearly all desire. We become dry, sometimes humorless, often self-righteous. The external conformity of shariat notices the shadow in others but not in itself. In that way, the good obscures the bad. (A corrective to this error will be provided in the invigorating *second greatest mantra*.)

The gradualness of longing's emergence, and the reflective self's enthusiasm for love—but impotence to create it—can develop in the mind an interesting twinness, the idea of God and the experience of God. Around the idea of God cluster texts, ritual, philosophy, images, names, even sometimes photographs and film (at least of the most recent Avatar, Meher Baba). Around the experience of God a growing silence begins. The experience of God is the experience of a presence, of the psychic being, of the inner master. Words can point—grace, warmth, freshness, lightness, love—but they fall useless at the threshold of experience.

The ego can sometimes form a fortress of ideation that prevents it from experiencing the juice of lived life where the work of disposition-unraveling surrender takes place. When one of Meher Baba's close ones experienced the loss of her son in an accident, she refused to weep, holding herself above grief with the determined thought that her son's death was Baba's will. Baba sent his women mandali to this mother with the instruction to remember aloud her son's kindliness and character until at last she began to weep the tears her ideation had repressed.

Because of the struggle, and because the process is delicate and gradual, one of the lessons for any aspirant—perhaps the chief lesson—is to find cheer in discontent, to patiently accommodate the limitation and error of the desire-disposition while striving toward the limitless. The self-loathing and even the depression ordinary to many seekers is a stage that must be recognized and surpassed. In essence, every moment of I'm-not-good-enough guilt is nothing but the power impulse of pride projected inwardly. Pride celebrates accomplishment and guilt regrets failure because both are equally bound to desire. Both result from the same mistake of egotism—everything depends on me. Which is why the solution to both is identical—the humility of surrender.

As humility establishes itself within us, we can begin to notice—without shame—our negativity, pettiness, guilt, grudging, pride. Those feelings can then be evaporated into the air of acknowledgment, inner relenting, and release. This is the essence of a humility which makes no claim, accepts no homage, neither fears nor boasts. This is not a station that can be willed. It is a station that must be wanted.

When the inner master is contacted, that presence is an ever-sustaining fountain of assurance that comfortably—sometimes blissfully—adjusts the yoke of existence so that instead of a burden, our bondage becomes the offering that creates withness. Meher Baba's prescription (reminiscent of Alcoholics Anonymous adage to "Fake it til you make it") is: *Though your heart is torn to pieces, wear a smile on your face.* This is not the false optimism of the weak. It is the resolution of the strong.

Aurobindo commented to a disciple (from *Letters on Yoga III*, page 18): "You speak of five and a half years as if it were a tremendous time for such an object, but a Yogi who is able in that time to change radically his nature and get the concrete decisive experience of the Divine would have to be considered as one of the rare gallopers of the spiritual Way." Impatience with gradualness has led to the proliferation of guides and gurus, meditation, crystal therapy, mediums, occult practice of all kinds, and on and on. These practices may have value—some more, some less, and always depending on the temperament of the seeker—but it is the relentless—yet, alas, gradual—emergence of longing that discards this, then this, then this as it plunges deeper and deeper still into the inner world. This gradualness must be faced with fortitude and has at least this consolation—unlike the bewildered farmer unable to direct the tourist to Chicago and the preacher who condemns, you *can* get there from here. Also you must—and also you will. Plus, slow as it may be, it's wonderfully interesting, and the gains you make cannot be lost.

In *The Discourses*, Meher Baba said: *The aspirant has been accustomed to derive zest in life from his limited ego, and an immediate transition from the life of egoistic action to that of ego-less action is impossible*. Discontent is not only inevitable, it is essential. It is a form of longing, the engine of all seeking.

Yet a secret every seeker eventually learns is that within discontent is hidden contentment. Discontent abides in our front self, and our notice of that discontent is the notice of our self's small desiring. Our refusal to pursue small desiring's endless and fruitless satisfaction begins the notice of the shadow self that binds us, and in that notice, faintly at first, but ever more clearly, we begin to experience the outline and then the body of the larger self beneath where lies real contentment. And in that notice is a profound encouragement which produces even more contentment. The small self, previously seen as natural and inevitable, seems more and more unnatural as a greater naturalness emerges. This emergence is not repression but is instead a welcome and a fond goodbye. It is a grounding. It is the foundation of faith, not in doctrine but in an unfolding process. Discontent prepares the soil from which contentment grows, and in contentment is the essence of both equanimity and surrender. The practice of so-called mindfulness can contribute to that surrender by calming and clearing, but it cannot create that surrender. Surrender is produced by need, and as Rumi said, "Without need, God gives nothing." Thus, looking past or repressing discontent (which is the face of need) is an error. Looking from it and beneath it begins the journey, at first perhaps through a desert, but eventually through a meadow. And meadows are beautiful, so who cares for the time the journey takes? Plus, the journey has a direction.

A few elaborations concerning metabolism and empathy

Now that Meher Baba's cosmology is better in tow, it's a good time to consider again two of the previous discussions that brought us to this point, namely, the miraculous brew of metabolism and the eerie marvel of empathy. Reviewing these two aspects of existence will more fully substantiate the architecture of the outer world and the vaster world within.

First metabolism. How odd, perhaps, to descend into biology from the spiritual stratosphere, but that descent is useful since it reveals a stubborn crudity in biological thought—and points convincingly to a hidden fabric of intelligence in life. Biologists have discovered an imagination-baffling intricacy in molecular life, yet under the ideation of physicalism, they have helplessly concluded that this intricacy must be somehow mechanical, functioned by the pushing and pulling of chemical—and now quantum—operations. After all, how else? Unless, oh no, it's God in there fiddling.

For those committed to the adventure of physicalist science, any God-conjecture seems fatuous. Yet in the same way that consciousness itself has become the central problem of philosophy, the working of life has become the central problem of biology—and for the same reason, the commitment to bumping-about particles as the causal process of all life and intelligence. A different supposing considers the matter bits we can experience and measure are not pushed and pulled wholly or solely by other matter bits, but instead by a force world as yet not experienceable (by most of us). This force world is the underlayment and foundation of the material world, and its supposition neatly solves the mystery of both metabolism and empathy—*and does not imply that God is a capricious interferer.*

Metabolism is unimaginable as a chaos of molecules, but is perfectly consistent with the view that beneath and controlling the matter-bits in cells is an invisible subtle-mental force world imbued with Infinite Intelligence. So that: those pieces of Infinite Intelligence called souls (us) get the body they need to develop their consciousness and fulfill their destiny. So that: the diseases we are immune or vulnerable to are part of our package. So that: nothing is accidental. So that: that toenail-bound carbon atom is not bumped randomly into place but rolled along by the invisible force-guidance of Infinite Intelligence. Utterly, incredibly, and laughably absurd! And perfectly sensible. After all, if Infinite Intelligence is making the world, is faithfully spinning the electrons of the most distant galaxy, it's not much of a leap to credit it with keeping tabs on your toenail molecules. In fact, it would be absurd to reach any other conclusion. The critical supposition is about whether God exists. Here we've supposed that because every other supposition fails in subtlety. After that, it makes sense to suppose that each soul is held perfectly in the delicate cup of God's palm.

In metabolism it's not the astronomically lucky bumping about of atoms that creates and functions life and evolution, not even the tiny command centers of DNA that somehow direct matter bits into their place in a living body, but is instead the sure guidance of the subtle and mental bodies.

Does this mean that all existence is somehow continually guided? It does, but not in the old-fashioned way of God dispensing destiny by inscrutable caprice. It is merely to say that there is order in the being of the subtle and mental worlds, and that, further, there is nothing miraculous in our development, not even miracles. It is also to say that there is nothing random in being. That's why teleology, with a bit of rubbing and scrubbing, can be reenthroned in thought.

For some, no doubt, science's current conception of metabolism, while not complete, is on the right track and will eventually unravel the last mysteries. Though we don't yet know it all, we have already discovered plenty of metabolic pathways, a host of anabolic and catabolic reactions, brownian motion, and thousands of enzymes and proteins. Thus, we can be assured that it's all an immense and marvelous self-cooking soup. Yet how 23,000 genes (the protein-coding human genome) manage and propel into place the 7,000,000,000,000,000,000,000,000,000 atoms of the human form by pushes and pulls remains unimaginable. What makes it more imaginable is the supposition that there is an intelligent force—so far unsuspected and thus unstudied—beneath and within genes, and that genes are merely the front-most physicality of the intelligent intention existing in the subtle and mental bodies of each living being, and that this intention is the causal force that somehow operates metabolism. The *somehow* is included in that statement, first, to grant that the working of this supposed subtle intelligence is, so far, mysterious, and, second, to submit to skeptics that, besides settling the grandest mystery of biology, this conception of metabolism opens a vast and waiting field of study. These bodies have been described, however obscurely and incompletely, by ancient texts from Egypt, China, and India and today are the study of a variety of thinkers and practitioners.

To forestall the distaste of atheists, it can even be granted that this intelligence need not be conceived as the benevolent will of an overwatching divinity. (Such a supposition may be inevitable but is not required here.) Just as genetic code is today considered a form of information, so too the subtle force-guidance beneath biological matter can be usefully considered as a companion form of intelligence/information. But if there is a subtle intelligence permeating the physical arrangement of genetic code, the elusive marvel of life processes is made comprehensible. It's not by random bumping that the toenail molecule gets home. It's by the somehow of an invisible force-guidance in the subtle and mental worlds described by Meher

Baba, Aurobindo, and many others. What form this guidance might take, whether through some so far undetected physicality, or through a form of energy or even a thought form—all this can be part of future conjecture and experiment.

It's worth noting here that science currently guesses that only five percent of the cosmos is apparent to instruments, and that the rest is composed of unknown dark energy and dark matter, hypothesized only from gravitational effects. The force-guidance in biological processes makes sense to suppose in the same way and for the same reason that the dark matter and energy of physicists makes sense to suppose—it explains the working of the universe. This supposed force-guidance within existence is, like dark energy and dark matter, invisible, so far at least, to instruments. Whether dark matter and energy and this dark force-guidance are associated or even identical may someday become evident.

A slightly separate but inevitable topic here is the advent of genetic engineering and the consequences for divine destiny or the will of God. On one hand, nothing that exists can possibly be outside the will (or being) of divinity. On the other, if we fiddle with genes, aren't we likely to upset the plan? Yet the argument that divinity has plans separate from our intention would constrict every human activity and would proscribe us from creating all medicines and even, for that matter, walking out of the paths of snakes. It takes high good sense to live wisely, and no doubt gene-editing will take some extra high good sense since its consequences are so immense. Before you cross a rickety suspension bridge, or edit genes, think deeply. Science and good thinking must progress together, and at the bottom of the best thinking is love, the welfare and unity of everything.

Now about empathy: how might this hidden world settle the mystery of empathy? As stated earlier, when we gaze at a human face and feel imparted to us the inner state of that person, we do not employ fierce and instantaneous logical calculation from physical premise-clues but instead experience the immediacy of recognition. A satisfying supposition is that this is possible in us for the same reason that genes are able to provide instruction to wandering molecules, that beneath the gross world is a world of a larger and guiding intelligence.

So that: *I see the invisible stuff of your being in the same way that I see and feel the invisible stuff of my own being—and a coffee cup*. The knowing that I have of your state and of my own is made conscious in me by mind recognition, not by physical clues. When I close my eyes my recognition of other people's mind vanishes, but that's simply because sight is the gross portal through which I am impressed across space by the subtle. When I open them, I see not only the physical, but also the subtle and mental bodies within people. These subtle and mental bodies, these meaning-fields, though mostly buried in unconsciousness, can be reasonably suspected by consciousness when we consider the reception of meaning from—well, anything, really. Bumping-about matter bits don't mean. Intelligence means. We are suspended in a cloud-lens of meaning every moment. When the face of another person means that person's inner being to you, that meaning is imparted not physically, by a thousand facial clues, but transmitted—somehow—by the meaning-stuff of mind emanating from the unconscious mind-penumbra of that person's subtle and mental bodies.

Empathy—and, in fact, any meaning whatever—can never be understood as the abacus-like fizzling of a billion neurons in the brain. No doubt, as neurology has shown, brain fizzling accompanies the meaning-states that pour through us, but meaning-states themselves, not neurons, are the primordial-most isness of our experience. For the physicalist at the lectern, the hard thing about the hard problem is granting the primacy of meaning, of the mind in which he is continually embedded. As the simple primacy of noticing the world begins to predominate, science will discard the interpretive scheme of physicalism as a bizarre hallucination. Given the invisibility of the most of existence, the welcome visibility of physicalism was natural and inevitable, but a different, more mature science must eventually take its place.

Empathy, then, is recognition, and what recognizes is not a fiercely calculating brain-computer (which cannot mean) but some sort of intelligence stuff we have always referred to, however uncritically, as mind. This is why Meher Baba's and Aurobindo's description of the universe as composed of three blended fields of being—the mental, subtle, and gross worlds—is useful in making sense of our existence. Whether these subtle and mental meaning-fields have a measurable physical aspect or a measurable energy aspect or indeed some hitherto unconsidered and immeasurable aspect of thought we may someday learn. Though we do not yet understand the how of its working, this three-part system explains the mystery of metabolism, that there is an undetected guidance in all matter, and also the mystery of empathy, that meaning is transmitted mind to mind.

No doubt our awareness of these hidden bodies is largely unconscious. Mediums, psychics, and advanced souls are less dependent on the gross world and are able to receive fuller subtle and mental impressions. (The first two, however, often swim in a vague soup of meaning, seldom agree, and can easily become victims of egotism.) Psychic phenomena, remote viewing, telepathy, and precognition are being studied world-wide and, as physicalism loses its grip on universities, will eventually yield more and more interesting results. Still, where any community decides to build a road or bridge must be decided by considering the group welfare and not by consulting psychics. (If a psychic could reveal that a contractor bribed the commissioners, that might be helpful...)

Lastly, this lingering conundrum: if empathy is indeed actually the reception of subtle and mental information, through invisible information-laden impressions, then how is it that we can empathize with characters on film, many of whom have long departed the earth? In that case, as also in the case of empathizing with living, but not present, actors in a movie, there is no present energy that somehow moves across space and through time to imprint our intelligence with information. This would seem to confirm that it must be subtle physicality—eyebrow raises, grimaces, half-smiles—that impart information. Further, seeing actors in a movie, where they can convey information via a forty-foot face, normally produces far more subtlety than live performance, where actors, since their faces are diminutive, must rely on voice and dialogue.

But since we have shown that physicality is too coarse a media to impart the subtlety of empathy, and since we have shown that we do not learn empathy by memorizing facial comportment—by studying our own face in a mirror, for instance—we must, perforce, conjecture that there is an intelligence within us, some organ, power, or meaning-field, that receives meaning from subtle, emotional, mental impressions. Which means: the vast, invisible, elusive soup of our interiority receives information from the vast, invisible, elusive soup of the interiority of others. And that, most marvelously, *this reception is not proscribed by time or space.*

This points, interestingly, to two further conjectures. Either, one, information of an actor's mentality (mood, emotion, etcetera) is somehow available in the physicality of light images on a screen (that persistent, invidious *somehow*), or two, an actor's face and physicality imprint the universal mind with information, which, when received even a hundred years later via images on a screen, is able to impress our minds with time-independent meaning.

The first alternative—that information is covertly *inherent* in the face of an actor independent of time—makes sense when we consider that the subtle and mental bodies, which contain and emit the information of mood and attitude in a face, are not separate from the physical but instead are its origin and support—and that the physical is their emanation, and that not only the physical but also the mental and subtle are somehow impregnated in film. After all, when we relive a scene from a movie, we are not intent on recalling the actors' mouth purses and eyebrow lifts, but instead we re-experience the feelings we felt.

The second alternative—that the actor's face imprints the universal mind (which we inhabit and which inhabits us) with information—means that we are, in essence, reading the mind of the cosmos.

Well, jeez, Louise! By exposing the absurdity hidden in our ordinary but crude presumptions concerning empathy, and by then innocently taking the hand of conjecture, we have been led to a land charged with enchantment, and at any moment might expect to see elves poking out of the shrubbery. We read the mind of the cosmos, for goodness' sake! But yeah. Indeed, we do. And, by the way, the above duo of conjectures are really the same conjecture, since however the meaning-getting intelligence installed in us goes about its business, whether by impregnating film with meaning independent of time or by preserving in the cosmic mind the meaning those faces embody, it's really all one thing, because faces and film are, after all, as is each of us, part of the cosmic mind which is the all of everything. We walk in gleamy-ness, and God, whatever or whoever he may be, is continually about his business of emanating and receiving meaning, and busy busy busy, now and now and now, everywhere.

The above conclusions interestingly do away with the ancient body-mind problem that has plagued philosophy for centuries—the what's-this-two-different-styles-of-stuff issue that was made prominent by Descartes. The conjecture of three interconnected worlds, gross, subtle, and mental, means that there is not some other-than-matter-stuff called mind and not some other-than-mind-stuff called matter, but that matter and mind are the same stuff in different forms, so that our minds, which see and move matter, and our bodies and the bump-into stuff outside us, which are seen and moved by mind, are emanations of the intelligence that is making the cosmos. The declaration of Meher Baba and Aurobindo is that the gross world is an emanation of the subtle world, and the subtle world of the mental, and that all three worlds are held, sustained, and emanated from Infinite Intelligence. The body and mind are distinct but not separate. Both are forms of the universal substance of God. However mysterious that substance must remain, their hidden identity settles the famous causation problem beloved and lamented by philosophers. Body and mind—the gross, subtle, and mental—can push and pull one another because they're conjoined at birth and built of the same stuff—the intelligence stuff of God.

Which means, as a sort of by-the-way, that all is well.

Why to give up bank robbery

Physicalism and its consequent atheism are full of talk about morality but have never yet proposed a good reason not to rob banks. Though most of us somehow restrain our bank-robbing inclinations through the vague guidance of conscience, we would be glad to understand our reticence as something more than cowardice. The dividend of a conception of the Self as the substrate of existence is that it makes bank robbery, and selfishness in general, a bad strategy. The reason is that, as Ramana Maharshi remarked when asked how we should treat others, *there are no others.*

This would not be true if Infinite Intelligence were somehow a mechanical and austere working of meaning, cause, and effect that produced numberless dispositions only to dissolve them into nothingness. In that case, the only requirement for good living would be to rob banks well. This is not the case, since inherent in the being of the Self is the force of love, the consequence and essence of oneness. Love is not an add-on attribute of God, a secret sauce he spiced the universe with so we won't get depressed, nor is it favoritism dispensed to the worthy by fiat. Love is the texture and glue of the intelligent isness that is creation—and also us, though in unconscious form.

The ontological fact that love's oneness is at the bottom of everything is why here in the knock-about world it feels good to be kind and bad to be cruel, good to be humble and bad to be proud, good to be generous and bad to be greedy. This sense of things isn't produced by the restraint of socialization. It is the emergence, however unconsciously, of a felt sense of the One in all. Which is why love produces equanimity. Which is why, as Meher Baba said, *real happiness lies in making others happy.*

Still, when we only believe that love is at the bottom and do not yet experience it, or experience it vaguely and not deeply, we can be battered by doubt. Humanity has always had difficulty with the God-is-love idea because, after all, if he's so loving, why—here name almost anything, from earthquakes to unsuccessful birthday parties to serial killers. If God is one and everything is God how to fit all that stuff under the God-is-good umbrella? It clearly doesn't fit under the umbrellas of the old religions. That's why they supposed devils, which, in the light of our understanding that choice is an illusion, means that an infinitely loving God must have incompetently, or vengefully, poisoned his hapless creation.

Earlier we encountered arguments about the nature of suffering—that one, there can be no accusation since the accused and accuser are identical, and two, from God's point of view, which is ours unconsciously, even suffering is a form of delight as God (as us) takes experience in order to develop the intelligence-consciousness needed to see himself.

Here's Aurobindo on the subject, from *The Life Divine*, Chapter 12:

> *In the first place, since in our depths we ourselves are that One, since in the reality of our being we are the indivisible All-Consciousness and therefore the inalienable All-Bliss, the disposition of our sensational experience in the three vibrations of pain, pleasure, and indifference can only be a superficial arrangement created by that limited part of ourselves which is uppermost in our waking consciousness. Behind there must be something in us—much vaster, profounder, truer than the superficial consciousness—which takes delight impartially in all experiences; it is that delight which secretly supports the superficial mental being and enables it to persevere through all labors, sufferings, and ordeals in the agitated movement of the Becoming. That which we call ourselves is only a trembling ray on the surface; behind is all the vast subconscient, the vast superconscient profiting by all these surface experiences and imposing them on its external self which it exposes as a sort*

of sensitive covering to the contacts of the world; itself veiled, it receives these contacts and assimilates them into the values of a truer, a profounder, a mastering and creative experience.

When we break off pieces of nature by wanting a banana split, a new girlfriend, fame (an endless list), we are given a nudge by pain—we get fat, the girlfriend vanishes, and so does fame. This is not a form of punishment for sin, and certainly not the justice of an ethical God. That idea of the cosmos is utterly inconsistent with good thinking. It's not only that villains sometimes die smiling, it's that that conception makes the all-creating divinity a kind of mad puppeteer, a maestro who charged creation with obsession for the sport of watching and judging. A more sensible conception is that the pain of desire, and desire's satisfaction too, is inherent in the structure of being, the structure in which we are all embedded, and the use of that structure is the greater and greater development of consciousness. Even if we die happy rascals in one life, and even if we perish miserably in another, happiness, success, misery, and failure are not portioned out as rewards or punishment but are instead the inevitable consequence of our incarnation as only part-God beings with the most of our natures hidden in the darkness of the unconscious. Life after life we are led through recklessness, hypocrisy, bewilderment—and finally to longing. And then to love.

Reincarnation, the guy that killed 99 people, and karma

At this point, it's worth more fully opening the topic of reincarnation, which, though accepted by half of the world's religions and dismissed by the other half, turns out to have mostly a sort of philosophical importance. The idea of reincarnation involves the idea of karma, of which we are unconscious, so why, you may ask, should anyone be good in this life so that 400 years from now some stranger (ourself in another body) doesn't break a leg or get murdered? While Meher Baba and Aurobindo both state that reincarnation is a fact, neither holds that belief in it is necessary for inner work. The concept is introduced in these pages to satisfy logic and emotion in three ways.

First, a life after life conjecture makes sense of the universe's architecture. Second, when we become aware of the Love that is drawing us, we needn't despair if we don't get home before we die. Third, since our bondage in desire makes eternal reward or punishment ontologically absurd, only an idea-system that includes reincarnation supports the notion that God is a loving fellow instead of a cosmic psychopath toying with his creation.

Though, yes, we can tick death off the list of things to despair about, few people go to work or feed their dog thinking, damn, death anyway. Death does come up from time to time, particularly out in that field at night, but after the no-death idea inherent in reincarnation nullifies despair, it has no leverage or function in the day to day. And it is in the day to day, in our own lives and in our lives together, that good living is found. The mandali of Meher Baba came from varied backgrounds, Muslim, Hindu, Parsee, and Christian, and as youths were concerned about which view was correct, one life or many. Meher Baba settled things by telling them they were both correct. The soul is born once into creation and dies once when it unites with God—and while it is in creation it wears many coats.

So this at least: you can't die. And this finally: you're headed home.

To understand how reincarnation makes best sense of the cosmos we need to understand the notion of karma. To understand that we must clear both ideas of their accumulated fancifulness. In reincarnation you don't go from human to cricket, ever. You go forward. Karma is not about getting your just desserts. You get those, no doubt, but it's not God's vengeance. It's the by-product of the thrust and nature of karma, your existence envelope. Karma is the sanskaric sheathe of your soul, the self-lens of your subtle and mental bodies that is developed day by day and is with you life after life. It is the mostly hidden (because unconscious) substance of you, the mood-giver, plan-maker, hoper, needer, wonderer that you are. It is the forward thrusting impulse of your very being. Though invisible to ordinary consciousness, it is realer than the material bits that make your body, and in fact its hidden intelligence is the sculptor of those bits. Though it is as inexorable as gravity, it is God's eternal withness with you and with all creation. It is the continual gift of God-conscious to God-unconscious. It must be neither feared, deplored, shunned, nor excused. It is desire's laddering in the psyche and, however wandering, it goes up.

To understand reincarnation and karma, the sorting and shifting of life after life intelligence, we must grant the existence of the so-far-invisible instruments of our subtle and mental bodies. It is these two which contain our past and develop our future. It is these two which account for the massive and unexplainable intelligence of instinct and the unconscious. In these two, the spending and accumulation of experience (impressions/sanskaras) produce the marvelously precise algebra of our development called karma.

From *God Speaks* (about human development): *...the impressions which were hard-set or dense get shaken up so thoroughly by the reincarnation process that their tight grip on consciousness becomes loose. These hard-set (dense or gross) impressions thin out or become feeble through innumerable and varied experiences of opposites.*

In *The Discourses* by Meher Baba, several chapters are entitled *Reincarnation and Karma*. In those chapters, Meher Baba notes, but does not make important, that in advanced aspirants past lives are often recalled. Bhau Kalchuri, author of the 5000-page biography of his Master, used to sit night watch outside Baba's bedroom and spent many of those hours reviewing—he called it filming—his past lives. An extensive research project from the University of Virginia has shown that numerous people, mostly children under seven years of age, have not only reported memories of past lives but can also name people in nearby communities where they had lived in a previous life. This occurs mostly in India, but some children, even those from the West, can name people from the distant past whose photographs they are shown. More than 1200 of these studies have been validated by on-the-ground research.

Still, reincarnation is a concept hard for science to accept—and for two good reasons. One, the popular conception of reincarnation—the only one science seems to be aware of—is fantastical, crude, and without explanatory context, and two, accepting reincarnation overthrows the entire body of their physicalist assumptions. As physicalism weakens, and as reincarnation's explanatory context is more richly elaborated, reincarnation will eventually be accepted by science and even by religion. It will remain, though, a fact true but mostly irrelevant to inner work. Past life memories can provide consoling information, but the bondage of those sanskaric patterns must still be overcome through the work of balance and surrender in the present life.

In the early days of Meher Baba's advent, his young mandali began to fret about sanskaras, wondering about the details of their accumulation, hesitating to act this or that way for fear of adding bad sanskaras. So Meher Baba told the story of an ancient murderer-thief (a tale also told by Buddha centuries before). This criminal was powerful and had killed and robbed 99 travelers. Finally, disgusted with his life, he found his way to the darbar of a Perfect Master. He prostrated himself, and the Master assured him that if he obeyed he would be given realization. He was told to sit in the middle of the road and wait for further instructions. Years passed, and still the murderer waited. He became a revered person in the countryside, and the villagers eventually made a path around him. One day one of the king's messengers approached on horseback, and, seeing this man blocking his way, angrily ordered him to the side. When he was ignored, the messenger struck out with his riding crop. The murderer's old sanskaras flamed within him, and he dragged the messenger from his horse and throttled him. And was instantly made one with God. The messenger had been sent by the king with death warrants for 100 men, and the murderer, by slaying him, had saved a hundred lives to balance the hundred he had taken. And thus settled his karma.

Oh well, sure, any fellow who could sit for years in one place in obedience to a Perfect Master is doubtlessly advanced. And sure, that's extraordinary karmic destiny and, if more than a story and actually true, it is likely a once-in-the-universe setup.

But the tale does point up the complexity of karma and reminds us as well that karma is generally held to be a vast compound of mysterious debt. Someone saves you, so you have to save them, now or in some future life. You feel natural warmth for this one and unexplainable mistrust of that one.

Whether you are assaulted now and celebrated eventually, or celebrated now and assaulted soon, your entire life is the just-what-you-need. You're not directing the play and mostly don't even know the script. But you have the starring role.

The girl in the bar

As the study of existence moves from physicalism and embraces the conjecture of an Infinite Intelligence both manifesting and noticing things, it will begin to understand more fully the intersection of the gross world with the subtle and mental worlds. This interplay will lead thinkers to titillating conjectures about how karma propels us through time. Is karma indifferent to the cards you are dealt if you're playing for fun, but when there's money at stake makes sure you lose or win? If someone wins in roulette and can thus pay his employees and save his business (which supposedly happened with the corporation known as FedEx) does God nudge the wheel or ball or inject the roulette operator's muscles with the just-right amount of energy to land the ball on 27? Did you go to that bar not because you wanted a beer but because your karma, the Infinite Intelligence that is continually making and sustaining you, effloresced a beer-thirst so that you would enter the bar and meet your future wife?

And even this: if you are destined to win at cards or roulette, wouldn't it violate the structure of being if Infinite Intelligence actually nudged the ball or changed the cards' arrangement? After all, that ball and those ink patterns need good reliable consciousness-evolving experience to develop their own subtle and mental bodies and wouldn't pushing them around by unnatural-to-law divine fiddling disturb their development? Or would they kindly be made unconscious of that fiddling and thus not be affected? Or maybe the ball itself is not embodied with a drop-soul but only the molecules that compose it, and they could care less what happens to their ride. Or maybe some roulette balls are embodied, but the ones whose course must be altered to fulfill someone's destiny are conveniently unsouled.

However things are arranged, it makes sense to conclude that at the instant of creation the destiny of each of the numberless souls created and to be created was already perfectly known by the Infinite planner so that the past, present, and future of each embodied thing is simply a working out of the scheme of creation, so that everything that happens to everyone is part of a just-right path which appears mechanical but instead is divinely ordained. After all, for Infinite Intelligence there can be no ignored or untended bits of existence. And so on. And on and on. No wonder that in the Middle Ages the Christian monks started thinking about the number of angels that could dance on the head of a pin.

But even if the universe—and our lives—unfolds with machine-like determination, it is not the purposeless machine of physicalism. It simply means that just as there is utter reliability in the seen world of gross objects (gravity, the speed of light, inertia), there is also utter reliability in the unseen world of thoughts and feelings and even who you run into on the street corner—or in that bar where you meet the stranger you end up marrying. The main problem of granting that karma is a must-be phenomenon is that our front minds, our conscious ego self, relies on the crudity of generalized thinking—ideas—to navigate existence, and ideas are always segments of Being, momentary snapshots of its fathomless working. Even close-noticing cannot see the action of karma, because close-noticing, while it can penetrate the tissue of crude ideas, cannot see beneath the veil of the unconscious—which is where the power of karma resides. The operation of karma depends on invisibility, otherwise it couldn't perform its function of directing things. You don't choose when you become interested in a beer. You just get-that-way. And at the just-right time. Because, hey, she's waiting for her husband.

The idea of karma, particularly in the West, has been smudged with simplicity and misunderstanding, and sometimes is even seen as cosmic vengeance. A better understanding of karma is that it is the unfolding-building of an infinitely delicate inner prism through which the soul sees existence, and that this unfoldment is not haphazard but entirely purposive. Each soul is a kernel of God that gradually, life after life, improves, widens, and deepens its prism-lens until it more and more purely refracts the rays of divinity that shine through it. (Shelley: *Life, like a dome of many-colored glass, stains the white radiance of eternity.*)

Given the discoveries in these pages, that supposition is not too hard to digest. What is more interesting to consider is that *nothing whatever can be accidental or random.* Every experience—whether you catch the ball or drop it, whether you were afraid to speak or spoke too rashly, whether you roll seven on your first roll or your last—is a destined gift of experience that crafts, with infinite patience, the prism of your inner bodies. There are no wasted days or wasted lives. Every moment is money in the bank. There is mechanism in this accumulation of experience, but the mechanism has a mandate that cooperates with and also supersedes physical law. This means then that the physical world is perfectly compliant to the need and unfoldment of the inner world—and yet so perfectly invisible that the doctrine of physicalism as the entire government of existence was natural to suppose. On a clock, we notice the second hand moving, and even, with patience, the minute hand—but never the hour hand. Yet it moves, and somehow that stranger in the bar agrees to marry you.

In *Beams on the Spiritual Panorama,* Meher Baba wrote:

> *The mystery of the universe is hierarchic in structure. There are graded orders, one supervening upon the other. The spiritual panorama of the universe reveals itself as a gradient with laws upon laws. Superimposition of one type of law over the other implies elasticity and resilience of lower laws for the working out of higher superseding laws. Instead of lawlessness, it means a regime of graded laws adjusted with each other in such a manner that they all subserve the supreme purpose of God, the Creator.*

> *The lower laws are subsumed under the higher laws. We have first the law of cause and effect reigning supreme in Nature. Such natural laws seem to be mechanical, rigid and inexorable. But by acting and interacting with life-force, they lead to higher laws of sanskaric or impressional determination and become superseded by them. Impressional determinism is not an exception to causal laws but is their finer and higher form. It supervenes upon mechanical causal laws.*

What is marvelous and assuring about this conception of the universe is that every instant of your being is the just-what-you-need.

The prison of dispositional context

It's interesting to note that the entire context of everyone's being is a point of view. As you bump about your life, meeting these, avoiding those, accepting this, refusing that, you are, in a sense that is enrichingly true to notice, nothing but a dispositional context. And so is everyone else. And, if the panpsychists, Meher Baba, and Aurobindo are right, so is the rest of existence—rocks and hydrogen atoms included. (Whether telephone poles are ensouled, and whether breaking a rock into pieces creates new soul homes, we may someday learn—or never.)

The shifting and interacting of dispositional contexts is the entire what of existence, so that the world, which seems to be made of clear-boundaried things like spoons and football games, is really an elaborate maze of shifting forms of meaning. Our attempt to create external clarities—this is my country, this is sacred, this wrong—is mind-work and creates maya. And emptiness. Life is meaning and desire and is a vast flow between drop-souls that cannot be cornered or understood with the concept-making mind. It must be felt for, deep, then deeper, and still deeper.

Wait—spoons and football games are unreal? Well, at least sort of. It takes only a small thinking to demonstrate their unreality as figments of meaning in our dispositional contexts, but a larger thinking grants their immovable seemingness. This seemingness is what we live and have our being in. It is what makes the gross world of bump-into stuff the limit of most people's perception and what has mesmerized physicalist science for centuries—and it is entirely natural and required. The pattern-imposing seemingness of everything issues from the unconscious within and provides the needed reliability and mutuality of intelligence.

As Well as Well

Although without, I am a stalk, a stone,
A dumb demand of space,
Within I have been
In Babylon
And seen a woman's face
Uplifting at the well
And felt my heart uplifting.
I have sat on temple steps,
Beaded with the rain,
And heard old Socrates
Snuffle and explain.
Why shouldn't this be true?
All knowing is a hue.
All thought mere overview.
Only consciousness is true.
The pebbles at the well,
Unnoticed by the watermaid,
I unnotice too.
And in the eye of gentle Socrates,
Which like a far bird winks,
I see as well as well,
The sky,
Far back,
Which thinks.

As the mind works the fingers of introspective thought into the hard shell of meaning forms, so-called reality begins to soften and reveal its elusive contextuality. Some Masters have given names to the inner geography that opens as we deepen—the intuitive mind, the illumined mind, this and that—and while names can clarify and inspire, the great friends and only lights of this inner deepening are honesty and its twin, patience. That's why, as noted in the thought experiment that opened this book, honest people must agree. Honesty and patience appear as the resolute companions of longing, and together they produce character, tolerance, nobility, purity—the entire train of virtue—and always see the same thing. Which, at bottom, everyone is.

Bottom-of-the-ninth—and the guy who was sent for water

How the hour hand of Infinite Intelligence gets things done is a fascinating (if idle) speculation. A fun example: it's the 2020 American baseball world series. The Dodgers lead two games to one. It's the bottom-of-the-ninth, Rays at bat, behind one run, runners on first and second, two outs. If the Rays can't score, they have to win three in a row to win the series. Which is almost never done.

The batter is behind in the count, two strikes, one ball. Here comes the fourth pitch, a fastball, and the batter hits a looping liner into right. An easy two bouncer. And the right fielder—amazing— muffs! The ball skitters off the edge of his glove, and as he darts to retrieve it, the first runner scores, tying the game.

Now the second runner rounds third and heads for home. The right fielder captures the muffed ball and pegs it to home plate where the catcher crouches, ready. The throw is like a frozen rope but maybe a foot high and a foot to the catcher's right. Still, an easy out, since the runner is halfway between third and home when the throw arrives. The runner rounds third, overextends, and loses his balance. And stumbles. And the catcher muffs the ball! As the ball skitters to the fence, the runner leaps to his feet and dives onto home plate, scoring the winning run. Two outs, bottom-of-the-ninth, two strikes. And the Rays even up the series. The right fielder and catcher feel rotten, the Rays are jubilant, and all across the world cash changes hands.

How did it happen? How did the hour hand of destiny perform its work, which work was, since the Rays won, to insure that they did? There were two runners headed home, and the right fielder muffs. Common error in ball sports, but not for this major leaguer. Except this time he muffs! Maybe he's thinking about the runners and briefly takes his eye off the ball. Easy for the hour hand of destiny to secretly divert his mind with runner-worry, since, after all, that diversion is entirely inner and invisible. He retrieves the ball and throws, and his throw is perfect for a catch and swipe. But just then the runner stumbles. (Divinity at work!) Now it's the catcher's turn for some will-of-God action. The catcher, feeling the runner close, notes the stumble in his peripheral vision, and this major leaguer too is injected with divine distraction, just enough so that when he stabs at the right fielder's throw, he misses and sweeps an empty glove toward home. The runner is up and dives to the plate. Game. An uproar of celebration and pain. Money changes hands.

Really? Well, because we have noted the mysterious functioning of empathy and metabolism, and because we have noted that unchosen and unchooseable desire propels us through the universe, and because we have recognized the place of humility, remorse, sameness, and love, we have (reluctantly or naturally) supposed that Infinite Intelligence not only underlies, but *is* creation, and thus it is natural to suppose that everything is from and toward this Intelligence, which is why it is sensible (if idle) to consider that the fielder's muff, the runner's stumble, and the catcher's distraction were not accidental but part of the infinitely complex, hour-hand-movement of God's will. How interesting! How seamless and couched in hour-hand concealment was the game's finale!

And yet, if the above suppositions are correct, this event is no more miraculous than what you have done so far today, and did yesterday, and will do tomorrow. If existence is produced by divinity, then everything is planned, or nothing is. Everything is sacred, or nothing is. If anything is alive, everything is.

The Withness never goes away.

Infinite Intelligence, besides being infinitely attentive, is infinitely patient. A delightful tale from the East: a young seeker came to the darbar of a Perfect Master to surrender himself. The

Master accepted him, then one day asked him to bring a jug of water from the public well. At the well, the young man met a beautiful girl, fell in love, married her, raised a family, ran a business, grew older. Eventually his wife died, his children moved away, and he recalled the aspiration of his youth. He found himself back in the court of the Master and again fell on his knees in surrender. The Master gently lifted his chin and inquired, "Have you forgotten the water?"

What next? and love

Here you are, awake each morning and out of bed. What now? Meditation? Prayer? Give all your money away and wander with a begging bowl? Get your family and misguided friends by the collar and cudgel them for their stupidity? Mostly those endeavors succeed only in adding to us, creating within us a more and more confident egotism. We must be subtracted from, not added to. We're trying to feel and think more deeply by reducing the thick texture of selfness that inhabits us. We are trying to reach a state of such absolute humility and inner surrender that the hidden infinite intelligence within us emerges. The way to God is the way of self-effacement, and without a sincerity produced by longing's restlessness, we can only restack the blocks of our banality. Longing cannot be meditated, prayed, or demanded into being. Time alone creates longing, time in harness to existence. After we've been a rich man, a poor woman, an acrobat, actor, and aviator, finally a yearning within says, all right, less of that, please. But once that yearning begins, it can be developed, groomed, encouraged, and made more and more intelligent and productive.

Meher Baba (from *Listen, Humanity*):

> *As the aspirant struggles through the obscuring fog of mental and emotional tension his consciousness becomes more one-pointed, forming a spearhead that eventually pierces through the curtain to the inner path of divine knowledge. Even the early glimpses of this knowledge which the pilgrim gets are a great advance over understanding that rests solely upon faith or reason.*
>
> *Poise of the mind born of the pilgrim's new understanding automatically and unwittingly brings about a readjustment of material surroundings, and he finds himself at peace with the*

world. Conservatism, intolerance, pride, and selfishness are shed, and everything takes on a new meaning and purpose.

A note that generates a useful new context of understanding is that it is not ourselves that we yearn to know, but our Self, the same Self within each of us, the Being that is making each of us and everyone else too, plus the mountains, rivers and stars. If then, as we have usefully and naturally supposed, there is this hidden Being within all, and if its nature, as we have usefully and naturally supposed, is the essence and source of love, then love too must be the hidden substance of every path to God. The reason for love's centrality is that the goal and urge within all paths is the Self within all, and the nature and being of that Self is love, the glue of all being, the one-thing-like-another structure of intelligence that facilitates meaning and desire, the oneness that makes existence sensible, knowable, and delightful. We can kick right and wrong to the curb but not good and bad. What creates love is good. What doesn't is bad.

Some form of love, however distorted and sentimentalized by ideology, has always been first on every culture's list of virtues. Love is the substance of the golden rule, the core of every great religion and high-minded philosophy. Without positing love as the foundation of virtue, all other virtues—selflessness, patience, and even courage—cannot be understood. It is the elusive scent of love that draws us from our isolation in egotism to a greater and greater sense of oneness in existence. It is the attraction of God for God. As love grows, we come to understand that egotism's compound of consciousness and unconsciousness has fragmented the Self with small desiring and small knowing. This is the essential beginning and leads to contact with the inner master. It is the right view. It is the way.

How to get through the day—and a life

The first step is noticing the cause of discontent, which is that tireless shadow self beneath our front self. Next, by more and more sensing that that shadow self is not some mysterious psychological stuff accidentally concocted from matter, but is in reality Intelligence itself looking through the "you" prism of our disposition. Next, by beginning the tortuous unknotting of that disposition.

That unknotting is the message of this thinking. It is the greatest adventure and the last one.

Earlier in these pages, the triad of love, obedience, and surrender was elaborated. Love begins things and is a gift of God, given not through divinity's caprice but because through long experience the soul has become capable of receiving. Something is lighted within, and the soul determines not to let that light fade. That determination is the essence of the next step, obedience. At first, a sometimes dogged faith in life, yourself, and God is required, but as the process continues, as an earlier poem put it, eventually everything "makes such perfect sense, that doubt is out of place." And so surrender comes, and with it come patience, equanimity, and courage, and behind everything, sustained by longing, comes the clarity of honesty which feels more and more the Withness of the inner master beneath everything. You can't demand this state from God as your due, you can't church or meditate your way to it, you can't reach it through drugs, complaint, or study. You must want your way to it.

Ages of human effort have been expended developing methods to aid the process of beginning the wanting that reveals the inner master. And ages have been spent justifying allegiance to the external form of some particular master as sufficient—and even required (Christ versus Mohammed, Mohammed versus Krishna, Krishna versus Zoroaster). It is not that ritual or that allegiance to a form is entirely detrimental. The mind can concentrate through ritual, and form can be a focus of initial longing. But both can stall the search by providing the comforting furniture of externalities. The seeker, made lonely and determined by the growing anguish of separation, needs contact. And contact is always internal. When the fish of the heart rises from its depths, it tastes light and has only a taste for more.

Report to Modernity

You've heard it all before,
The soul talk and God talk and la la la.
You said, fine, but whoever who made all this
Is certainly a prick.
Cancer kills the kids, you said.
Armies kill the poor.
Besides, you're busy,
And if next door they're lost in hatred,
It's nothing you did.
It's vexing though,
And the questions end in silence.
Anyway, everyone says it's just one thing after another.
You're already your parents' age,
And so far that's true.
It's been lots of talk and a long blank stare.
At least the silence doesn't accuse you anymore.
At least disappointment doesn't disappoint you anymore.
What you mostly need is courage now.
What you mostly want is rest.
But listen to this hopefulness—
I scratched a hole in my heart.
Deep in the dark, behind belief,
I found a wall made thin by fifty years of need,

And on my knees, I wore away a hole.
First warmth, then light.
Now I have company.
I know you're busy,
But I'm making this report, in case.

So how to get through a life? Become convinced—and eventually aware—that you are completely surrounded by, continually manifested by, and ultimately destined for divinity. After that, as Meher Baba famously said, "Don't worry, be happy." The rest is a growing naturalness. If you like to meditate, why not? But learn to long.

The interesting how of longing and the divine name

Most contemporary writing about spirituality, whether thought of as philosophy or psychology or esoterica, is—alas, or oh well—from the pen of intellectual thinkers. The intellect may declaim to itself that it wants nothing, that existence is one without a second, that consciousness is infinite and that therefore the self is the Self, but unless the disposition supporting that thinking is restless with longing, it is all talk-talk, finer and finer finery in the monkey dance of egotism.

Mere belief has always been a frail and wavering flag hoisted over the desert of inner emptiness, and the central problem of the search has always been how to get from belief to love. The failure to reach love has littered the religious landscape with war and persecution—and the personal landscape of many seekers with doubt and despair.

Longing alone provides the light of inner honesty that enables the desire-disposition, however grudgingly and cantankerously—but finally steadily—to devour itself and open the way to the Self. It is the resistance of the desire-disposition that must be addressed in spiritual effort, and entry into and dissolution of that resistance cannot begin without need.

There is a fascinating secret behind longing's power, and that secret is: *longing alone is acquainted with the enemy*. Longing alone possesses a pass to the stronghold where the disposition is arrayed in its myriad defenses. On that ground, piece by piece, longing alone has the power to recognize the enemy, penetrate its fortress, nullify its armament, and even win over its soldiery. Longing possesses this power because longing is a form of desire, a form of the same energetic stuff as the disposition, so that smaller desires, sometimes truculently, sometimes willingly, when they hear the voice of longing, respect its authenticity as a brother-in-kind—and eventually become willing to follow its lead. Thought, even spiritual thought, though it may be an attendant to longing, arrives from a different space, a reflective space unfooted in the rough and tumble of life-living. Its admonitions and exhortations the disposition is happy to hear, happy to feel allied with, and happy to ignore—giving Ovid to comment, "I see the better and approve. I do the worst."

It's edifying to consider the opening of Chapter Twelve, *The Yoga of Devotion,* in the *Bhagavad Gita.* Arjuna asks Krishna which sort of devotee has the best grasp of yoga, and Krishna replies, "Those whose minds are fixed on me in steadfast love, worshiping me with absolute faith, I consider them to have the greater understanding of yoga." (from the Swami Prabhavananda and Christopher Isherwood translation)

Krishna then mentions that those who concentrate on the unmanifest God can also approach him, but their path is arduous: "But the devotees of the unmanifest have a harder task, because the unmanifest is very difficult for embodied souls to realize." Krishna's unmanifest God is what Meher Baba describes as one of the original Beyond states of God, a state in which God is conscious of himself as Infinite Reality but unconscious of creation. Meher Baba in *Listen, Humanity* says much the same thing as Krishna:

> *Although God is more easily accessible to ordinary man through the God-Men, yet God also reveals himself through His impersonal aspect, which is beyond name, form, and time. This mode of experiencing God is not only difficult but dry. Progress is more realistic and enjoyable when there is an ample play of love and devotion to God.*

The inner search may begin, and even for some continue, in the higher ranges of mind and intellect, but is most efficiently and effectively pursued in the heart, the home of longing, which then becomes the maestro of the process. When longing senses the inner master, by whatever name your destiny prescribes—Mohammad, Buddha, Jesus, or Meher Baba—the inner process becomes natural and clear.

Humankind has developed numerous methods for so-called spiritual work, and here we encounter names from the East, the yogas known as *bhakti, dnyan, karma,* and *raj.* Though foreign-sounding to the Western ear they are not foreign to the psyche, since they are inherent in the values of all cultures—Western, Eastern, or Polynesian. Meher Baba, in *The Discourses,* mostly avoids their use (that book is for all cultures), but the ideas expressed are familiar, and incorporate devotion, mental discipline, and service.

Early in his advent, Meher Baba observed: *The contact of a saint, service to humanity, and the repetition of God's name—these three combined mean the highest possible yogas and religious practices. If this much is done, all religions are observed.* (from the *Combined Diaries* of Meher Baba's early mandali, May 17, 1926)

Seeking contact with a saint is always problematic, since both the East and West are full of pretenders. For that, though, we have the God-Man, who, said Meher Baba, is the highest of high roads. And selfless service is available everywhere.

Why the repetition of the divine name should be effective in spiritual work is interesting to consider. It is a form, however mechanical in the beginning, of remembrance of the Self. When we consider that the body of God's being is an infinite body of meaning-links (oneness shattered into manyness), it makes sense that any of the names of God, however initially barren of feeling, can reveal an inner richness that, once tasted, stirs even greater effort. The seeker who discovers that silent repetition of the divine name brings relief from anger, lust, envy, or pride has found a powerful tool for inner work. Though thinking of God by simple remembrance or by the repetition of his name may seem dry at first, eventually a stage is reached when each impulse of egotism—a coloring of pride, a whiff of resentment, a pulse of blame—creates an inner revulsion that itself is a reminder of the Self.

In *The Discourses* Meher Baba describes what he terms the *provisional ego,* a center of consciousness the aspirant can develop that initially imagines, but more and more feels, that the Master himself is working in and through him, working not only in the aspirant's service or so-called devotional acts, but in walking, bathing, eating. That's a truth discovered in these pages—that, given our bondage, it makes sense to suppose that it is always Infinite Intelligence that is experiencing through us. When this is merely an ontological conviction, its practice can be effortful remembrance. But eventually, as surrender deepens and contact increases, the aspirant feels within the ever-flowing presence of the Self.

Meher Baba:

> *The fire of divine love alone can destroy all impressions once and for all. However, remembering Me can keep down the impurities in the impressions in your mind, as alum catches hold of dirt in a vessel of turbid water. Therefore when you feel angry or have lustful thoughts, remember Baba at once. Let my name serve as a net around you so that your thoughts, like mosquitoes, may keep buzzing around you and yet not sting you. In that manner you can prevent unwanted thoughts turning into unwanted actions, and thus eventually bring your heart to the purification required for me to manifest...*
>
> (Quoted in Charles Purdom's *The God-Man.*)

The road, if you can walk it

Americans fondly recall the reply of Benjamin Franklin to the woman that stopped him outside the constitutional convention to ask what sort of government the delegates had created. Franklin replied, "A republic, Madam, if you can keep it." Spirituality, as it is called, offers a similar reply to the seeker: a road, friend, if you can walk it.

Involution depends and is begun by desire itself, the drive for moreness that was installed in every soul at the beginning of its journey. Desire, as noted, is the conjoined-at-birth twin of its sister, meaning, and not only leads each advancing soul through the grades of form that develop consciousness, but leads also to the final desire, the longing that begins involution and the journey home.

There are numberless souls, numberless destinies, numberless paths. The issue before all of us is how to get on the Path. The problem of good living has never been how to be the smartest person in the room (the ego's cherished goal), but rather how to be the most humble, most patient, kindest, most receptive, most thoughtful, most unreactive, most benevolent, most welcoming. Water, the Tao says, flows to the lowest place. Infinite Intelligence, and its manifestation as the inner master, is that lowest place, the fountaining source, the abiding isness within all ises, the ever-present consciously-making maker of all being.

It's not through the talk-talk of the intellect (this book, for instance) that the inner world is illuminated. Meher Baba and Aurobindo have said plenty about that world, but for those without experience—or the longing for it—all that is like a map of the ninth planet circling some distant star. Who cares! For those whose inner world is ripening, no doubt a welcome mat of explanation can be helpful, and that explanation is most fully given in *God Speaks* and *The Discourses* by Meher Baba. Of course, psychics, mediums, and plenty of minor gurus (many fraudulent and self-important) can offer descriptions of the inner world involving auras, astral visions, all that, and you can spend lifetimes sorting through the glitter of their explanations. That sorting will no doubt be part of the search for some. But when the emptiness refuses to abate, longing develops. That's when everything else is cast aside as a bylane—arresting, fascinating, and worthless. Longing wants love and nothing less. It doesn't even want religion. It wants the deepening of the inner being. It wants God.

Letter to Myself

Eventually, you'll get a taste for God.
Maybe you'll get everything you want someday,
And you'll say, why, it's just the same as if I didn't get it.
Maybe you'll get old and tired of being stubborn.
You'll say, all right, then, what?
Maybe what I'm saying now will turn a key in your heart.
But I know better than that.
The longing you are longing for
Must come most naturally, like hunger and courage,
And simple as sight,
The way shyness from a young girl falls
When love makes up her mind.
That's true, but also this,
That God is standing across a green field,
Shouting and waving his arms,
While you're munching like an ox with your head down.
Well.
Everything is simple
Because everything is true.
Every lie knows the truth it hides.

Therefore, eat.
Make a trail of dung.
Love has made God patient.
Time is his caress.
Still, take this good advice—
Make your trail straight.
Don't make it complicated.
And if you see something bright
Waving its arms from across a field,
Stop chewing for a minute.
Try to notice it.

The wasps of self and the Self

Even if the close-noticing in these pages has cleared for you the intellectual debris of the physicalist ideology or reinvigorated an incomplete theological system, it's still only thinking. For experience, as the poem *The Forest* given earlier suggests, you must "tear out all your chest bones to let the water in." As longing develops, we begin to build into our being the forces of honesty, patience, and the indefatigable resolve needed for the inner work. This work is destined for all, whether in this lifetime or another, and it will be done by each differently, with unique stresses, failures, and successes. If there is any enjoyment for God (other than his eternal infinite bliss!) it must be in guiding the numberless selves into which he has fractured back to the radiance of the Self. (That, plus jokes, which, said Meher Baba, lighten his load as long as they don't hurt anyone.)

The question becomes then, how to get to inner experience—which, by the way, is not a one-time event. You don't get enlightened and you're done. It's a process, like swimming up from the depths of the ocean into more and more sunlit waters.

We sometimes think of the self as that corrupt aspect of our being that wants little things, that scampering-about fellow in us that opines this, demands that, proclaims this, boasts that, and so on. He is the rascal always eyeing the last slice of pizza, and must be reproved, repressed, and guided. And true enough, sort of, except that he is also the fellow that repents, grieves, laments, laughs, weeps, and feels transports of freeing humility. The admonition of much modern psychology—learn to love yourself—can be confusing, since lots of our self is that first rascal, and he's already got plenty of self-love. Which is why psychology will eventually capitalize the *s* of Self.

The question then becomes not so much how to get rid of the self, which comes in infinite and conflicting flavors, but how to get to the Self, which comes in one flavor. For that, it makes sense to consider the self as the vehicle, not the problem. The problem is what the self wants, its clinging to habit, its defense of opinion, its reluctance to listen—in short, its desires. Inner noticing begins with longing, and longing begins when you've had enough triviality, emptiness, disappointment, and all-round frustration with trinket life. Longing rejects difference and condemnation because it sees the maddest, most improbable truth—all beings, great and small, are slaves held in the cupped palm of divinity. For everyone, the only hope and only solution is to go deep and big. Which everyone, when their time comes, will do. As we tumble down the long pipe of existence, however much we may bump against its walls, gravity draws us deeper and deeper and home.

So how to get deep and big faster? How to subdue those small desires that swarm like wasps from the hive of the unconscious? For starters, it's good to note that you've earned those wasps, not earned as a punishment (that's morality talking), but earned as a consequence of having painstakingly evolved your current consciousness, earned as a consequence of having been a plant, a bug, a bird, a baboon. That's the way you got *here,* and here, wherever here is for you, is where you start and the way home. You get angry a lot? You get depressed? You feel envy and pride and greed and lust? That's the waiting field of your adventure.

If you hold the door shut to the world within, you're guaranteed to keep those desire wasps clustered at the windows, beating their wings against your resistance. Better is to open the door and let them take a seat. (Don't offer them refreshments though!) That's how you see them—and then see past them. Because a secret those wasps don't know, a secret only longing can sense, is that the wasps of your desires are messengers. They are teachers produced by Infinite Intelligence to confuse, exasperate, and finally make tender some deep patience within. When that softness begins, you bounce less and less off the walls of the existence pipe and more and more fall centered toward home.

Meher Baba: *For the purification of your heart, leave your thoughts alone, but maintain a constant vigil over your actions. Let the thoughts of anger, lust, and greed come and go freely and unasked without putting them into words and deeds. Then the related impressions in your mind begin to wear out and become less and less harmful.* (from *The God-Man* by Charles Purdom)

The rest is time, the continuing gift of Existence.

Here's an apt poem from Vijay Seshadri (winner of the Pulitzer in 2014). It's called *The Long Meadow* and mentions "one of the old poems," the *Mahabharata*, which Vijay reimagines to suit his purpose. His purpose comes most beautifully in the last seven lines.

The Long Meadow

Near the end of one of the old poems, the son of righteousness,
the source of virtue and civility,
on whose back the kingdom is carried
as on the back of the tortoise the earth is carried,
passes into the next world.
The wood is dark. The wood is dark,
and on the other side of the wood the sea is shallow, warm, endless.
In and around it, there is no threat of life—
so little is the atmosphere charged with possibility that
he might as well be wading through a flooded basement.
He wades for what seems like forever,
and never stops to rest in the shade of the metal raintrees
springing out of the water at fixed intervals.
Time, though endless, is also short,
so he wades on, until he walks out of the sea and into the mountains,
where he burns on the windward slopes and freezes in the valleys.
After unendurable struggles,

he finally arrives at the celestial realm.
The god waits there for him. The god invites him to enter.
But looking through the glowing portal,
he sees on that happy plain not those he thinks wait eagerly for him—
his beloved, his brothers, his companions in war and exile,
all long since dead and gone—
but, sitting pretty and enjoying the gorgeous sunset,
his cousin and bitter enemy, the cause of that war, that exile,
whose arrogance and vicious indolence
plunged the world into grief.
The god informs him that, yes, those he loved have been carried down
the river of fire. Their thirst for justice
offended the cosmic powers, who are jealous of justice.
In their place in the celestial realm, called Alaukika in the ancient texts,
the breaker of faith is now glorified.
He, at least, acted in keeping with his nature.
Who has not felt a little of the despair the son of righteousness now feels,
staring wildly around him?
The god watches, not without compassion and a certain wonder.
This is the final illusion,
the one to which all the others lead.
He has to pierce through it himself, without divine assistance.
He will take a long time about it,
with only his dog to keep him company,
the mongrel dog, celebrated down the millennia,
who has waded with him,
shivered and burned with him,
and never abandoned him to his loneliness.
That dog bears a slight resemblance to my dog,

a skinny, restless, needy, overprotective mutt,
who was rescued from a crack house by Suzanne.
On weekends, and when I can shake free during the week,
I take her to the Long Meadow, in Prospect Park, where dogs
are allowed off the leash in the early morning.
She's gray-muzzled and old now, but you can't tell that by the way
she runs.

We are all on this journey, and, whether in the ancient Himalayas or in Prospect Park, whether alone or accompanied by a crack house mutt, we have come to solve the riddle of existence.

In a sense, the question is always about method. If you open the door of your awareness to the within, if you admit, as it were, the swarming wasps of your inner nature, how to endure their stings? How not to respond with anger, or hopelessness, or indulgence, or fall back into repression? It's intricate, confusing, and often, in the beginning, a fairly dry undertaking. In the East, in Vedanta, a term used to describe the early stages of the search is *tapasya*, meaning struggle, aridity, and sometimes thankless effort (what the "son of righteousness" endures in Vijay's poem). With persistence, the period of tapasya ends. And what follows is absorbing.

It's as if a prisoner gripping the bars of his cell finally turns to look behind him and finds there is no back wall, that beyond his cell is a meadow. And over the meadow is the sun. Are there mountains in the distance? So what? You were born for this journey.

The roads

As mentioned, there are plenty of yogas, practices, gurus, and self-help guides. Each soul that is drawn by longing will sort and sift through these, sometimes, say the Masters, for many lifetimes. This is called the spiritual search. Many begin in religion, and as the work deepens and that mapping begins to fail in subtlety, many turn to this or that guru, to meditation, some to hallucinogens, to parapsychology, to spirit helpers, to so-called ascended masters, to retreats, sweat lodges, this and that, on and on.

Though a formal notion of a consciousness-unconsciousness junction is fairly recent in psychological and philosophical thinking, it has been supposed, however vaguely, for millennia. It's always been natural to guess that something is going on the underside of everything (those forces called gods—more recently called archetypes and the collective unconscious—are part of that guess), and if we could just know what this something was, by any means whatever, we could know better and do better. Of course, our folk tales—the sorcerer's apprentice for one (the subject of a poem from Goethe but with ancient roots in many cultures)—are full of warning about knowing too much, knowing too soon, or knowing too little, and we all recognize in our own lives the blunder of rushing in with half-baked understanding.

But inner darkness is not the only issue. The other issue is inner complexity. We are hunting for our Self, and, even after longing arises, some part of our Self—our self—doesn't want to be caught. The small *s* self, our disposition, is built of a sanskaric desire-sheath that means to express itself, and therefore must protect itself—and find outlets—as this busybody aspirational search for the Self proceeds. Pride smuggles itself into selfless service. See what I did for them! Generosity is spoiled by resentment. See how ungrateful they are? Kindness becomes lust. We are both lonely so why not? Thus a battle begins, and since everything in the battleground is invisible and shape-shifting, and since the flags of morality meant to mark our inner geography are complacent and crude, as we begin we are wandering lost, sometimes for a long time.

But though the Infinite Intelligence peering through our sanskaric sheathe can seem dark and indifferent, it has another part that is infinitely light. And we can contact it. In Sufism that part is called the Friend, in Christianity the Christ, in Hinduism Krishna or Rama or Vishnu. The names of the Friend are many, but the Friend is one. The Friend is the inner master that is endlessly making the world.

Approach to this inner master is sometimes thought to be available solely through meditation, a practice which, starting when the *Bhagavad Gita* was rediscovered in the West in the early 1800s, has come to dominate the Western mind. (And, of course, there are plenty of atheist practitioners and teachers who declare that though meditation may not lead to God, since there isn't one, it's still good for calming down and mind-clearing.)

Meditation and mindfulness are popular because, for one thing, you can do it, and, for another, you can sell it. No doubt it also has the welcome property, for some at least, of clearing the mind. But a mind that is clear is not necessarily a mind that longs. Meher Baba once remarked that there were numerous yogis meditating in the Himalayas but said, "I do not go to them." When Mani, his sister, expressed admiration for a group of wandering mendicants, Meher Baba remarked, "You have passed that stage long ago."

Meditation is an act of will, and humility cannot be willed. Though meditation can calm the mind so the process of notice can begin, deeper forces must arise before the inner master appears. Honesty, which is courageous submission to what is, must develop. Patience must come. Insofar as meditation can begin notice of the shadow self, it can be of use. It can also, alas, become in the unready a focus of egotism and self-assurance, particularly in those whose contact with the inner realms is unguided by surrender and humility.

It's evident that many of the practitioners and guides of meditation and mindfulness are themselves beginners in the inner world. One such instructor wrote that when he and his colleagues met with the Dali Lama they all confessed that egotism, competition, and feelings of unworthiness were rampant among them. Ah, well. And so what? All this is natural, inevitable, and temporary. The vast and various practices associated with the spiritual search—many with a lineage that confers authority—can be considered, and employed or discarded. The soul takes its stand on need. And then on devotion. The soul is searching for its knees.

From Meher Baba's *Listen, Humanity:*

> *God does not listen to the language of the tongue and its japs, mantras, devotional songs, and so on. He does not listen to the language of the mind and its routine meditations, concentrations and thoughts about God. He listens only to the language of the heart and its message of love, which needs no ceremony or show, only silent devotion for the Beloved.*

One phase of Meher Baba's advent was his New Life period. Beginning in 1949, Meher Baba wandered, often on foot, for 30 months throughout India with twenty of his mandali. About that phase of his work, he said:

> *This New Life is endless, and even after my physical death it will be kept alive by those who live the life of complete renunciation of falsehood, lies, hatred, anger, greed and lust; and who, to accomplish all this, do no lustful actions, do no harm to anyone, do no backbiting, do not seek material possessions or power, who*

accept no homage, neither covet honor nor shun disgrace, and fear no one and nothing; by those who rely wholly and solely on God, and who love God purely for the sake of loving; who believe in the lovers of God and in the reality of Manifestation, and yet do not expect any spiritual or material reward; who do not let go the hand of Truth, and who, without being upset by calamities, bravely and wholeheartedly face all hardships with one hundred percent cheerfulness, and give no importance to caste, creed and religious ceremonies. This New Life will live by itself eternally, even if there is no one to live it.

A last note about meditation: according to Meher Baba, in Avataric periods, which last from 100 to 200 years, the path of love is made widely open by the Avatar's inner working. In those periods, meditation is less important or required.

Meditation may help clear the mind's clutter, but longing alone has the visa required for the trip. The question the seeker confronts is not so much how to obtain such a visa, since everyone has one. The question is how to locate it in the cluttered cabinet of your heart. Eventually, and more and more, the visa to the inner world takes shape as longing clarifies. And the journey begins.

The occult!

Earlier it was noted that even the most infinitely intelligent psychologist cannot effect change in a client by offering even the most precise map of their interior world. That's because though true maps reflect the what-is of experience, they are themselves *not that experience.* That's why psychoanalysis takes so long, and why the terms resistance, transference, reaction formation, projection—all the verbal paraphernalia of the profession—stand outside the event of one human being kindly and unreactingly feeling toward the within of another. That kindness and unreaction, the province of only a few of psychology's practitioners, is a form of love and welcome that encourages the hidden feelings of the patient to emerge from the mind's attic and integrate themselves with the psyche's conscious self. The term *resistance* in the above catalog reminds us that somewhere in his or her depths the patient must *want to change,* must long for integration. Neurosis may be an initial obstacle, but when it relents the real work of maturing begins. Aurobindo called his method the integral yoga because it called into consciousness not merely the excluded neurotic impulses of the attic mind, but also the lower vital impulses of lust, greed, and anger that protect the ego—and because his yoga did not insist on asceticism, fasting, or meditation, but instead, through submission and inner equality, was the work of gathering the fractured selves of the aspirant into the Self.

Spiritual practice is a struggle with our egotism. The Friend is the power that makes that fight luminous and provides an all-well-no-worries assurance. In the Friend alone do we find the infinitely subtle intelligence of divine love.

So what about psychics? What about ouija boards, astrology, mediums, remote viewing, ESP, spells, amulets, crystals, all the clutter of occultism? *The Discourses* by Meher Baba has several chapters on the occult, and points out that though the subtle and mental worlds are real, in fact realer, and supportive of, the gross world we are conscious of, information from those worlds gained from occult practices cannot be usefully integrated into our walking-around self, and so for the seeker is mostly superfluous. If a medium reveals that the birthmark on your stomach resulted from a spear wound that ended your life as a French knight five hundred years ago, interesting!—and so what? Also, the medium is getting paid, either in money or prestige, and may have an incentive to imagine—or lie.

While the study and experimentation with the occult can be useful in dislodging scientific dogma from the citadel of physicalism, and thus aid humankind in drawing a more accurate map of reality, for the seeker intent on integrating his or her own inner being, it's all a bit of the sorcerer's apprentice dilemma. Really, it's the same dilemma that psychoanalysis confronts—the integration of the invisible into the visible, the unconscious into the conscious—and depends on the welcome of sameness, which is, in essence, the welcome of love. We enlarge by recognizing sameness, but that process, because of the trillion-handed texture of our being, is an inch-by-inch accumulation that occurs now and now and now as we chug through the day. The insights that accumulate may seem like mouse-sized treats, but they are connected to the Self itself and require ever-deepening patience to assimilate and digest. The inner world is an infinitely complex layering, a mix of high-mindedness and self-excusing, where, as an earlier poem expressed, "loud-talking anger struts in the palm of love." Worse, occultism can plunge the too-green seeker into a world where the energies are powerful, enchanting, and sometimes subversive. Instead of swallowing mice-sized insight, the seeker can get lost.

Here's Aurobindo from *The Life Divine*, page 553:

> *We find that the contradictions and the struggles of our surface consciousness are largely due to the contrary or mutually discordant tendencies of our mental, vital and physical parts opposing and unreconciled with each other and these again to the discord of many different inner possibilities of our being and even of different personalities on each level in us which are behind the intermixed disposition and differing tendencies of our surface nature. But while on the surface their action is mixed together, confused and conflicting, here in our depths they can be seen and worked upon in their independent and separate nature and action and a harmonization of them by the mental being in us, leader of the life and body—or, better, by the central psychic entity—is not so difficult, provided we have the right psychic and mental will in the endeavor: for if it is with the vital-ego motive that we make the entry into the subliminal being, it may result in serious dangers and disaster or at the least an exaggeration of ego, self-affirmation and desire, an enlarged and more powerful ignorance instead of an enlarged and more powerful knowledge.*

No doubt the inner world must be entered, but it must be entered gradually, gently, patiently, and intelligently. If you think it would help, find a good shrink. But definitely get a good master. By whatever name, there's only one of those, the inner master within every soul, who, by the way, doesn't charge for his endless supply of mice.

Miracles, angels, parapsychology

Every religion has plenty of talk about miracles, talk which regrettably tends to reinforce the view that God is a fickle dispenser of boon to the favored. A better understanding of so-called miracles, one more in keeping with God as the infinite and continual emanator of the mental, subtle, and gross worlds, is that the superseding of physical law occurs from time to time when more mundane law is inadequate to perform the karmic purpose of the moment.

Here's a tale from *Lord Meher* concerning Sheriar, Meher Baba's father. As a young man, Sheriar left Iran in search of God, wandered to India, and eventually got lost in the Sind desert (now part of Pakistan). Soon he was dying of thirst and barely conscious. A man and young boy appeared with skins of water, revived him, then disappeared. Shortly afterwards, as Sheriar was again on the point of collapse, they reappeared, gave him more water, and this time the man directed him to a hermit that would feed him and also gave directions to a nearby town—and, incidentally, admonished him for troubling God with his foolishness. When Sheriar looked up to thank them, they had disappeared again.

A man and a boy mysteriously appear with water and vanish? Since that happening is out of the keeping of earthly law, we tend to pedestal it in our thinking as a special dispensation of God's favor. But while it is out of the keeping of mundane law, it is not out of the keeping of divine law. Sheriar's destiny was not to die in the desert, and, since there was not a good Samaritan available for divinity to inspire, God manifested a couple of *abdals*, or spiritual agents. But if this was somehow done by a special I-like-this-guy divine fiat, that makes God a meddler, subject to him-but-not-you caprice. It makes God subject to desire, instead of its creator. Which is inconceivable.

It makes better sense to consider everything—physical law, karmic law, and everything in between—as the precise, continual, and entirely ordinary grace of God, who is, after all, and who must be, after all, precisely, continually, and most ordinarily manifesting the oneness of creation as infinite love. So that: really speaking, there are no miracles in the you-but-not-me sense. Instead there is only and always the withness of God, the eternal miracle. So that: when God needs to quench your thirst in a good-Samaritanless desert, abdals manifest. (Also so that: if you're meant to die of thirst, he won't send abdals, and if you're meant to drown, he'll kindly direct you to a well.) And either, both, and everything are no-big-deal aspects of the eternal biggest deal, which is the creation, which is existence. This is useful to grasp, since that way, when you come across a miracle, or a coincidence, or some fascinating synchronicity, you can take it in stride. It's just the universe working to get you home. And no big deal.

The no-big-deal aspect of existence is also good to think about when it comes to parapsychology. Parapsychological experience is definitely different from our ordinary experience, and it means, yes, that the world as we receive it in gross consciousness is vastly superficial. The excursions this thinking has taken into the working of empathy, humility, and even metabolism point conclusively to ranges of being out of the notice of ordinary life, and also mean that everyone, ourselves included, are mostly dodging around the deck while the boat is being steered—with uncanny skill—from beneath the waves. When we become convinced of that steerage, the first and natural impulse is to find-the-controls and start steering ourselves. The market for these controls is burgeoning these days and includes meditation, mindfulness, precognition studies, remote viewing, extra sensory perception, psychedelics, yoga—all the variety of disciplines and methods for revealing and benefiting from the world beneath the world. As the subtle and mental worlds begin to open to humanity, we will naturally begin to find uses for the forces there and the fields of psychology, philosophy, physics, economics, ecology, politics, medicine, and even archaeology will be immeasurably changed—and hopefully enriched.

So are the possible adventures there cause for celebration? Sort of. The *sort of* is because exploration of the inner worlds, unless inspired by aspiration for the Truth beneath truths, can excite, bewilder, and even pervert. No doubt, the discovery of the hidden worlds can develop a more useful science of the universe. No doubt, discoveries there can confirm and elaborate the Path to the Self. But those worlds have always and notoriously been a distraction for the unprepared. When such efforts are only a dabbling at the shore instead of a dive beneath the waves, the conjectures that result are always incomplete and usually misleading. Rare indeed are those truly able to dive. Rare indeed are those who want to. But as longing ripens the soul, entry into the inner world is natural and automatic. The seeker's business is that ripening, and that business can be transacted everywhere and every day because, hey, here comes your worried spouse, or crabby child, or the next tired clerk.

And, by the way, here's a bit of interesting esoterica—the process of ripening, when you're in the keeping of a perfect one (the Avatar or a Perfect Master), does not normally involve the growing awareness of occult forces, called siddhis. It does always involve honesty and deepening poise, but Masters usually keep their close ones under a veil and out of danger.

The carnival of drugs

Now then, what of psychedelics? What of the modern vogue for mescaline, psilocybin, DMT, LSD, ayahuasca, and the like? Meher Baba's views on psychedelics are contained in a pamphlet from Sufism Reoriented entitled *God in a Pill?*:

> *To a few sincere seekers, LSD may have served as a means to arouse that spiritual longing which has brought them into my contact, but once that purpose is served further ingestion would not only be harmful but have no point or purpose.*
>
> *Medically there are legitimate uses of LSD. It can be used beneficially for chronic alcoholism, for severe and serious cases of depression and for relief in mental illnesses. Use of LSD other than for specific medical purposes is harmful physically, mentally, and spiritually.*

Psychedelics are powerful drugs which can sometimes, said Meher Baba, provide a glimpse of a shadow of the subtle world. They can provide a sense of being-becoming unmediated by thought and thus reveal the contours of our hidden selfness. After its effects are gone, though, consciousness is once again deposited into the drab world of stick figures and surfaces, the intricately-evolved theater of the desire-disposition with its trillion-handed, delicate, and insistent penumbra of impressions. Psychedelics, like exploration of the occult, are a too-crude opening of the vast delicacy of the psyche. That's because, as noted, only the highest desire, longing, is respected in the inner world and possesses the visa for entrance and exploration.

The vividness of psychedelics can be inspiring, no doubt, both for the seeker and for those stricken with obsessive desire formations. But their continual use is dangerous and futile. It's the sorcerer's apprentice all over again, the dumping of nonintegratable contents into consciousness. The growth of useful insight is in essence the growth of character, the plain-seeing from the now that develops honesty, kindliness, and love. That growth occurs only in the soil of a growing humility, and the pass to humility's chamber is need.

In the 1960s, when some of the young ones asked Meher Baba why psychedelics weren't worthwhile—after all, many had come to him after their use—he replied, "Airplanes bring you to India, but when they land, you disembark."

Longing is the only friend of the search and, when it becomes inexorable, crucial, and finally agonizing, everything else is tossed overboard. Longing is nothing but the anguish of God lamenting the darkness of his imprisonment. This is when humility becomes the steady receptive station of our being, the sole force that can adequately address the teeming desire-disposition. Through deepening humility, we more and more realize that we have never lived our own life, but that it is lived through us by the One in all. This is the state of surrender. Many are its counterfeits that obscure and distract, and one by one they must be confronted and rejected.

Reporters from the front

Early in the twentieth century as psychoanalysis developed—beginning with the work of Sigmund Freud with sexuality and continuing with Carl Jung's work with the deeper layers of the psyche—it became known that larger, deeper, and richer desires hidden in the unconscious could emerge and subsume a clutter of neurotic desires. Somehow the mysterious osmotic pressure of the talking cure, as it was called, made possible the emergence of hidden feelings in the patient so that at the end of analysis he or she felt within the emergence of a brighter, more integrated self. For many psychologists, the term *integration* has become indispensable in describing their work.

In his thirty-eighth year, in 1913, Carl Jung broke from Freud and began to explore his inner being using a method he termed *active imagination*. It was a method in which he permitted his fantasies to bloom and be overtaken by powerful imagos from within, personages with which he could converse and interact. He transcribed these explorations in a folio he called *The Red Book* (also called *Liber Novus*—the new book). This work continued for several years, and he reported that all his subsequent theorizing was based on those experiences. In essence, *The Red Book* contains the meeting of his conscious ego mind with the numinous personifications of his unconscious mind. The book is not philosophy and not even an organized psychology, but is instead a mythic travelogue. (Some of his biographers considered these years in Jung's life a kind of psychotic break.)

Jung did not publish his folio, and it was kept private by his estate for 48 years, finally reaching print in 2009. It's a book full of intricate paintings and careful calligraphy, and though Jung showed the book to only a few, he evidently lavished much attention on its contents over his long career. Yet in an important sense, the inner work of *The Red Book* was simply a figurative delineation of what we all experience in daily life—the tumult of egotism, the fraud of tissue-thin ideals masking hypocrisy, the chaos of fear, opinion, and self-justification—all made luminous in vivid personages that swarmed from his unconscious. The value of this exploration to him, and to the world, was that from it he developed a comprehensive psychology of the unconscious, a psychology, in fact, that knew well that there is a Self beneath the self. All neurosis, he held, can be understood as the self separating from the Self. Though his capitalization of *Self* was principally psychological—that is, not meant to posit the residence of divinity—he did consider the Self to be not only the home of his famous universal archetypes but also the home of all spiritual feeling and thought. All inner effort—whether intent on removing neurosis or in slimming the desire-disposition to encounter the inner master—is goaded and fueled by the same force, the longing that wants a richer experience of life. (Jung reported that when his patients discovered a reason for living their neurosis usually dissolved.)

After these explorations, Jung spent the rest of his life writing books and letters, seeing patients—and editing and refining *The Red Book.* He was an adventurer who could endure the turbulent meeting of his conscious mind with the shadow world within that invisibly guided him—and that guides us all. As he formalized these explorations into a psychology, his work was to find and advocate for a method of making the unconscious conscious. Though Jung was a psychologist, not a spiritual master, in 1959, when a BBC interviewer asked him if he believed in God, he replied, *I don't need to believe. I know.*

It's interesting to note that Bill Wilson (founder of Alcoholics Anonymous) wrote to Jung that Jung's statement to one of Wilson's friends inspired the development of the twelve-step program, a program that begins with surrender to a higher power. (Jung, it seems, had told this friend that his case was hopeless without a religious conversion.)

Most of us, of course, have little or no facility with active imagination, and those that do—artists, writers, and poets—are notoriously inept at finding the Self amid the multitudinous selves that arise from their inner debris. Jung was partly successful here, but his thinking rested content with revealing the contours of the unconscious through the study of symbols and dreams. More successful was Aurobindo Ghose, whose realization was greater than Jung's and whose psychological geography offers detailed phenomenology instead of symbolism. (He chronicled his early inner exploration in his *Record of Yoga.*) He discovered within himself an emanation of the Supermind of God, the Self. He discovered the force-presence of what he termed the psychic being, the inner master.

The disembodied—and prayer

A side effect of more widespread inner exploration will likely mean more conclusive contact with disembodied souls. For some, such contact can support faith and produce new insight. For most of us though, it's mostly time-wasting. If it's your loved ones you miss, be patient. You'll see them again. If it's knowledge of the invisible world you want, know that disembodied souls are not necessarily advanced (though many pretend to be). Most of them don't know which horse will win the Kentucky Derby anymore than the local tout. Maybe one or two know where your great-grandfather buried the gold, but they don't know who you should marry. Besides, here in our current embodiment is all the guidance we require, and we know that without consulting the disembodied. Figuring things out through introspection, through intuiting for the inner flavors of our feelings and thoughts, is our work. Blindly following even good advice, whether from priests or the disembodied, cools the heat of longing by imposing a gauntlet of thought-opinion. If in our occasional emptiness we need some short-form guidance, we have plenty: be honest, except to the Nazis, don't shout in the library to get yourself noticed, be kind to the next on-his-feet-all-day clerk you meet. In short, we have the golden rule, which perfectly fits the God-is-all view of existence. This is a key truth of creation and, at least for longers, it's plenty.

Unpacking the structure of these layered, nuanced, invisible, and mostly unconscious inner bodies will be the scientific labor of centuries—and may remain frustratingly obscure except to the experience of travelers in the inner worlds. But at least two features of this cosmic working are now worth considering, the use of prayer and the nature of maya, or illusion. A discussion of prayer leads to the always interesting, and plaguing, and baffling, idea of destiny or the will of God. A discussion of maya leads to the nature of knowing itself.

About prayer: the usefulness of prayer—about which university studies are so far equivocal—deserves careful attention. Since in these pages we are considering Infinite Intelligence as the actor and producer of his own play, the question comes: does he indulge in rewrites? Can we change anything with prayer? Rivers of ink have been spent considering that question. The idea that God can and should be solicited imagines him as outside the universe, overwatching on a celestial throne, ready to reward the deserving and punish the scoundrels. But this is the bad mapping of the olden religions and for modern thinking is off-puttingly absurd, since it implies a capricious interference in the established law and pattern of existence.

Besides, the question about God's interference in creation is misguided, since God, as the manifester of creation, is a continual and complete interferer. Any apparent deviation from so-called natural law is odd to us but natural to God—and as compulsory as the natural law it seems to disturb. So-called miracles are as natural as gravity and both issue from God's devotion to his creation.

Since karma is the perfect recording and effect of what we do and think and feel (on our subtle and mental bodies), prayer for an otherwise would seem to violate the law of being. Still, Meher Baba wrote this in *Beams on the Spiritual Panorama: If you pray with a motive to do good to someone, your prayer may actually bring about good both to him and to yourself.*

Yet he also said many times what he made clear in his Highest of the High message given on September 7, 1953 in Dehra Dun, India:

> *If I am the Highest of the High, my Will is Law, my Wish governs the Law, and my Love sustains the Universe. Whatever your apparent calamities and transient sufferings, they are but the outcome of my Love for the ultimate good. Therefore, to approach me for deliverance from your predicaments, to expect me to satisfy your worldly desires, would be asking me to do the impossible—to undo what I have already ordained.*

And yet he wrote this too, again from *Beams*:

> *Through repeated sincere prayers it is possible to effect an exit from the otherwise inexorable working out of the law of karma. The forgiveness asked from God evokes from Him His inscrutable grace, which alone can give new direction to the inexorable karmic determination.*

How to reconcile these seemingly opposed ideas—one, that prayer can help others, even change our own sanskaric disposition and affect our fate, and two, that God does not alter the divinely ordained working of the universe? They are reconciled by the notion that all existence is meaning and desire, the linkage-context of sanskaric patterning, and further, that the deepest patterning within us is the patterning of the sixth plane, the plane of feeling. When we move our attention to others in loving support we link our being-context to theirs in the invisible feeling world, and both our own being and theirs is enriched, because in the inner world there are no physical boundaries. When we move our attention to God, to our feeling-longing for the developing inner master, this contact too alters our inner disposition as blocks are dissolved and energies released—and hence our karmic patterning is altered as well. Again, from *Beams*: *The ideal prayer to the Lord is nothing more than spontaneous praise of His being. You praise Him, not in the spirit of bargain but in the spirit of self-forgetful appreciation of what He really is.*

The efficacy of prayer is not in altering the will of God, but in tuning ourselves to the presence of God. That presence automatically dissolves the habitual formations of neurosis and lower desire through the magnetism of higher desire, which is the Self, which is God. When we change the way we feel, we change our lives and destiny, because the deepest system of meaning-links that we are is altered by contact with the deepest, widest, and beginning link.

The dilemma and task of psychoanalysis has always been how to lever our deepest feelings into the light of consciousness. The cry of the existentialists was authenticity and was a cry for depth. Religion too, however formalized by doctrine, is an efforting toward depth. The thinking in these pages conjectures that our deepest feeling is the longing for the One in all, that the highest prayer is the expression of that longing (usually in silence)—and that through longing itself we are transformed.

Head work has its place in clearing the debris of bad thinking, but heart work is the real work. It alone can knead tenderness into the stiff knotting of the lower nature. In a sense, every moment of your suffering, every disappointment, every discontent, is that heart work.

The More You Give

The more you give,
The up you be,
The true you grow,
The more you free.
The free you dream,
The wings you lift,
The high you fly,
The sweet you gift.

The more you feel,
The tear you fall,
The soft you go,
The love you all.

Heart work prepares the path of longing. It leads to the inner master and real prayer. In discussing the head and heart, in mentioning the residence of feeling on the sixth plane of consciousness, we allude to the unknown and vastly complicated inner world. The structure of that world has been mapped by both Aurobindo, Meher Baba, and numerous psychologists, but not in perfect detail. In days to come, that detailing will likely become more and more clear, but entering and walking it will remain an inner adventure. The intellect can offer maps, but the heart alone can travel the within as it unrolls inch by inch.

So the question of whether God interferes is really a question about the nature of creation. In the truest sense, God is continually interfering, now and now and now. He is making all the stuff we see and is making the intelligence in us that sees. Everything, in short, is the will of God. The universe is the will of God. We are the will of God.

Which is why God doesn't remove the problems. The problems are the path.

When the question comes, did the Rays win the game so they would feel good, or so that the fielder and catcher would feel bad, or that some bets would be lost and others won, who can say? It's no doubt entirely orchestrated, and speculation about how and why is fascinating—and trivial. Because while no leaf turns without his will, none of us turning ones can know the deep cause inherent in that will. Those who claim God has directed them to do something are right, but not because he directed some particular thing and not others. Everything is directed or nothing is.

Wondering about the structure of the inner world is an effort to guess the will of God and is a task dangerous, futile—and important. It's dangerous because some fool is always saying he knows what Infinite Intelligence wants, and he can't, so he's deluded or lying, but now and then believed. It's futile because infinity is always out of reach for the merely human mind. It's important because the patient delicacy of thinking about such matters refines our sensitivity to the mystery of being.

We could spend lifetimes considering the intricate working of destiny, and in a sense all study—history, psychology, philosophy, even science—is that study. It's important to concede, though, that no notice of the past, however full that past may be of coincidence or synchronicity, can demonstrate we have found at work some special intention of God's will. The deep working of creation is magnificently and necessarily hidden. The sprinting right fielder can't be wondering about whether he's destined to muff the ball. As the saint said, if you want to know the will of God, consider the past. To believe we know the will of God for ourselves or our nation is egotism. God has no favorites. He's on everyone's side.

The important consideration is how to get home. From Coleman Barks' Rumi:

Only full overhead sun diminishes your shadow.
But that shadow has been serving you.
What hurts you, blesses you.
Darkness is your candle.
Your boundaries are your quest.
I could explain this, but it will break the
glass cover on your heart,
and there's no fixing that.

Let the glass cover do its work. Learn to long.

Finally this: every thought offered about the working of the inner world is best considered a how-about-this conjecture. This is what the best science has been doing for centuries in the physical world. As science turns its careful thinking to the subtle and mental worlds, no doubt a multitude of discoveries await. Since those worlds are hard to measure and require introspection to receive and conceive, thinkers whose longing has mastered their desire will have an advantage.

Maya—and mutuality

We have described received meaning as caught somehow in the catcher's mitt of already-established meaning, and this insight turns out to have a long history. It was described by the Master, Adi Shankara, as maya, as the mapmaker of mind superimposing a wrong pattern on experience, as when someone sees a coiled rope and thinks it's a snake. The world we experience is just that, a vast seamless superimposition of mind-forms, a catching of the oncoming in the mitt of already-established mind-forms. This is why we are urged in school to think outside the box. The boxes that confine us are exactly these mind-forms that obscure the truth (accurate mapping). The watchword of modern education is critical thinking, the thinking that notices the beneath penumbra of the mind-forms it holds.

This concept of maya as mind-forms leads us to a consideration of the first mind-forms that arose in intelligence as it evolved, and leads too to a fuller understanding of our imprisonment in the great mutuality that produces the evident-to-all universe.

Mutuality means that we read the same world, so that my impressions of existence are not an elaborate guesswork mysteriously coincident with yours. It would be only by some ten to the millionth improbability that all of us happen to make the same guess. Somehow the same near-enough meaning arises in everyone, and, though uncertain, bedeviled by error, and unhappily invisible, it contains a hand-off-the-rudder mutuality. Which is why honesty compels agreement.

Mutuality has always been one of the knottiest problems of philosophy—how do I know you and I see the same yellow, the same tree? After all, the only experience we have is our own. Maybe our experiences are utterly different, and we disguise that by using the same words. How to account for mutuality?

This way: the subtle and mental bodies that developed by long evolution began with the finest gaseous forms, which eventually gave rise to stone, plant, and so on. Since all meaning forms are compounds of previous meaning forms (we receive the new in the arms of the old) these experiences create the deeply embedded meaning forms that produce the trillion-handed gestalt-penumbra of all the meaning that inhabits us. Our top-of-the-mind sense of things developed from the ancient and most-primitive meaning forms of our earliest evolution—and in that early state is a vast and dependable sameness. (The Baskin Robbins of electrons has only one flavor.) Which means that the mutuality of our present noticing is founded on the fathomless mutuality of our beginning noticing. This is why psychology's idea of the collective unconscious—and the mystic's idea of cosmic consciousness—makes sense. The lens of our intelligence is produced not by materiality but by the dispositional structuring of our subtle and mental bodies through evolution. Only after long evolution, as the mind divisions imposed by culture and thought begin to oppose and contrast, do we seem to see things differently. Beneath difference though, and in fact supporting and manifesting it, is the unconscious infinite sameness of our beginning—and of our end.

As noted earlier, certainty is never a legitimate property of thought, but the supposition that your yellow is like mine makes good-enough sense to get on with painting the house, and the mutuality supposed by this view of evolution assures, however uncertainly, that we're both painting it the same color.

First-most knowing

Our earlier discussion of empathy invites thinking about the structure of the inner world, about the receiving and transmitting of inner moods, feelings, and intentions, not only from others but also from our own interior to our conscious front self. It's clear that some of us are aware of more of the inner world than others, and we call them sensitive, intuitive, and deep. As we consider how the psyche must be configured to account for states of depth, and how the back-and-forthing of inner states occurs, it's useful to recall how all knowing is configured. We have shown that mind, our meaning-station (whatever it may be), somehow receives new meaning through sameness. As in: I recognize that's a tree because it's like the trees I know. This is the law, property, and structure of knowing.

As noted before, if what I come to know is always in terms of what I already know, to break from the sameness-staleness inherent in the structure of knowing, we need the elder sister of desire. Desire opens us to newness, while the sterility of stereotypes creates the confinement and suffering of boredom. So that, alas, a main dilemma of living is that all freshness (a new car, wife, or pocketknife) eventually becomes the new stale as the desire that acquired them is made restless by satisfaction. This is why longing is the last and greatest desire. Longing has caught the scent of the Within that enlarges as we progress and thus never stales. Small desire for small freshness neglects the great freshness beneath every freshness, a freshness that only the deepening psyche can scent. Just as every meaning is a participant in the sameness of the One (Aurobindo described *knowledge by identity* as the understructure of all meaning), every desire is a fragment of the greatest desire, the desire for completist withness, which is the desire for God.

Now comes a discussion for the philosophically minded.

A question earlier posed in these pages was this: if all knowing is knowing by receiving the new in the arms of the old, how was the first knowing, in say, the electron state, possible since at that moment there existed nothing old to embrace the new, nothing for the new to be like?

This problem of first-most knowing turns out to be not merely the problem of first knowing, but the problem of any knowing whatever. In these pages the terms *intelligence* and *consciousness* have this difference: intelligence is meaning-getting-and-holding and consciousness is the on-or-off light of its manifestation. Both are primordial, without penumbra, and hence unexplainable. The meaning we get and the desires we feel are somehow *in* consciousness and intelligence, which is why we say "I have an idea," not "I am an idea." In that sense, consciousness-intelligence is partly the mind in which Being manifests, and partly the Being outside each mind, the stuff of the cosmos with its numberless particles and laws and the invisible (and mostly unconscious) subtle and mental worlds that underpin and structure the gross world.

When I say I see a tree, this *I* business that I unthinkingly proclaim does the seeing, is not the tree and not the tree-meaning in my mind and not the tree thought-memory I carry away after seeing the tree. All these are meanings that I have, not what I am. What I call my *self* seems to be some always-back-there intelligence and not any of the meaning forms it holds or presents. (When we consider expressions like "I am embarrassed," it's evident that we do not mean to say that we have become embarrassment. The expression is simply a pardonable convenience of language that shortcuts the more accurate expression, "I feel embarrassment.")

All meaning and desire then are the something-that-is-impressed on this always back-there intelligence, which helplessly—and interestingly—I continually concede that *I am*.

As intelligence accepts larger and larger meaning forms and larger and larger desires, it grows, and the amplitude of its consciousness grows, which, from the inception of every intelligence-bit into the universe, is what every intelligence-bit has been doing.

Returning to the issue of first-most knowing: when consciousness registers the first, most-faint meaning-impression that appears in the so-far unimpressed meaning-station of virgin intelligence (at the first moment of creation), intelligence did not envelope this first impression in a meaning-field already in intelligence (because in this most-unique case there was no waiting meaning-field already in intelligence). The essence of that first meaning (that first impression), *is meaning itself,* which, from this thinking, is the essence of Infinite Intelligence. Meaning can appear in consciousness without being received in an already-established meaning-field because *existence itself is intelligence which is meaning*. The existence of any meaning whatsoever—that the cosmos means itself in intelligence-consciousness—is the central and initiating fact of all existence. (And, by the way, the solution to the so-called hard problem.) This is why the first-most arrival of meaning in consciousness is possible without being received in an already-established meaning-field. After that first arrival, it is natural that every subsequent meaning form arrives in the arms of—and amplifies—prior meaning forms.

The Old Testament captures this beginning moment of creation in the phrase, "Let there be light." In the New Testament, John opens with "In the beginning was the word, and the word was with God." John and Genesis could have begun, "In the beginning was meaning." Though all meaning, after the first meaning, is received in the catcher's mitt of the meaning that preceded it and is, as it were, layered onto that more primary meaning, meaning itself is preliminary to all catching and layering, and is, in fact, the originating isness of God, the

Infinite Intelligence that God is and that we unconsciously are. We are, from the first moment, created, embedded, structured, and conscious of the meaning of divine intelligence. We exist in the mind of God.

It's interesting to note that in *Infinite Intelligence* Meher Baba describes the goal of creation as a return to that first meaning state—the stone state, as he calls it, the first most-primordial isness of meaning. That state is the least encumbered-by-impressions state of being, and the return to that state is a return to the originating isness of God. But now with full consciousness. In *Little Gidding,* T.S. Eliot said it well: *We shall not cease from exploration/And the end of all our exploring/Will be to arrive where we started/And know the place for the first time.*

Which is the purpose of creation.

The second greatest mantra

Alas, all this talk of God and purpose has a tendency to hush the voice and fold the hands. But hushed voices and folded hands are often—often mostly—masks of helpless hypocrisy and concealed agony. So gird your loins. It's time for the second greatest mantra.

The perfect master, Upasani Maharaj (who brought Meher Baba back to creation-consciousness after he was awakened by Babajan—a seven-year process), said the greatest mantra was: *Be as it may.* In that statement is the essence of surrender, the recognition that all existence is produced by the hidden will of divinity, and that coming in tune with that divinity is the goal of life. Upasani was what is known as a jalali type Master, often rough and abrupt, as opposed to the jamali type, who is rather more sweet and mild. Upasani went naked except for a gunny sack around his waist, sometimes drank the water with which he had washed the feet of lepers, commented that family life was all shit (in the next life your father might be your son, your enemy your brother). When Gandhi came to visit him, Upasani exposed his genitals to him and rebuked him for his worldly fame. Gandhi was alarmed and left in dismay. In 1931, on his way to attend the Round Table Conference in London, Gandhi met Meher Baba aboard the SS Rajputana and sat with him three hours each day. Baba assured Gandhi that Upasani was a God-realized Sadguru, a Perfect Master.

Therefore, we now present, in keeping with the jalali nature of Upasani, the second greatest mantra: *Om, motherfucker, om. Om* at the front because we come from God, and *om* at the end because we all get home. But in the middle, friends, sometimes it's a motherfucker. And sometimes it's us.

Really? A descent into obscenity in a spiritual discussion? But deeper reflection reveals hidden health here. Indeed, the alarm most of us feel at such a provoking term is a symptom of our isolation. Our prohibition against obscenity is too often a cover for a greater obscenity within.

For millennia humankind has been content to consider half of its existence as outside divinity, as too repellant for notice—even though, as it is said in the East, we are born between urine and feces. No doubt there's practical wisdom in some degree of moral conformity, since for the majority of people the strictures of propriety can keep the lower self at bay. That's why we cover our genitals, and why some cultures cover their women. Yet such conformity can obstruct introspection, and more, provide an umbrella of hypocrisy to hide and make palatable blame, indifference, and relentless competition. The penalty of conformity for seekers is that as they begin their journey they are often timid to question or oppose the exoteric institutions they have dutifully accepted from youth.

For those with little inner aspiration able to redirect their lower impulses the confinement of cultural mores make sense. But those who begin the inner search eventually find within themselves a welcome that excludes—and fears—nothing.

Since the passage to the Self is through the self, the self must be known. And so our spotless hands, scrubbed by aspiration and devotion, by meditation, prayer, and ritual, must be thrust into the mire of our selfness and come to grips with our inner nature, a good portion of which seems, at least at first, fairly loathsome. This coming to grips is challenging, because first, it's hard to admit it's required, second, it's hard to want to do it, and third, it's hard to know how to do it.

Thus morality becomes a mask that protects hypocrisy. Meher Baba:

> *With me, no one can live what the world considers a moral life. Here, we are concerned with spirituality, not morals. A spiritual life is not ruled nor bound by any principles. In a virtuous life, evil*

> *is suppressed and good surfaces; but the evil is still there. The bad sanskaras remain and have to be worked out, if not in this life then in the next or the one after. In the spiritual life, both good and bad sanskaras express themselves, and both get nullified. A spiritual life leads one toward naturalness, whereas a virtuous life, in the guise of humility, inflates the ego and perpetuates it!* (from Lord Meher, page 3668)

Padri, one of Meher Baba's stalwart early mandali and headman at Meherabad in his later years, was an inveterate cusser. When asked what Baba might think of that, he replied, "Where do you think I learned it?"

It's not that everyone must learn to cuss. It's that fear and timidity must be overcome. It's not that the shadow self must be welcomed and expressed. It's that it must be known. A well-scrubbed face immunizes the aspirant from inner contact.

No doubt the second greatest mantra may be unnecessary for the mature, but for those who come in search of God with hushed voices, it's therapy. Its courage dislodges obstruction and reveals external morality as a pale imitation of value. Such courage recognizes a higher chamber within where we stand surrendered, naked, and fearless before the measureless tenderness of love. Meher Baba: *True love is no game for the faint-hearted and weak; it is born of strength and understanding.*

Therefore, oh hushed-voice, folded-handed spiritual seekers, om, motherfuckers, om. Which, besides being happily lurid, has the further distinction of being true. Between the oms, sometimes things are hard.

And yet

And yet, Meher Baba also said: *The illusory values of usual things become insipid through familiarity, and the mind then has a tendency to transfer the illusion of value to those things which are not usual instead of trying to discover true and lasting values.* The second greatest mantra is not itself those values. It's only an exuberant knock at the door of Truth. It reminds us that when someone asks who it is, it's sometimes healthier to reply *an asshole* rather than *an aspirant*.

No doubt for those not yet awake to the inner world, superficial decorum, however formal and empty, maintains civility. And while the second-greatest mantra musses the hair of this civility, and is meant to, real decorum is natural to the maturing psyche. Real decorum is a kindly master of ceremonies reminding us to form lines so we can live together more agreeably. Real decorum is graciousness, and graciousness is love. Decorum's counterfeit, sanctimony, is lamed by repression and avoidance and is not wise, wide, or large. It is a mind-imposed unnaturalness, and is why the youth, artists, and comedians of every culture are in continual rebellion. No one rebels from love.

It's easy to see why real decorum gets confused with sanctimony. The conscious part of the disposition, the ego, is a master of masking, producing a train of eerily plausible but false front selves. These masks are useful—likely even mandatory in our long evolution—as we maneuver through our disposition's vast and conflicting desires. When the disposition says yes to this, it must often at the same time say no to that. Yes to feeling good about being pretty and smart, but no to vanity, so a splash of modesty across my smart pretty front, please. A splash of this, a dash of that, and over time the front self mask is a jumble of evasions, confusions, excuses, and uncertainties—in short, of bullshit.

The target of the second greatest mantra is that bullshit. When the bullshit is recognized, the inner orchestra begins playing.

And dancing starts.

Do a Little Dance

Oh, you holy ones,
Cut your hair,
Ask God's forgiveness,
Live in the forest.
For a hundred lifetimes,
You have trod his patient back
While grumbling of neglect.
Though you have forgotten him,
He cannot stop remembering you,
And though his loyalty binds you both,
In the forest neither kept nor keeper are to blame.
Broken friendship caused this ancient quarrel.
That friendship is more ancient still.
Live in the forest.
Let honest holiness begin,
And do a little dance while you cook your food.

Poetry, by the way

These pages have had recourse to poetry, so poetry's nature (and the rest of art too) is interesting to consider in the light of this thinking. Without launching a full inquiry into aesthetics, we can at least wonder about its use to the Self. We can learn that by examining how it works.

Anyone who has ever read a poet's work in an anthology and then thought to read more by reading his or her collected works, usually suffers disappointment. That's because everyone generally likes the poems chosen for anthologies better than the ones in collected works (undiscovered gems are sometimes found, of course), and this is because anthologized poems are the ones that have most and widely touched the human heart. Anthology editors possess those human hearts, and, like fishermen, make trophies of the best.

With fish, trophy selection is simple because you can weigh a fish. But how to weigh poetry? The best in poetry—sometimes that there can even be a best—is generally granted but always debated. That's not just because the response to poetry lies in the invisible within but because that within-response is buried beneath thought, mood, attitude, mentation of all kinds—and hard to get at and hard to agree about. But everyone who scents the Self agrees, and true poetry has caught that scent.

The scent of the Self pierces the layers of our externality by bypassing the mind-forms that construct and populate our front selves. True poetry is the Self's voice and expresses what we know and feel deeply but do not know or feel in stereotypical forms. What we know consciously is held in those front-of-the-mind-forms that create our intellect, attitudes, and opinions. What we know deeply *is felt and known always vaguely.* After all, the Self is beyond form. When that knowing becomes unvague, it means that it has been captured in the aridity of a thought, which is why poets and writers dislike writing that is too "on-the-nose." Adages, aphorisms, and bad poetry may point to a world of richer feeling but do not have the power to produce that feeling in us. Longing yearns for the substance beneath the sterility of ideas, and real poetry (and all real art) awakens that substance within us. Poetry comes when the house is empty and leaves a note on the door: *gift inside.*

Poetry works partly by technique—always with the satisfaction of rhythm, sometimes with the charm of rhyme—and partly by compression, the kindly service of swift meaning-delivery. But its real power lies in its resonance with and evocation of our many-flavored Self, the Truth beneath truths.

Rumi's line "Whoever brought me here will have to take me home," utters an entire theology.

The last stanza of Robert Burns' *To a Mouse*—"Still, thou art blest, compar'd wi' me!/The present only toucheth thee:/But Och! I backward cast my e'e,/On prospects drear!/An' forward tho' I canna see,/I guess an' fear!"—perfectly expresses the dilemma of our press-on-regardless ignorance.

Emily Dickinson's poem that begins *"To fight aloud is very brave..."* praises those who undertake the lonely inward fight against the lower self and ends with: "We trust, in plumed procession/For such, the Angels go—/Rank after Rank, with even feet—/And Uniforms of snow." The three-word phrase *with even feet* compresses with supremest brevity the regard of the soul for the silent self-effacement of the inner work.

Aurobindo Ghose wrote an entire book, *The Future Poetry,* elaborating the progression of English poetry through the ages. He concludes that the coming poetry will be colored more and more by the Self as the psychic being, the soul force within all, emerges in consciousness. The form-evading and depth-touching nature of poetry, and of all the arts, will remain one of the most valuable and essential guides of humanity.

This poem then, half verse, half poetry, half joke (so 150% of something):

Bag of Lions

Sometimes I think I should go on out to Africa,
Go on out into the wild Serengeti and get me some lions.
Get me a bag of, say, twenty, thirty lions,
Strong fresh lions!
Next thing, I haul that bag into some place like MacDonald's,
Just let it go.
The patrons will feel hesitant.
Is that lions in that bag?
Pretty soon they know the truth—
Lions in the bag!
Everything straightens out in no time.
Jealousy and anger?
Racism and belittling?
Ha!
Lions in the bag!
Not enough lions in the whole wide world to do the job right though.
So I send out poems.
Dum de dum de dum.

Those rascally others

As each soul moves along the path of its involution, it looks about and sees that others are still stuck in the hard-shelled gross world. And these people need a good talking to! Except that everyone's heard it all before.

But shouldn't we be trying to change the world? We should, if *should* means that we deeply and naturally want to. But the way that change occurs is bottom up, not top down.

Everyone knows that talking to an atheist about God—or to a preacher about a better idea of God—is like talking to a french-fry loving kid about spinach. It's hard to generate spinach interest by discoursing on nutrition. A kid's appetite, and everyone else's too, depends on taste. Someone whose appetite is ready, who is restless for largeness, can perk up, if only at the tip of their tongue, when they taste good ideas, but in the end God is love and moves taste by taste from heart to heart.

Here's Meher Baba on the subject, from *The Discourses*:

> *Love and coercion can never go together; but while love cannot be forced upon anyone, it can be awakened through love itself. Love is essentially self-communicative; those who do not have it catch it from those who have it. Those who receive love from others cannot be its recipients without giving a response that, in itself, is the nature of love. True love is unconquerable and irresistible. It goes on gathering power and spreading itself until eventually it transforms everyone it touches. Humanity will attain a new mode of being and life through the free and unhampered interplay of pure love from heart to heart.*

The separation we feel from others has all to do with front-of-the-mind opinion, and when we try to change opinion with merely better opinion, we inevitably encounter obstacles of pride, jealousy, and anger. It is the elder sister of desire that directs thinking, and only the force of love can prompt that sister to listen.

When the longing of humanity deepens, the nobility, tenderness, and self-forgetfulness that begin to shine from us are the forces that will change the world. So what about feeding the poor? What about working to vote those fools out of office? Feed them and vote, of course, but for the seeker all that is offhand work, forever incomplete, and can sometimes become a harbor of self-righteous ill-will. When Ali, grandson of Mohammed, was spat on by the man he was about to kill in battle, he sheathed his sword because he could kill in service to God but not in personal anger.

Given this dangerous world, of course, even though it doesn't make sense to hate Hitler, it sometimes makes sense to shoot him. Yet, alas, the effort to not-hate Hitler—and not-hate disease, cruelty, and death—is normally so unnatural it merely plasters on the face an unhappily frozen smile. In the poem *The Long Meadow* given earlier, this was the son of righteousness's dilemma. At the door of heaven he found his worst enemy exalted at the throne of God. As the poet said, *"This is the final illusion, the one to which all the others lead."* The world spread before each of us, so full of despair, injustice, and seeming imperfection, is God's embodiment, the infinite working of the dispositional contexts that produce creation. The heart of God is hidden from all but seekers. What is visible of his being is the pandemonius world. No wonder theology had resort to demons.

We all know love is best. But only some of us know it cannot be willed. Those who don't produce the thicket of thought we call political correctness, the mind-in-advance-of-heart conundrum that plagues a changing world. Political correctness builds an impenetrable world of ideation that justifies enmity. At bottom, political correctness is an impassioned condemnation of impurity, and its angry justification is equivalent to a child's cry, "But he hit me first!" But hating hate is still hate. Like an earthly parent, the divine parent within counsels tolerance, patience, and love.

Still, though the inner world changes only through longing and surrender, the outer world changes through new institutions. As Martin Luther King said at UCLA on April 4, 1965, "It may be true that the law cannot change the heart, but it can restrain the heartless. It may be true that the law can't make a man love me, but it can restrain him from lynching me, and I think that's pretty important also. So while the law may not change the hearts of men, it does change the habits of men. And when you change the habits of men, pretty soon the attitudes and the hearts will be changed."

So definitely vote. After long centuries of illusion and disconnection from the within, the out-there world is pretty much a mess.

Ah well, politics

At the Meher Center in South Carolina, Meher Baba gave several specific orders. One was to wear covered shoes because of snakes. Another was not to discuss politics. The feet can be protected by leather, but even the Avatar prescribed silence to protect against the fierce bite of politics.

The psyche is vulnerable to political dissension because all knowing in our press-on-regardless existence is fragile, and that makes us easy to fool and persuade. Political dissension persists because egotism is impelled by pride to protect its front-self thinking. In every psyche and society there is a contest between higher desire and thinking, intent on expressing the Self, and lower desire and thinking, intent on expressing the self. It's easy to agree that selfishness is the problem, hard to agree about the solution. The contest between the aspiration for new and less limited institutions and the preservation of however-limited-at-least-workable past institutions creates the opposition between progressives and conservatives, as they are called. In a pure world, a habitual preference for either position is easily seen as error. When rain is plentiful on Coconut Island it makes sense to liberally share the coconuts. In a drought, it makes sense to be conservative.

Still, natural good sense agreement between political opponents is possible and even inevitable when the deep mutuality within every psyche and society is revealed. Thought experiment: after the apocalypse, the last two people on earth meet beside a brook and discover they are on opposite sides of the political spectrum. Would their hearts be frozen in hostility? Or would their loneliness and grief unite them? After all, all they wanted in their old life was love and companionship, and that at last they have found. Would they not gladly let their political ideas slip into the water and, like everything human, wash to the sea?

If a conservative and progressive were each asked to make a graded list of human virtues, their lists might be ordered differently but would be generally the same and at the top of each would be love. Love wants to share the coconuts. Love wants fairness because it sees oneness.

Yet progressives and conservatives have always fought. At bottom, this fight persists because of the natural opposition between those who have and want to keep, and those who have not and want more. And alas, when the less-havers get more they too usually want to keep, which, say the more-havers, sanctions their own keepingness. Though the more-havers seem more selfish and less Selfish, they argue that they are in fact more Selfish than the selfish less-havers, since it is on their ingenuity, industry, and wealth that the welfare of all havers depends. And besides, those less-havers are lazy. Except that no one moves to the ghetto so they can be lazy.

Another complication is that the more-havers are always fewer in number than the less-havers, which in a democracy means that the less-havers have more votes, so the more-havers must find ways to get the less-havers on their side, which they usually can't—because usually won't—do by distributing their wealth, so they do by the emotionality of so-called culture wars, which broadcast that though the less-havers are not rich they are at least right. This makes the fight not so much about wealth as about esteem. There the fight can be long and malevolent, since hidden in the scolding attitude of both camps is the self-protection of proud egotism.

At its best, politics is simply thinking about the best way to live together. At its worst, it is the sanction of hatred. In an interesting sense, democracies are marketplaces where the currency is votes instead of money. Votes, like prices, are leveled by competition, which means that in a democracy if elections are not close, one or more parties have come to market with shoddy goods. It is the public's wanting that creates what politicians sell, and that market creates a nation. Statesmen, who help the public recognize true value, can change a nation—but only if the nation is able to listen.

When the discussion turns to politics, or even to economics, people whose temperament a moment before was generous and well-meaning, can become unforgiving, contemptuous, and derisive, reactions amplified by the self-interest of the media. The ferociously protected ideas of each side create a funnel through which humanity can pour the teeming venom of its shadow self. It would be an interesting experiment, and one useful for voters, if simultaneous with any political discussion or decision, each side would be required to argue convincingly for the position of the opposition. Failure to argue convincingly would reveal at least a lack of understanding and at worst a lack of scruples.

The justification for conservatism is that a hearty selfhood is best developed in a people freest from top-down management. The best justification for progressivism is that top-down management is needed to spread prosperity and reduce harms. The truth of both those points of view is simple to see, and if emotional allegiance were set aside, decisions by public servants would be no more troublesome than deciding where to build a bridge—consider the traffic and the public welfare.

Political thinking is always intellectual combat, and while such combat may sharpen ideas it is helpless to produce agreement. No one in a public forum, especially given today's social-media badgering, can afford to say, hmmm, I didn't think about that. Few are those who can wonder together even in private. In most political argument, however high-minded and smiling, as opponents listen to one another, each is alert for that fatal *but,* as in, "I like your thinking, but..." Too often, that *but* echoes down the dark hallways of egotism where sits pride with its feet dangling fretfully over the void of its ignorance—and reputation.

In an important sense, politics is always about the cause and remedy of inequality—in short, about poverty. Poverty is easy to deplore in foreign countries, but in one's native place the issue plucks at the heartstrings of self-interest—if they get more, I'll get less. Besides, the question reasonably comes whether a society should permit poverty so that the poor are incentivized. Yet any society which permits poverty without first making provision for the children of the poor is perpetuating the problem it is trying to correct. Poverty creates far more hopelessness than ambition. No doubt, as Jesus said, the poor will always be with us, and clearly, sometimes the cause is within the character of the poor themselves. But recognizing that fact without also acknowledging that economic hopelessness produces emotional hopelessness is short-sighted and self-serving. Further, the cause of poverty is just as clearly sometimes in the character of the wealthy. If some are destined to be poor as their soul's corrective—the well-known sanction of caste that has paralyzed India for millennia—does destiny also sanction the indifference of the rich? The leper outside the ice cream shop asks for more than rupees. He asks for recognition. The sense made in these pages is that every form of selfishness is a mask concealing the Self, and the solution for all, poor and rich alike, is the discovery of oneness.

Change is coming, but its slow pace can be torturous, especially for the young. Yet the changes Self-recognition produces are usually permanent. Consider the institution of punishment. The historical movement of criminal punishment has been from public torture-to-death to public execution to hidden execution to no execution. Some countries now even provide prisoners rooms with TVs, good food, education, and considerable freedom of movement, conditions which are found to reduce recidivism. Perhaps some future prison, instead of being hidden in the countryside, will be a compound of glass rooms built inside factories and offices so prisoners are isolated but not excluded. This would produce two salutary effects, first in the public, who would no longer see criminals as entirely other, and second in criminals, who would better understand their commonality with the world they had offended.

The political solution awaiting humanity is not perfect social institutions, but a more perfect society. Institutions evolve only as a people evolve. In a society of scorpions, everyone must be jailed. In a land of saints, laws are not needed.

The current political turmoil in the West is why Churchill commented that the worst form of government is democracy, except for all the others, and why Jefferson said the government you elect is the government you deserve. Democracies are notoriously vulnerable to demagogues—the first democracy killed Socrates—and our age of clamorous electronic communication gives the talk-talkers of both sides a megaphone. The media, whose income depends on the let's-you-and-him-fight formula, is mostly helpless to rise above its own interests. In politics, the smart money bets on hatred because that force is always the most accessible—and because what hatred promises it can deliver. Love, though the top of everyone's list, manifests slowly and at first can only wring its hands and squeak. Whether some form of more enlightened democracy prevails in world government, or a less restrictive socialism, or even Plato's leadership of the wise will be determined not by argument but by the inner emergence of the deep commonality natural to the soul.

Meher Baba:

> *When the worker launches upon his spiritual work he enters a field of divisions to which people cling desperately, which they accentuate and fortify, and which they strive consciously or*

> *unconsciously to perpetuate. Mere condemnation of these divisions will not enable the worker to destroy them. Divisions are nourished by separative thinking, and they yield only to the touch of love and understanding. People must be won to the life of truth; they cannot be coerced into spirituality.*

Here and there the voice of the Self is heard. Here-and-there noble spirits speak, and more and more their voices are welcomed. There is a fluid currently rising through the tangled veins of modernity—so say the seers—that will transform everything.

The finest time to be alive

Here's a bit of cosmology for the interested—and because awareness of the vast cycles of time in creation point both to God's imperturbable patience and our own frenetic impatience.

According to Meher Baba in *God Speaks*, each Avataric age consists of eleven periods from 65 to 125 years so that the Avatar appears on earth every 700 to 1400 years. Yet this cycle is itself part of a far vaster cycle. From Meher Baba's Final Declaration:

> *My next advent, after I drop this body, will be after 700 years, and that will mark the end and the beginning of a cycle of cycles. All cycles of time in illusion end and begin after 700 to 1400 years. There have been and will be millions and billions of such cycles in a cycle of cycles. Thus, there is no end to illusion, which always remains illusion.*
>
> *When I speak the Word, I shall lay the foundation for that which is to take place during the next 700 years. When I come again after 700 years, the evolution of consciousness will have reached such an apex that materialistic tendencies will be automatically transmuted into spiritual longing, and the feeling of equality in spiritual brotherhood will prevail. This means that opulence and poverty, literacy and illiteracy, jealousy and hatred, which are in evidence today in their full measure, will then be dissolved through the feelings of the oneness of all men. Prosperity and happiness will then be at their zenith.*

Avatar's work is always to release into the world a flood of divine sanskaras so that an invisible force of oneness-recognition begins to rise and consolidate in world consciousness. The current political squabbling, self-righteous anger, and even war are merely the ever-more-shrill protests of those unmoored by changes they cannot trust and absorb.

In one of the chapters of *The Discourses, The New Humanity,* Meher Baba wrote:

> *In the light of the Truth of the unity of all life, cooperative and harmonious action becomes natural and inevitable. Hence, the chief task before those who are deeply concerned with the rebuilding of humanity is to do their utmost to dispel the spiritual ignorance which envelops humanity.*
>
> *Humanity will attain to a new mode of being and life through the free and unhampered interplay of pure love from heart to heart.*

Things are changing, but our dispositional contexts develop so subterraneanly that change is difficult for most to notice. After all, even as we gaze at our own childhood photos it is rare that we can empathize with the child we were. The work of historians is to pry at the fabric of the past and wrest insight from a world submerged in memory and relic, but from them we mostly learn the dates of battles. Only sometimes, and then confusedly, do we sense the mindset of past ages. It's hard enough to see the mindset of our present age.

Today, though, we have film and audio, and even in the short time we have possessed those two we can see the evolution of consciousness. When we watch movies from the fifties they seem stilted, sentimental, and rote (though now and then, of course, we find masterpieces). Those films were attuned to the dispositional contexts of those living then and can no longer move the developed sensibilities of today. This alteration in mindset has been invisible yet came about in a mere half century.

Depth is coming. The Avatar has done his work. The supermind, as Aurobindo wrote, is pressing into the world's consciousness. The age of intuition, said Meher Baba, is beginning to ripen. We are repelled by the simplicities of religion, but the angst of the modern world is generating acute need. Gurus and guides abound. The idea of a higher power has rescued millions from the grip of addiction. Phrases like *don't be a hater* and *it's all good* are in common parlance. According to Google's Ngram viewer, which records word frequency over time, the words *conscious, unconscious,* and *intuition* have been dramatically increasing in use since the last half of the twentieth century. We have even come to explore, through the James Webb telescope, the genesis of the universe itself. New ideas and a developing science are stirring the pot. But the heat that cooks comes from elsewhere. And is building.

Though the highest path may be through the most recent Avatar, we will all follow what path we can. Some will remain atheists yet still celebrate nobility. Some will hold this Avatar dear but not another. Some will fall under the sway of this guide, some of that. As Meher Baba's spokesman, Eruch Jessawala, said in Mandali Hall, "We have not come to search for God. We have come to pursue him."

The scent of God is powerful today and is coming from our own depths.

The Rose Caravan

This book began with a thought experiment and ends now with a folk tale.

During the devastation of a war, Adi, a young boy, is separated from the father he barely remembers. One day in the busy city market he is aided by an old woman who gives him a rose meant for his father, a mantra meant for his soul, and a daring task.

We are all Adi. All of us bear the same rose and the same mantra, and all of us have been set the same task.

The Rose Caravan

A small boy, barefoot and wearing only a dingy loincloth, made his way through the crowded bazaar. His eyes, though they saw a good deal, seemed fixed on the ground—a boy who does not see much is also not much seen. And he was hunting his breakfast.

He had only two possessions, a wooden flute he had found some years earlier and which he kept tucked into his waistband, and a worn gunny sack into which went the day's forage—a piece of fruit, a few sticks for the night's fire, a piece of bread. Except for the pale heart-shaped birthmark on his shoulder, his skin was sun-browned, and he was brown-eyed and wore his long brown hair tied behind with a piece of string. His overall brownness was another advantage for a boy seeking his breakfast, because a brown boy blended well with the brown city and its brown shops, brown streets, brown people, and dusty brown sun.

As he walked and dodged through the crowd, from the corners of his eyes he watched for an untended banana, a mango, an apple. He did not steal, not in the sense of taking someone's purse or wallet as some of the lost children had learned to do, but if a banana had detached itself from a bundle of bananas on some peddler's cart or shopkeeper's stall, and if that banana was lying close to the passing crowd, was offering itself in a sense, why then, yes, it might slip or tip or slide into his gunny sack. Yes, that was permitted by his conscience, which was a practical conscience and understood that if it did not permit this bit of fruit piracy, the boy might starve. And if the boy starved, his conscience would starve as well.

His name was Adi. He was twelve years old, though he himself did not know this, nor did he know how he had come by the name Adi.

There was, however, a disadvantage in keeping one's eyes downcast, and the disadvantage was that policemen, whose brown uniforms also blend well with brown streets, are hard to notice. Then suddenly they are on top of you, drawing back their hand for a slap or reaching out for your neck, as the one directly ahead of Adi was now doing. But Adi, seeing the policeman's brown boot, lifted his eyes in time and ducked. The hand missed its grip, and Adi darted away through the crowd, leaving in his wake a shout and several irritated glances from the townspeople.

Life in the city became more risky every day. The king's marriage was close at hand, and the king wanted nothing to spoil the arrival of his new queen. Though the dust brown city could not be made white, at least it could be cleared of riffraff, at least the lost children could be swept up and confined in the orphanages.

There had been a war, and the war, as usual with wars, had been a clumsy harvester, taking a parent here, dropping a child there, tumble jumble. The army of the enemy had retreated, but the army of orphans remained.

Adi heard tales of the orphanages from children who had escaped. It was not only that they were filthy, with scanty food and cruel masters. It was that they were hidden away in the forests—why should the busy townspeople have to witness such misery?—and there Adi knew all hope of finding his father would end.

His memory of his father was so worn by daily use he was no longer sure what was memory and what had been added by loneliness. But when he brought the memory out, as he did from time to time during the day and at night playing his flute for the other children under the bridges or in the fields—then in his mind he saw a tall man with broad mustaches, clear deep eyes, and a bright smile. Was it truly his father? Did he truly believe he would find him one day? It was a dream from which he could not afford to awake. Without hope, he could not have endured.

An oxcart piled high with sugarcane came creaking and cracking down the stony lane, its ox pulling hard, parting the crowd with its broad horns. Adi, mindful of his bare feet, scampered to the side. And as he did, he tripped on something soft and small, something which gave a short irritated cry.

"Ho, boy! Have you eyes?"

Whether or not he had eyes no longer mattered, since he was falling, and falling directly onto this soft, irritated something. At the last second, he twisted and came down with a plop beside it. It was an old woman in a tattered gray robe, sitting in the dust of the lane. She was more than old, she was ancient, shriveled and shrunken like a mummy. Her hair was a white halo and flecked with bits of leaf and straw, so that Adi's first impression was that it was infested with insects or spiders. He drew back.

She seemed to be smiling, but it was hard to tell, since her lips were thin and nearly lost in her many wrinkles. But her eyes, blue and watery and set deep in her brown face, sparkled like gems, and when she spoke, her voice was clear and strong.

"Good you have found me. But you might have broken me in pieces, and where would we have been then? You lost and me in pieces!"

"Please excuse me," said Adi, getting to his feet. "I'm very sorry." Though the old woman seemed kindly, he had no time for a crazy person. He had a breakfast to get.

"Going?"

"Yes, I—I have—yes, I'm sorry. Goodbye then."

He turned and threaded his way through the crowd. He felt the old woman's eyes on him, and for some reason had a powerful desire to look back. But he resisted. The city was full of peculiar people, each with a life and a tale, but a lost boy, if he meant to eat, had to tend his business.

At last, behind a tea shop, he found three rice cakes that had slipped under a crate. Though they were a bit dusty and one partly eaten, they would make a fine breakfast. He deposited them in his gunny, then went back up the lane toward the central well to wash them.

Then something odd happened. Again, an oxcart, this one laden with bags of grain, pushed through the crowd, and again Adi moved to the side. And again he stumbled on something soft. And again the soft something cried out.

"Ho, boy! Do you mean to crush me?"

He came down with a plop at the side of a stall and stared at the old woman. He was frightened now because definitely there had been no old woman in his path an instant before. So that meant here was a witch! Or a goblin! What to do? Run? No, a witch that can appear anywhere, how can she be outrun?

As these thoughts flashed through his mind, she said, "Not a witch. No, no, not a witch."

Had the old woman read his thoughts! Or had he spoken aloud in his fright? He stared at her. Then, taking courage, he sent out a thought: who are you?

But she tilted her head and with a slight frown said, "Not like that. You are the boy Adi who is looking for his father?"

Adi nodded. Then he felt something warm, like a warm fluid, or a force like a fluid, flood up from his feet and through his legs and into his chest and out the top of his head. And his fear was gone.

He heard himself say, "Yes, I am Adi." He was suspended in the fluid, floating in it. In years to come, he would recognize the feeling as love. The old woman smiled, and the warmth that came up from his feet and out the top of him pressed two tears from his eyes.

The old woman's smile faded, seemed to draw back into her. Though he knew that he was not moving, he felt himself drawn toward her, and her face, now serious, glowed brighter.

"Listen well," she said. "There is a caravan leaving from the eastern gate at noon. It will take you to your father."

"My father? How could—how will—"

"No time for talk! It's nearly noon!"

Adi's mind could not seem to form thoughts. He said, "At the eastern gate—"

"Have you a gift for me?"

A gift? What gift? Adi tried to think. Nothing came.

With a swift motion—a motion extraordinarily swift for such an old person—she reached forward and lifted Adi's gunny from his back. As she did, her nail scraped across the heart-shaped birthmark on his shoulder, and bright flecks of blood appeared. She scooped the sack onto her lap. Then from the folds of her garment, she produced a rose.

"The rice cakes are for me," she said. "This rose is a gift for your father. Mind you give it to him. Now up!"

She rose quickly to her feet. Adi also got up, lifted lightly by the warm force.

She gazed intently into his eyes, then said, "This thought keep with you: Give all and you will get all."

With that, she turned, and walking nimbly, an instant later was lost in the throng of townspeople.

Adi stood, trying to think what had happened, but his mind was useless. Gradually and by degrees, the warm feeling drained away, and thoughts began to form again until at last he was himself, a hungry child, alone in the bustling city. Had it been a dream? Was the old woman a witch after all, a spell-caster? Was she a swindler after his rice cakes? But she had known his name. And she had known about his father.

But it was not these facts—not facts at all—that made up his mind. It was something else about her, something hard to name, something in her smile or in the air around her. He trusted her. His heart began to pound. His father! The caravan would take him to his father! Holding the rose before him, he set out for the eastern gate.

The rose was dark red and perfectly formed. It spread its scent around him like an invisible cloud. A gift for his father! He bent his head to inhale its fragrance, then instinctively drew back. It was a gift. To enjoy it for himself would have been unfitting.

The sun, he realized with a shock, was nearly overhead. The caravan was leaving at noon! He began to run, only trotting at first, weaving in and out of the crowd, then ran faster and faster as he reached the end of the bazaar. He passed through street after street, his feet flying now, his breath coming in ragged gasps.

At last he entered the caravan muster grounds. And his heart sank. It was empty! No camels, no drivers, no heaped goods.

But there! Across the grounds, passing through the eastern gate, were the last camels of a caravan. There was no time to beg passage or watch for a chance to stow away. In an instant, he saw his only chance—the city wall!

He raced across the grounds and up a flight of stone steps. Then he was running across the rooftop veranda of a home.

A shout! "You, boy! Stop there!"

A family, a man and woman with two children near Adi's own age, looked up from their lunch. The woman shrieked. The man rose, seizing his walking stick.

Adi reached the edge of the veranda, and without breaking stride, leapt onto the low stone wall and sailed into space. He soared over an alley that separated two houses and landed in a rolling heap on another veranda, still cradling the rose at his chest.

In the center of the veranda, an old white-haired woman sat under the shade of an umbrella. She was dressed in shining silks, her hair set with gold combs. As he raced to the opposite wall, she turned toward him. Her smile was bright and piercing, and he stopped, astonished. Was it she? Was it the witch! With a flick of her wrist, a lift of her chin, the old lady motioned him on, as if to say, Hurry! No time!

He leapt onto the wall at the verandah's edge. Below him passed the last camel of the caravan, heaped high with carpet-covered goods, the driver nodding sleepily under his red turban. Adi crouched and placed the stem of the rose between his lips. He glanced behind for a last glimpse of the old woman, but—amazing!—she had disappeared.

He leapt! He landed on the bundle not three feet behind the driver, who continued to nod sleepily. Quickly, Adi wormed his way under the carpets, curling his body around the rose. A moment later, exhausted and lulled by the camel's rolling stride, he was asleep.

He opened his eyes. The camel's motion had stopped. He listened, then slowly lifted an edge of the carpet. Night had fallen. The camel had settled onto the earth to sleep. The driver had disappeared.

Then Adi caught the pungent scent of wood smoke and more—food!

He slid down from the camel. A sea of sand stretched away under the moonlight like frozen waves. A line of five small campfires burned in the night.

How long it would take to cross the desert to his father he had no idea. But this he did know—without food and water he could not survive. Perhaps, if he were careful, he could creep close, and while the people slept, find what he needed in their stores.

He crouched and moved silently toward the nearest fire.

As he drew closer, he saw the three men sitting before the fire were not sleeping. Still, the fire would make them night-blind. He could move close unseen.

He placed the stem of the rose between his lips, then sank to his belly. He crawled, keeping his face to the sand so his eyes would not gleam in the firelight, and was soon near enough to hear their conversation.

One of the men, a small man whose bony shoulders poked into his cloak like sticks, laughed heartily.

"Ha! With the epidemic raging, I'll make a killing! Did you hear? With the epidemic, I'll make a killing!"

Adi recognized the man across the fire from the small man as the driver of the camel he had stowed away on. His hands were studded with jeweled rings, his tunic draped with golden chain, and his black beard tied neatly beneath his chin. He said, "Oh my, not only is our friend an apothecary, but also a comedian! A killing, eh? Ho ho!"

Then the jeweled man made a serious face, as men often do when they are preparing to utter a boast. He said, "No doubt your herbs and medicines have some worth, but if you threw aside the carpets of my camel, your eyes would dazzle. The jewelers are panting for my goods! Need I say more?"

"No, indeed!" said the apothecary, suitably impressed.

But the third man, a tall young man who sat hunched over his knees further back from the fire, said nothing, and was perhaps not suitably impressed. The jeweled man reached to prod him with a forefinger.

"Eh, brother musician? What have you to say? What is your cargo?"

The young man, whose simple shirt and worn turban spoke either of indifference to money or a lack of it, stared moodily into the fire and was silent.

"Speak out," said the merchant. "No shame to be poor."

The young man made a quiet smile. He said, "I carry a substance brighter than gems, my friend."

"Oh, ho!" said the merchant, with a broad wink at the apothecary. "And what can that be? Perhaps he has bottled sunlight! Something brighter than gems!" The merchant glanced at the apothecary, who rewarded this wit with a chuckle.

The musician said, "My camel carries only my worldly goods. But in my heart—" The young man touched his breast and spoke without embarrassment. "—I carry love."

"Ah," said the apothecary, suitably impressed.

The merchant glanced irritably at this turncoat apothecary, then addressed the musician. "And who is the object of this bright love?"

"Her name is Mehera."

"Mehera?" cried the apothecary. "The sardar's niece!"

"Yes," said the young man. "It is my misfortune to love the niece of the caravan master."

The merchant sneered. "How easy to profess love for what is so far! You're a dreamer! This is fantasy, not capable of fulfillment."

The young man's expression did not change. In a tone that caused the merchant to frown and the apothecary to raise his head, he said, "What has love to do with fulfillment?"

The apothecary nodded thoughtfully.

The musician continued, "Love's joy is in it's being. Whatever it touches, it enriches. Whatever is offered from the heart has more worth than jewels."

Suddenly the musician sobbed, and his head dropped forward.

"What's the matter with him?" demanded the merchant.

The musician did not speak.

"What is it, brother?" asked the apothecary softly.

Now the young man lifted his head, and they saw an expression of piercing misery. "I told Mehera I would bring her a rose tonight as a seal to our love. All day I searched the city without finding one."

"Alas, brother," said the apothecary. "All the flowers have been claimed for the king's wedding."

The merchant sneered. "Good you didn't find one! The sardar would have had your head on a spearpoint. Haven't you heard that his niece is already promised?"

The musician did not reply.

"Besides," said the merchant. "Did you think a mere flower could capture the love of such a beauty?"

The musician raised his head. "The rose was meant to express love, not to capture it, my friend." With that, the young man stood abruptly and strode into the night, passing not ten feet from where Adi lay in the darkness.

When his footsteps faded, Adi lay quietly for a moment, then crawled toward the fire. His heart beat heavily, charged by the young man's words and his own daring plan.

The merchant and apothecary stared moodily into the flames, each occupied with his thoughts. When Adi reached the musician's seat, he brought the rose to his lips, then laid it on the young man's blanket.

At that instant, the old woman's face appeared in his mind. She had told him to present the rose to his father, and he had disobeyed. But her face was smiling. With a throb of joy, he recalled her words: "Give all and you will get all."

Now he heard footsteps and crept quickly into the darkness. The steps passed nearby, then at the fire, they halted. He heard the musician cry out, saw him stoop, then straighten, staring at the rose as if dazed. Both the apothecary and the merchant had risen to their feet. Their faces revealed their astonishment.

The three men stood silently as tears gathered in their eyes.

The merchant spoke first. His confidence had vanished. His voice was thick. "It seems we have witnessed a miracle."

"Yes," said the apothecary.

"Yes," said the musician.

The merchant turned and walked to his camel. He returned with a golden silk sack which shimmered in the firelight. He said, "I confess this: I sought happiness in riches but remained empty. Tonight a rose has filled my heart with love. Into this cloth I discard my old life as an offering to the Maker of All Miracles."

The apothecary nodded. He said, "I like this," He went to his camel and returned. "I have cured men's bodies, but tonight I have seen how souls are cured. I too make an offering from my old life."

The musician brought the sack to his blankets. They saw him unwrap something and place it inside. He turned to them, his face glowing. "I will leave these offerings in the wilderness. Then I go to Mehera's fire. I have a gift for her tonight!"

The musician strode into the desert night. Fifty feet from where Adi crouched, he stopped and placed his burden on the sand. He folded his hands, bowed low, then turned and set out across the desert.

Adi, his heart pounding, crept to the sack. Give all and you will get all! How quickly those words had come true! He fumbled for the sack's opening, excitedly feeling its bulky contents. But then, as his fingers found the drawstring, he stopped. Give all and you will get all! Had his father's gift been traded merely for the contents of a sack? Was this—all? Across the desert, he saw the second fire and understood in an instant what he must do. He hoisted the sack onto his back and set out.

At this fire, there were also three men gathered. One, a short, burley man whose brow was wrapped in a flowing red bandanna, paced and gestured as he spoke.

"How I dread this desert crossing. Nothing but sand and silence. I am a man of the city. I am not used to..." But here he was interrupted by a fit of coughing, and his face darkened in the firelight.

A thin man, sitting erect under his cloak as if attending a lecture, or giving one, said, "You must have your cough looked to, friend."

"You can't kill a Roma with a cough," said the burley man. "For that you need a knife!" He stopped in front of the third man, who sat hunched like a huge boulder under his blanket. "Eh, brother? I suppose you have slaughtered your share of gypsies?"

The big man looked up. His hair was cropped short and a ragged scar ran from his forehead to his chin. "Soldiers do not require the histories of those they fight," he said quietly.

"Indeed not!" said the Roma. "Soldiers are not trained in humanity. Only in killing."

"As gypsies are trained to steal," said the soldier.

The Roma's eyes narrowed. "Not all gypsies, brother." Then he laughed. "But I admit it—I am a thief! But no ordinary thief, I assure you!"

"No," said the soldier dryly. "An arrogant thief as well."

"Friends!" said the thin man. "Why quarrel? Keep your tempers, the trip is long."

The Roma sneered. "As you keep yours, perhaps?"

"I practice self-control," said the thin man.

"And how easy for you, Scholar! When have you felt passion or anger? But this fellow and I are men of action! We..." But here another fit of coughing interrupted him.

The scholar's face showed that the Roma's words had struck home. "It's true," he said quietly. "I have neglected the emotional life. I sought the truth in books and found emptiness. Indeed, I envy men of passion."

The soldier lifted his scarred face and spoke intently. "To envy men of passion is to envy slaves."

"Why envy anyone?" cried the Roma. "Live! Take what you want, then die. It's enough!"

"A good plan!" said the scholar. "In fact, I have left the city in search of what I truly want."

"And what do you want?" asked the Roma.

"Poetry, perhaps. Or music. Water to moisten my dry soul."

The Roma coughed long and hard. "My soul will be satisfied when I get rid of this wretched cough!"

"And what will satisfy your soul?" the scholar asked the soldier.

The soldier smiled and shrugged. "A farm."

"A farm!" cried the Roma. "On a soldier's pay!"

"It's a dream," said the soldier. "But a dream that has consoled me in a life of hardship and struggle."

The huge man's words stilled the conversation. The black sky above them, which before had been held at bay by the firelight, seemed to draw closer and press a familiar grief into their hearts.

Then, from the darkness, came three notes from a flute.

The men froze, listening. The soldier drew the scimitar from his waistband and strode toward the sound. He stopped, listening. Then his eyes fell on the dim outline of a golden sack.

At the fire, the soldier opened the sack and on a blanket laid first a setar, a beautiful long-necked stringed instrument; next, an apothecary's medical chest; and last, from the bottom of the sack, he poured forth a glittering cascade of gems.

As usual, the Roma found his voice first. "Well, now!" he said. "These seem to be gifts from the Unseen." He affected a careless tone, but his voice trembled. He lifted the setar and handed it to the scholar. "Surely this is meant for you, brother. Water for your soul."

As the scholar took the instrument, two tears coursed down his cheeks.

The Roma knelt and let the gems trickle through his cupped palms. "And who might these be for?" he asked.

The soldier replied. "We must share."

The Roma smiled. "No, brother. What the Unseen gives, who can challenge?" The last gem dropped from his hands. "With these, you will buy your farm." He lifted the chest of medicines. "And for a gypsy's cough? Is this chest of herbs the least of gifts? Not at all! It contains two remedies. One to cure my cough, the other my faithlessness."

With that, the three men wept openly, and their tears dropped onto the sand.

Then the soldier said, "I am moved to offer something in return." The others nodded. Each went to his camel, and each placed something in the sack. The soldier returned it to the desert.

With the sack across his back, Adi crossed toward the next fire. His heart beat fast. Lightness had entered his being. His mind was still. Like the atmosphere at the center of a hurricane, at the center of the miraculous there is silence.

He drew near the third fire and saw three more men and heard their conversation.

"See how it is!" said a man whose round face, bald head, and pot belly gave him the appearance of balls lumped together. "A cobbler, a tailor, and a jeweler. We who work with our hands are thrown together. And why? Because we are every man's inferior!" He thrust a stick at the fire, and sparks mingled with the stars.

The tailor, a lean man with a gaunt face, sat erect under a fat purple turban. "Speak for yourself," he said irritably. "I am no man's inferior because of my occupation!"

The jeweler, cheerful and rosy-faced, was stretched on his blanket gazing at the night. He puffed a large, sweet-smelling pipe. He said, "We are not considered inferior because of our work. We are inferior because of our poverty."

The round cobbler returned, "And why are we poor? Because the rich will not pay a fair wage!"

"You crave money," said the gaunt tailor, "and so you are discontent. But money cannot buy contentment or dignity."

"And you have dignity?"

The gaunt man was silent for a long moment. Then he quietly replied, "I have lost it."

"Ah!" said the rosy-faced jeweler. "Here's a tale! Let's have it!"

The gaunt tailor said, "I have no tale worth telling. I have only shame. The war came, and I could not protect my family. My wife and children are the slaves of mountain bandits. I have neither the ransom nor the means to free them."

The others were silent. The firelight danced on their faces like golden water and seemed to amplify the blackness around them.

The pot-bellied cobbler said, "I too have lost my dignity. But I lost it long before the war. It vanished slowly, year by year. In my youth, I longed for knowledge. But each year I found a new excuse to avoid the labor of learning. I feared I was too simple, so I didn't try. Now I have lost hope. Probably my brain has shriveled anyway. Learning was not my destiny."

The jeweler emitted a cloud of smoke. "Until you are dead," he said, "your destiny is not written. If the Lord wants you learned, He will provide the means."

The tailor said, "And what is your destiny, jeweler? We have spoken our hearts. Speak yours."

"You would be alarmed to know my heart."

"Alarm us!" said the cobbler.

The jeweler smiled. "I would like to be a thief!"

"Oh, lord! Another tale!" said the cobbler.

"A simple one. All my life I have worked for the rich, designing trinkets of gold and silver. Beneath their pomp, I have seen their greed and selfishness. While they parade in finery, children starve." His cheer vanished, and his face grew stern. "If I had the means, I would..."

But here they fell silent. In the darkness of the desert they had heard three notes from a flute. The cobbler strode forward.

"Who's there?" he cried. He advanced a few steps, and his foot struck something soft.

A moment later, the cobbler emptied the golden sack onto a blanket. Before their astonished eyes lay a bow and quiver of arrows, a dozen leather bound books, and a ring of more than a hundred keys and lock picks.

The tailor lifted the bow and quiver. "The One Who Hears All has responded!" he cried. He raised the weapon above his head, clenching it fiercely. "Now I have remembered courage! I will free my family!"

The cobbler fell on his knees and poured over the books. "Botany, history, mathematics! Tonight the Invisible One has granted my heart's desire."

The jeweler lifted the ring of keys and laughed long and loud. "It seems I am meant to serve as a thief!"

And they began to weep.

Then the cobbler said, "For years together I have been working on a single piece, thinking one day to find a wealthy buyer. I am prompted to sacrifice this treasure to the Giver of All Gifts."

"I too have such a piece in my carpets," said the tailor.

"And I," said the jeweler.

And so the sack was again filled and placed in the desert. Adi threw it across his shoulder and set out for the fourth fire. He had forgotten hunger and thirst. He had forgotten himself. He moved across the sand like a spirit.

There were three young women at the fourth fire. Two were beautiful in the ordinary way—luxurious hair, fine-featured, lyre-shaped. But the third young woman was more than merely beautiful. Her face was radiant with love. In her hand she held a rose.

One of the girls exclaimed, "Ah, Mehera! If I were you I would run away from this uncle! I would fly like the wind!" To dramatize this advice, she whirled in a circle, and her skirt spun like a colored top.

The other girl laughed and sang in a sweet voice:

"And like the breeze that blows so meek,
I would caress my true love's cheek."

Mehera smiled at their merriment. But her voice was sorrowful. "It would break my uncle's heart."

"Has he a heart, to marry you to one you do not love?" said the dancer.

The singer said, "Ah, but that was before she met her musician."

The dancer added, "Before he overwhelmed her heart with a rose!" She spun again, making a flower of her skirt. "For love I would give up everything!"

"Your bangles, too?" exclaimed the singer.

"Nearly every one!" laughed the dancer.

The singer sang:

"Oh, for love I would presume

To give up even my perfume!"

Mehera laughed. Then suddenly she sobbed. "What am I to do!"

"Tell your uncle, the sardar. He has a noble heart."

"I feel I have betrayed him. I am ashamed to have fallen in love after he has arranged my marriage to another."

"And which is greater, your shame or your love?"

"My love!"

"Well, then," said the dancer. "Never fear! The Lord of Love provides for his own. Already I imagine he has instructed his angels to sew the most beautiful wedding gown for you!"

"And for me," said the singer. "A silver tambourine to play at your wedding!"

"Why not?" laughed the dancer. "And for me, golden slippers to dance for you and your musician!"

All three embraced, and even Mehera, though her face was wet with tears, laughed merrily.

Then their laughter stopped. From the silent desert they had heard the sound of a flute.

It was the dancer who brought the golden sack to the fire. She brought forth from it a white gown, richly embroidered with gold and silver thread and bedecked with gems. In silence, she presented the gown to Mehera who held it to her shoulders.

"The Lord of Love has not delayed, dear sister," said the dancer. "It seems you must marry your musician."

Mehera said, "Look further. There will be slippers and a tambourine."

And so they drew out a pair of golden slippers (which perfectly fit the dancer's feet) and a jeweled tambourine from which the singer brought forth a cascade of silver sound.

The singer and dancer burst into tears.

"My heart will burst from this!" cried the dancer.

"I am too small for this love!" cried the singer.

Mehera embraced them. Her face shone. She had gone beyond tears. "How else should we feel, dear sisters? Love fills the earth and stars, and beyond the stars there is only love."

"Oh, sisters!" cried the dancer. "We must return something for this good fortune!"

Again the sack was filled. It was Mehera who returned it to the desert. She laid it on the sand, then knelt beside it. She said, "Oh Love, who has given me all, I surrender my all to you." She laid the rose on the golden cloth and returned to her friends.

Adi knelt and lifted the rose. He held it to his heart as he brought the sack to the fifth and last fire.

There sat a long-haired man with wide mustaches, his arms wrapped about his knees, a golden scarf wound about his head like a crown. A second man, short and fierce-looking, dressed in white cotton, paced and gestured angrily as he spoke.

"You are my master, and I am your servant! Your company has shaped my heart! I remind you of this first, so that you may keep your temper when I tell you I am disgusted with you! I want to kick you!"

"Kick me," said the other with a smile.

The fierce man threw open his arms. "He is gone, my lord! He is lost! Grief will not bring him back!"

"Perhaps that is why I grieve."

"You are a madman! How many hundreds of twelve-year-old boys have we examined this year, and how many thirteen-year-old boys will

we examine next! I am finished with it! Are we women to grieve so long? I tell you, I would wear perfume and bangles if it would restore your son, but this is a life of hopelessness!"

And with that, the servant stalked into the desert night. After ten steps he stopped. His foot had struck something on the sand.

The sardar stared into the fire. Perhaps his friend was right. Perhaps his search was futile. But how else could he live? His longing was his life, and for years he had kept it alive with remembrance. It was his pain and his joy together. One day, he was certain, love would draw his son back to him.

Now in the darkness he heard a tinkling sound. He lifted his head and peered into the night. The scent of roses drifted across the desert. Then, in the firelight, his servant appeared. On his arms, he wore silver bangles. His cotton garment was drenched in rose perfume. His cheeks streamed with tears. He held his hands open to the sardar.

"Forgive me, master," he said. "Then let him appear."

The sardar rose and stared into the desert. Adi stood in the night with the rose clutched to his heart. He saw the broad mustaches, the flowing hair. He walked into the firelight and bowed before his father, then offered him the rose. As the sardar took the flower, his eyes fell on Adi's shoulder and the heart-shaped birthmark he had sought so long. Father and son fell into each other's arms. From each burst a flood of joyful tears.

The remainder of the night was full of wonder and exclamation as the members of the caravan learned how the miracle had touched them all. Each had given what was most precious and received from the Unseen a gift that opened their hearts. They freshly wept and could not embrace each other tenderly enough. The next day, the wedding of the sardar's niece and the musician was celebrated in the desert with dancing and song and lunatic joy.

The miracle of the rose caravan was told and retold from city to city and back again a thousand times. For years, Adi and his father searched for the old woman to offer their gratitude, but no trace of her was ever found. Eventually they built a school and home for the lost children, and from time to time, their secret benefactor, a certain jeweler-turned-thief, appeared with an amazing amount of cash. But all this can be guessed or imagined. What else could they do with such joy?

Adi grew, married, and began a family of his own. Daily, like a bright light, he saw the old woman in his heart and to the end of his days held precious her words, "Give all, and you will get all."

The story doesn't end here, but what story ever ends? So enough of these rascally words. Life cannot be caught in their net. It must be lived. So good you have one, my friend, an adventure of a life!

Off you go!

About the author and the book

I studied philosophy in college, became dissatisfied with its emptiness, and began to prowl the library for books about the inner world. Eventually I discovered the work of Aurobindo Ghose. A year later, in 1969, I was introduced to Meher Baba. I traveled to India more than a dozen times to visit Meher Baba's tombsite and speak with his mandali, those who lived their entire lives under his direction. *Everything Makes Sense* is a distillation of 50 years of thought and living, and is, in a sense, a letter to the youth I was when I began my search for Truth.

I have written several books of fiction. One of them, *Bhajan*, is the tale of five characters in a traveling zoo who encounter a tiger that was raised in India by a mast, one of the God-intoxicated. The tiger, Bhajan, purrs, and the purr has the mysterious property of awakening the inner being of each character, even of the nearly mad antagonist, JJ. The novel is a fictional development of the themes presented in *Everything Makes Sense*.

A last note: this work is not scholarship, that is, not a looking through the thought-lens of other thinkers. I am widely read in philosophy, science, and spiritual traditions, but the thinking of *Everything Makes Sense,* when unattributed, is the product of introspection. It's hardly conceivable that at this stage in human development there are any new ideas, but where mine coincide with previous thought I leave for others to consider.

I can be reached at timgarvin.com. For those interested, I have invented an absorbing card game, *Caravan,* based on the folktale *The Rose Caravan* that ends this book. The sixteen characters of the tale will be illustrated by the artist Girish Adannavar. The game and a tutorial explaining the rules will be available soon (perhaps now) on my website.

T.V. Garvin

O-BOOKS

SPIRITUALITY

O is a symbol of the world, of oneness and unity; this eye represents knowledge and insight. We publish titles on general spirituality and living a spiritual life. We aim to inform and help you on your own journey in this life.
If you have enjoyed this book, why not tell other readers by posting a review on your preferred book site?

Shine On

David Ditchfield and J S Jones

What if the aftereffects of a near-death experience were undeniable? What if a person could suddenly produce high-quality paintings of the afterlife, or if they acquired the ability to compose classical symphonies? Meet: David Ditchfield.

Paperback: 978-1-78904-365-5 ebook: 978-1-78904-366-2

The Way of Reiki

The Inner Teachings of Mikao Usui

Frans Stiene

The roadmap for deepening your understanding of the system of Reiki and rediscovering your True Self.

Paperback: 978-1-78535-665-0 ebook: 978-1-78535-744-2

You Are Not Your Thoughts.

Frances Trussell

The journey to a mindful way of being, for those who want to truly know the power of mindfulness.

Paperback: 978-1-78535-816-6 ebook: 978-1-78535-817-3

The Mysteries of the Twelfth Astrological House

Fallen Angels

Carmen Turner-Schott, MSW, LISW

Everyone wants to know more about the most misunderstood house in astrology — the twelfth astrological house.

Paperback: 978-1-78099-343-0 ebook: 978-1-78099-344-7

WhatsApps from Heaven

Louise Hamlin

An account of a bereavement and the extraordinary signs — including WhatsApps — that a retired law lecturer received from her deceased husband.

Paperback: 978-1-78904-947-3 ebook: 978-1-78904-948-0

The Holistic Guide to Your Health & Wellbeing Today

Oliver Rolfe

A holistic guide to improving your complete health, both inside and out.

Paperback: 978-1-78535-392-5 ebook: 978-1-78535-393-2

Cool Sex

Diana Richardson and Wendy Doeleman

For deeply satisfying sex, the real secret is to reduce the heat, to cool down. Discover the empowerment and fulfilment of sex with loving mindfulness.

Paperback: 978-1-78904-351-8 ebook: 978-1-78904-352-5

Creating Real Happiness A to Z

Stephani Grace

Creating Real Happiness A to Z will help you understand the truth that you are not your ego (conditioned self).

Paperback: 978-1-78904-951-0 ebook: 978-1-78904-952-7

A Colourful Dose of Optimism
Jules Standish
It's time for us to look on the bright side, by boosting our mood and lifting our spirit, both in our interiors, as well as in our closet.
Paperback: 978-1-78904-927-5 ebook: 978-1-78904-928-2